Trading the World's Markets

Interviews with the Great Global Investors

Trading the World's Markets

Interviews with the Great Global Investors

Leo Gough

John Wiley & Sons (Asia) Pte Ltd

Singapore   New York   Chichester
Brisbane   Toronto   Weinheim

Copyright © 2000 by John Wiley & Sons (Asia) Pte Ltd
Published in 2000 by John Wiley & Sons (Asia) Pte Ltd
2 Clementi Loop, #02-01, Singapore 129809

This publication is designed to provide accurate and authoritative information in regard to the subject matter covered. It is sold with the understanding that the publisher is not engaged in rendering professional services. If professional advice or other expert assistance is required, the services of a competent professional person should be sought.

Other Wiley Editorial Offices

John Wiley & Sons, Inc., 605 Third Avenue, New York, NY 10158-0012, USA
John Wiley & Sons Ltd, Baffins Lane, Chichester, West Sussex PO19 1UD, England
John Wiley & Sons (Canada) Ltd, 22 Worcester Road, Rexdale, Ontario M9W 1L1, Canada
John Wiley & Sons Australia Ltd, 33 Park Road (PO Box 1226), Milton, Queensland 4064, Australia
Wiley-VCH, Pappelallee 3, 69469 Weinheim, Germany

Library of Congress Cataloging-in-Publication Data

Gough, Leo.
    Trading the world markets: interviews with the great global investors/Leo Gough.
        p. cm. — (Wiley traders' quest series)
    Includes bibliographical references.
    ISBN 0-471-83861-6
        1. Capitalists and financiers—Biography.   2. Investments, Foreign.   3. International business
enterprises.   I. Title.   II. Series

HG172.A2 G68 2000
332.67'3-dc21   99-055788

NOTE

All investment markets are volatile and subject to fluctuations which cannot reasonably be foreseen. Any investment may result in losses as well as in gains. The publishers, author, individuals featured in this book, and their respective organizations cannot accept any responsibility for any loss suffered by any person acting or refraining from acting as a result of material contained herein. The material in *Trading the World's Markets* is for information purposes only.

Typeset in 11/15 points, Garamond by Linographic Services Pte Ltd
Printed in Singapore by Craft Print Pte Ltd
10 9 8 7 6 5 4 3 2 1

For Elena & Gonzalo

CONTENTS

PREFACE

Not since the late nineteenth century have global trade and investment been so open, yet most investors still keep their money within their own countries. The reason? It takes extra effort to invest abroad — an effort which, in many cases, will be richly rewarded, but which serves as a deterrent to many people.

The *Wiley Traders' Quest Series* sets out to show how successful global investing is done, by interviewing top professionals in many different fields of finance and business.

The first book in the series, *Trading the World's Markets*, looks at the general issues involved and investigates the nuts and bolts of conducting stock transactions in far-off foreign markets. Other titles delve more deeply into specific topics and industries, helping to put the everyday torrent of market news into a broader context and giving readers the opportunity to interpret events in more insightful ways.

Whether you are a novice or a seasoned professional, a buyer of mutual funds or a dedicated short-term trader, you should find much of interest here. The people interviewed are not only excellent in their chosen specialties, but are generous enough to talk openly — and amusingly — about the ups and downs of global investing in the major leagues.

No-one can predict the future precisely, and only one thing is certain in investment — constant change. As a global investor, the world is your oyster; take the trouble to master your craft and you will not be disappointed.

Leo Gough
Series Editor

INTRODUCTION

We're told that we are in a great age of globalization and international investment. Relatively speaking, it's true — the last time markets were this open across the world was before the First World War. But is globalization really affecting your personal investment program directly? Unless you are a bank, the answer is probably "no."

There are reasons for this. Even if there were no barriers at all to investment abroad, the chances are that most private investors would keep most of their money in their own country's stocks. This has been true in the United States, in part, because of growth and opportunity at home, but it is also the case elsewhere. When I have spoken to groups of private investors abroad, I've found a similar attitude almost everywhere, from Seoul to London. The fact is that investing abroad seems more risky to many people and there are various administrative barriers. Your broker is quite likely to discourage you if you want to buy stocks in, say, Vienna — you may be told that the transactions costs are ridiculously high, that the rules of the exchange are different, that you're taking a crazy risk, and so on. The majority of brokers are geared up to sell domestic stocks. For many of them, small purchases of stock on foreign exchanges entails too much work to make it worth their while — so they tell you not to bother.

Most stock exchanges, these days, will allow you to purchase shares as a foreigner — and you will normally be able to find a local broker to act for you. You will probably have to pay upfront and you are unlikely to be given any margin. You may have trouble following the stocks. So yes, there are indeed barriers to trading in foreign stocks, but nothing that you can't overcome with a little time and effort. What's more, the existence of these barriers is a hint that many overseas markets are not "efficient" — that is, their prices get out of whack with the fundamentals — which is what an aggressive investor wants.

Many U.S. investors try to solve the practical problems of foreign investment by purchasing American Depository Receipts (ADRs), which represent foreign stocks but are traded in the United States. In this book I canvassed interviewees' opinions about this strange class of security. Their responses were remarkably varied — from the "Great American Scam" view of Jim Rogers (see page 41), to the "can be appropriate" argument of Paul Melton (see page 55). ADRs may be the best way to trade in certain stocks in certain countries — indeed, they may be the *only* way to do so at times — but they do represent an additional level of cost and therefore should not be seen as a universal solution for foreign investment.

This book is for investors who want to make above-average returns. Isn't that everyone? No — conservative institutions often prefer safety to high rewards, while many private investors have other considerations that, to them, are more important than profits, such as so-called ethical investing or the need to feel safe (even if the apparent "safety" of their investment choices is dubious). Some people won't consider putting money in foreign stocks out of a sense of patriotism — which is misplaced, in my view. It's a matter of opinion, maybe, but I don't believe that loving your country has much to do with investment.

In writing this book, I set out to find investors who had a proven record in international investing and to discover how they do it. While their methods differ greatly, they all turned out to have enormous enthusiasm for their subject and to enjoy the manifold uncertainties that active investors must live with. Most of them are highly cultured individuals who have wide-ranging interests, both inside and outside the markets. Investment, to them, is not merely the miserable accumulation of money but is an activity full of meaning — it's a way of understanding world affairs, of active participation in current events.

Can you, as a private investor, learn from these masters? I believe you can. While your resources may be smaller than theirs, the principles of making profits remain the same — understanding how to think about markets, and developing an adaptable, yet individualistic attitude is all-important. Blindly following the herd into the latest stock craze is unlikely to make you rich, since you'll be caught in the crash, but that is exactly what most amateur speculators do. In contrast, the investors interviewed here are people who think for themselves.

Investment is an art as well as a science. You don't have to be a born investor — whoever you are, and however much or little you have, there is always more to learn. Even more importantly, it's a way of life, even if you only have a few hours a week to spend on it. A lifetime's success in investing will make your retirement more enjoyable, since you'll have more money, and, better still, you'll have decades of experience to draw on as you continue to invest. Given mental clarity, there is no reason why you shouldn't still be investing actively in your nineties. Time is on your side, so don't waste it by impatiently taking suckers' risks. Steady returns will compound over the decades into substantial wealth. I hope that this book helps you to achieve this.

1

Jim Rogers:
Indiana Jones
Investing

Jim Rogers is a truly remarkable investor. Between 1970 and 1980 he partnered George Soros in managing a hedge fund that not only appreciated 4200% during the period but never had a down year. How did they do it? By taking views on broad political and economic factors in countries and industries across the world, they successfully anticipated many huge price moves in their favor. Subsequently, Rogers has continued to pull off many coups on his own, including, for example, investing in the Austrian stock market in 1984 — it moved up 145% in the following year — and at the same time shorting Swedish blue chips which dropped between 40% and 60%.

Born a "poor boy" in Alabama, Jim Rogers went to Yale in the early 1960s and then to Oxford, in England, on a scholarship. After working on Wall Street, culminating in the heady period with Soros, he "retired" to pursue his own interests and manage his own money. His career has been documented in several books, including the excellent The New Money Masters, *by John Train (Harper & Row, 1989), and Rogers' own, the highly entertaining* Investment Biker *(Random House, 1994), which documents a round-the-world trip by motorcycle, larded with opinions and anecdotes about international investing.*

He doesn't like being called an "Indiana Jones," but few other investors have been as intrepid. When I contacted his office I was told that he was on the road again — this time in a custom-built

Mercedes car with a team to run his website following in a Mercedes G Wagon (see page 46) — and that he was somewhere in Central Asia. Perhaps I could interview him in Korea or Japan in a month or two, they said. We finally met in Xi'an, China, the first major city he had reached after a grueling trip across Kazakhstan, Uzbekistan, and the wilderness of western China.

It was supposed to be a short interview. I talked to him and his partner, Paige Parker, as they worked out in their hotel gym, but our mutual enthusiasm for investment topics took us, still talking, on a ride out to the site of the ancient terracotta army, then on to a Buddhist temple, now fully functioning after decades of neglect, and finally to dinner at a Xi'an restaurant.

Throughout our discussion, Jim Rogers frequently made the point that it is hard to get rich by investing. There are no easy answers, he says — you have to work at it. To be able to grasp the significance of current events — and then to interpret them successfully — clearly takes an enormous amount of effort. The Rogers investment method is not for everyone, especially if you only have a few hours a week to spend doing it. Yet, if you are truly inspired by the opportunities available to the internationally minded, here is a man who has done it successfully for decades — and can explain how.

LG: You have written that two basic principles for growth are finding something that's cheap, and then looking for somewhere where there is going to be a dynamic change.

Jim Rogers: The reason you want to buy something cheap is so that you don't have much risk; if you're wrong, you're not going to suffer too badly. Buying something cheap doesn't do you any good on its own; it might stay cheap for years. You've got to have a reason why it's going to change and why something is going to get better. But it's not just a matter of finding things that are cheap; it's also a case of finding things that are expensive and selling them short. There is more than one way to make money in the markets. If there is something that's too expensive and there's a negative change coming, you can sell it short and make money that way too. But yes, for most people, buying cheap when there's a change is the best way to make money. It's the way *I* make money, anyway.

LG: Should the little guy, the smaller investor, really play around with selling things short, considering margin calls?

Jim Rogers: Well, yes, one should. It teaches you a whole lot about the market. It gives you discipline, if nothing else, and it teaches you how to sell. A lot of people know how to buy, but to make money in the markets you've got to buy and sell. The world is littered with stories, including my own, of people selling at the wrong time, so one does need to know how to sell, and selling short is certainly a good way to learn how to sell. You don't have to do it, but I would remind you that markets don't always go up; in fact, markets frequently go down for long periods of time. Knowing how to make money on both sides of the market is good. Since most people, including me, are not very good at judging the direction of the market at any one point in time, being able to sell short, at least in my experience, gives you a good hedge. I have longs and shorts, and if the market goes up the theory is that my longs are going to go up more than my shorts. My shorts may go up, but I've got the protection; and if the market goes down, then hopefully I'll have shorted bad companies and marginal companies, so those stocks will go down much more than my longs will go down, so that I can make money when markets go up or go down. Recently in Western markets we've mainly had markets that just go up all the time. I hasten to tell you that that's not the norm and anybody who thinks it is should certainly know how to sell short because they're going to find out the hard way that stocks don't always go up.

The best way to learn is to do it yourself; there's nothing quite like it. I've read a lot of books (I've written books myself) and talked to a lot of people, but I'll tell you there is nothing quite like *doing* it. You can even invest on paper and learn that you're a great investor, but when you actually *do* it, it's a whole lot different. I don't know of any other profession where it's quite the same — you've got to do it in order to know whether you're good at it, because your emotions, your passions, and your thought processes are a whole lot different when you've got real money on the line and the market's open, and you're sitting there trying to figure out what to do.

LG: You once wrote that there was never a "good old days." Could you talk a little bit about that?

Jim Rogers: I constantly have people tell me how easy it was in the old days. I don't remember when it was ever easy, because when you're in it at the time there are always scores of things that you're worried about — at least *I* am. I can look back on some of my great triumphs and they may seem easy now, but at the time I'm sure I was sitting there sweating and wondering, and saying, "Oh, my God. Is this right? Am I doing the right thing?"

Protectionism

LG: You have written at length about the evils of protectionism. Do you think it's something that will always be with us?

Jim Rogers: Yes, I'm afraid so. Anybody who stops and thinks about it will see that protectionism is totally irrational — it doesn't do the world any good, it doesn't do the great mass of people any good. We have just come from Kazakhstan, and you can see how they would all be so much better off if they just opened their borders, their economy, and their society. I have seen no instances where protectionism should be encouraged. Even in America there is this ludicrous rationalization that we protect our sugar industry because of national defense. When they can't think of any other argument to defend protectionism, they always resort to "national defense," but why the sugar industry helps national defense is a mystery to me.

The worst part of it is that protectionist measures are never temporary. They get put in place and then they just stay there. People forget why they're protecting such an industry, but they go on doing it. In Kazakhstan we were told we couldn't mail undeveloped film out of the country. Nobody knows why. They said you can take it out with you on a plane, you can drive across the border with it, take it on a train or a bus, but you can't mail it out of the country. It's some leftover rule that some bureaucrat came up with once upon a time that's totally dispensable but it's still there. That's the worst of it — these things get a life of their own, and thirty years later it's very difficult to get them changed.

LG: So, given that you think it's always going to be around, what do you say to the people who are talking about a brave new world of globalization and free markets?

Jim Rogers: That's all wonderful — when everything is going well, people talk about globalization and about opening their markets; but as soon as things start going wrong, somebody goes and squawks to the politicians or to the dictator and says, "You must protect us." It sounds fine: we're just going to save it for all the Kazakhs, or for all the Ethiopians, or whoever it happens to be, but they don't understand the big picture and why it's actually going to hurt them in the long run. As long as things are going great, markets do open up. It happened in the nineteenth century, it happened in the twentieth, it's happened repeatedly; but when things start going bad and somebody starts getting hurt, they start pulling back.

Unfortunately, we can see it happening already. Look at what happened in Malaysia, for instance. The Malaysians themselves were the biggest sellers of their currency and sold it before others did. The politicians blamed it on the evil foreigners, rather than acknowledge that they themselves had followed bad policies.

During the Asian currency crisis of 1997, currency speculators were able to conduct complex deals on the international foreign exchange markets which had the effect of forcing already weak currencies, notably those of Thailand and Malaysia, down even further. Speaking at a political rally in October 1997, Malaysia's Prime Minister Dr. Mahathir, said that there may be a Jewish "agenda" behind the recent attacks on his country's currency and stock market. In the same month, an effigy of George Soros, a prominent currency speculator, was burnt in public in Kuala Lumpur.

Jim Rogers: When things were going great they were shouting about opening the markets and how terrific all this is, but then they started thinking how smart they were. Eventually they started to believe they were smarter than anybody else, but then they found out that they weren't. That makes it worse, because when they react they've got to blame somebody else. It's never themselves, it's always the "evil foreigners" or the "evil financiers." That's how wars start. When you have problems, you look for somebody to blame. It's because of the blacks, or the whites, or the Jews, or the Christians, or the Muslims; you know, it's not *my* fault, it's somebody else's fault. It's always easier to blame it on the foreigners, and that leads to protectionism.

LG: Do you think it may happen in the West also?

Jim Rogers: Oh yes, absolutely. Always has. Do you think we're smarter than everybody else? When things are going right we *think* we're smarter than everybody else. In the 1980s everybody thought the Japanese were smarter than everybody else. People said, you have to understand that the Japanese market is always going to go up because they're smarter. They do things differently than we do. They don't put their trousers on one leg at a time. They wake up in the morning and, somehow, their trousers are already on.

You can sit down and say, look guys, why don't we just take all the steelworkers in America and close down the inefficient steel factories? We'll teach them new businesses, we'll give them $50,000 a year; whatever they feel they need, we'll give it to them for as long as they want and we'll teach them something new. And if we can't teach them something new, fine, we'll give them fifty grand a year for the rest of their lives and a Chevrolet. Whatever they want. They'd be better off and we'd be better off, the country would be better off. You can explain that, you can even do the numbers, but then you go out and talk to the steelworkers and they get all emotional and they talk about "their culture, their way of life."

In Japan they tell you that they have to protect rice because it's the soul of Japan and Japanese culture wouldn't be the same if they didn't have those rice farmers out there. They say, "We can't eat imported rice because our digestion system is different. We can't digest foreign rice." They really say that, and they mean it! I don't know whether we should hope they mean it or don't mean it, because if they do believe it then they're nuts.

People come up with these outrageous reasons and rationales for protectionism when things go wrong, and then they develop a life of their own. Japan wouldn't be Japan if it didn't grow rice; the South wouldn't be the South if it didn't grow cotton. Well, the South doesn't grow much cotton anymore, but the South is still there; it still has a way of life and somehow we've all survived even though not a lot of cotton is grown in the South now.

LG: So, how do you cope with the things you hate?

Jim Rogers: There are lots of things I "hate" because they aren't good for the world, they're irrational, or they shouldn't happen. Forget that. You can't be an investor and say, "Well, I don't like that, so I'm not going to invest in it." You have to understand, and invest in, the world as it is.

We would all like the world to be the way we want it. I mean, I would love it if everybody lived to a hundred and never had cancer. If I sat there and said, "Well, I'm only going to invest if everybody in the world lives to be a hundred and nobody has cancer," I wouldn't make a whole lot of dough. So, you have to understand the world and take it as it is, and you certainly have to understand the changes that are coming in the world.

What to buy in Europe

Jim Rogers: This is April 17, 1999 and anything I say today I may change my mind about by the end of the year. But I'll tell you what I'm doing. Take Europe — there are a lot of things wrong in Europe, but it doesn't mean that there aren't ways to make profits from the long side in Europe. I'll give you three examples. Actually, all of them are things that I don't like, but there are going to be changes and so they are ways to make money. For instance, right now American oil companies are not allowed to do business in seven or eight major oil sectors of the world. That's nuts. It's costing America jobs, it's costing America profits, it's costing America income, it's costing America lots of stuff — prestige, balance of payments, and so on. I say, "OK, what does that mean?" What that means is that the non-U.S. oil companies are going to make fortunes in those places around the world.

If you look around the world, you'll find that the big non-American oil companies are mainly in Europe. So, I own shares in nearly all the European oil companies because they are being handed a gift on a platter. Remember that when there's a dramatic change taking place, you've got to buy something that's cheap. Oil is cheap, so even if you're wrong and it doesn't go up, you may lose some money but you're not going to go broke. All these European oil companies are very cheap and they're being handed gifts by the American State Department, by these thirty-two-year-old know-nothings in Washington. Since these companies are cheap, and they all realize they have to compete with the Americans, they're all merging. That wasn't part of the plan when I bought these things, but it's now happening — lots of mergers are taking place. But that's what happens when you buy something cheap and there are changes taking place: good things happen which you don't expect, which makes it even better.

If you look at Europe, defense spending has been declining for years for a lot of good reasons. Several things have happened in the last couple of years. First, defense spending has bottomed out; it's not declining anymore, it's actually started up again. So that's a big change for the better if you're a European defense company. The American defense industry is all consolidated, and the Europeans suddenly looked around and said, "Oh my God, we've got to compete with the Americans and there are a hundred of us and now there are only the big five of them." So the governments of Europe, the defense industry in Europe, and the European Union have all said, "Thou shalt consolidate." You don't have to be too smart to figure out it's an industry which hasn't been overpriced, because spending has been coming down for years. So, you buy the small ones because they're going to be bought out. They know they have to be bought out. It doesn't matter if they want to be bought out or not, they're going to be bought out because if they aren't they're going to disappear.

This is one of the few times in world history when governments have actually said, "Consolidate. We'll encourage you, we'll help you." So, I don't see how you can lose buying European defense companies because they're cheap, the industry is turning around, and the small ones are all going to be bought out. Even the big ones will look good because they'll buy the small ones.

Third, many nations, including China, are starting to re-arm. Some of them will avoid buying armaments from the U.S., since they are afraid that the rug could be pulled out from under them at any time by the U.S. State Department. China has decided to buy from foreign suppliers for the first time, but they'll buy from Europe, not America. So, that's the industry where you can make money. Forget war, but if war happens that'll be even better for them.

Look at the European banking system. Denmark has only five million people, but it has ten banks. I don't know why it needed ten banks, but they are now into consolidation. This equitization, or equity-mania, that's taking place in the world is causing the European banks to realize that they have to consolidate. So, I buy all the small banks. I must own twenty small banks in Europe, and two or three a year get bought out from under me. I hope I have two or three bought out every year for the next five years. And again, when a small one gets taken over, the accounting methods that are used make the bigger one look better for a while.

Those are scenarios in Europe where, despite the problems I see there, you can make money. Whether or not you like the situation, they are cheap and you're not going to lose money even if something goes wrong.

LG: Continental Europeans, particularly the French, are generally quite scared of capital markets. Don't you think there might be a backlash in a few years' time?

Jim Rogers: Yes. When you look at the world, you have to look at the way the world is, not the way you want it to be. I'm fully aware of that and I always prepare for the backlash. I'm always afraid that I might be trapped in some countries because they're going to change the rules suddenly. I was short Russian rubles last year — even I get something right once in a while — and I was ecstatic when the whole thing started to collapse. I covered sooner than I would have otherwise, because I was afraid they would suddenly change the rules. They might say, "You guys who sold short, go to jail and we're going to confiscate your money." So I covered, but not because I'm not incredibly bearish on Russia. Russia as we know it is going to disappear. It doesn't do you any good to be brilliant if you lose money because they change the rules. So yes, I'm always worried about that factor.

We talked earlier about how when things start going badly, everyone looks for somebody to blame. When things start going badly in Europe and in America, they're going to outlaw a lot of things. In the 1930s, for instance, we had the economic collapse. Commodity prices collapsed — cotton went to half a cent, and oil went to a nickel a barrel. The American Congress, in its wisdom, outlawed options on commodities. They said the reason the commodity prices had collapsed during the Depression was because of options. I'm not making this up; I wish I were. Commodity prices would not have collapsed if there hadn't been those evil guys in Chicago and New York buying and selling options.

In England about seventy years ago it was an act of treason to use anything except the pound sterling as currency. All the country's problems were blamed on people using other forms of money. For a while, you could be hanged for trying to use gold or U.S. dollars or Bank of Japan notes in your transactions.

So, there will be a reaction and they will come up with all sorts of things. And yes, before it's all over, exchange controls will be in place in the U.S. The rules will also be changed in Europe, especially in the anti-equity countries such as France. But that's OK as long as you know it's coming and can invest accordingly.

When I say that's OK, I don't mean that I approve of it, but as long as you know that such things are possibilities and invest within that context, you'll probably survive. You may even figure out a way to make a profit if you know that the French are going to do something ludicrous. The Americans did this crazy thing about American oil companies, but that creates opportunities for other people.

Indonesia

LG: You've written that, as an investor, you wait until wars are fought, the borders are redrawn, and a newly elected democratic government is eager to do something. But take a country like Indonesia; that wasn't the case there, yet everybody was investing and making money.

Jim Rogers: I wasn't one of those people in Indonesia. I invested in Indonesia in, I think, 1985 and sold out long ago. Indonesia isn't a real country — it's not going to survive as a country. It's going to split up into — *you* pick a number. It comprises around 15,000 islands (nobody really knows the exact number), but the Dutch sort of put them together and said, "OK, guys, you're now a country." Then, when they gave them independence, they said, "Now you're on your own."

One of the reasons I'm not buying Asia yet in any meaningful way is because it is inevitable that Indonesia will collapse. When it does collapse, I'll want to rush in, but I'll probably rush into other parts of Asia, or I may just buy into parts of Indonesia. Let's see how it splits up. It usually takes a while to sort out what's going to happen next.

I try to understand history. I don't know if I'm any better at it than anybody else, but in my view Indonesia basically isn't a real country. It's going to collapse in the same way that the Soviet Union did. I don't have any plans to invest in Indonesia for years, maybe decades, maybe never.

It's the reason I've stayed away from Russia and Central Europe. When an empire collapses, the reverberations go on for a while. You don't wait a year or two and then send some kids off to Columbia Business School or the Harvard School of Democracy and say that everything is now fine. Look at the collapse of the Ottoman, British, Spanish, and French empires. The reverberations don't just wind up in

a year or two, but when the collapse comes, that's when I like to go
in. But don't go in just because something has collapsed. Indonesia
has collapsed, but you ain't seen nothing yet.

Each country has its own historical situation which we have to try
to figure out and understand. We won't always get it right, but we
have to be prepared for these things. It's the same in Russia — I know
it's not going to work.

Central Asia

LG: And Central Asia — is there any hope there?

Jim Rogers: No. I just came through Central Asia. The Americans rant
and rave to me about the Chinese being so repressive and dictatorial,
and then they rant and rave about their great allies, Turkmenistan,
Uzbekistan, and Kazakhstan. But talk about police states — I've never
seen anything like it. We were stopped by the police ten times in 150
kilometers in Georgia. There are police everywhere in those countries.

We were at a market in Turkmenistan, video-taping the goings-on.
It was a great big Asian market with vegetables, plumbing supplies,
and the rest. The KGB came up to us, took away our camera, and
confiscated our film. I don't know what kind of wonderful state
secrets they thought we were getting there among the vegetable stalls
and the rug dealers. They gave us the camera back eventually, but they
took the film. Fortunately, I was able to get to the KGB general and say,
"Look at the damn tape." They watched it and then returned it. There's
no accountability with our famous allies, the Turkmenistanis. Half an
hour later they came back and said, "You know that part where you
were filming and our KGB agents came over and started hassling you,
would you cut that part out?" The only thing that they were
embarrassed about was their own behavior. And these are our allies!

In China, no-one ever stops us. The police wave to us. We've
traveled over 3000 kilometers. We walk freely around the streets.
People do what they want to do. We were riding through the
countryside yesterday, riding down this fabulous road — the best road
I've seen since Austria, or maybe Turkey — and all of a sudden over

here on the left there's this gigantic church with crosses at the top. At first I thought it must be some leftover Russian Orthodox church or something, but it's not. We pulled over at this huge Christian church, 20 meters off the highway. It's not as though the Chinese authorities have said, "OK, you Christians have got to go hide in the corner" — it's right beside the autobahn. The whole town is Christian; it's a bunch of Chinese farmers and they're all Christians. The government pays the minister's salary. This is in a country that Americans worry has all these oppressed people, but in Turkmenistan they're meant to be our great friends.

None of the 'Stans are going to make it. None of Central Asia is going to make it. Stalin drew the borders, and they're absurd. When the Soviet Union fell apart, the local communist guy was the only guy there, so he took over. They're hopeless, they don't know anything; they are dumb guys and it's all going to fall apart. It's all going to be worse than Russia. Get out of there if you can.

China

LG: And China?

Jim Rogers: I'm wildly bullish on China. I'm back here for the first time in nine years and I can't believe it. There's no question that the next century will be the century of the Chinese. The nineteenth century was the century of Britain, the twentieth century was the century of the U.S., and the twenty-first century will be the century of China.

I don't have any investments in China at the moment, and the reason I don't is because — back to the big picture — all of China's neighbors have devalued recently. China is now in a difficult competitive position, whether it knows it or not. They keep denying this, and say they're not going to devalue. Maybe they won't, but somewhere along the line they are going to have to float the currency if they are going to be in the WTO [World Trade Organization] and be a real country to realize their potential. At that point the currency will probably go down, whether they like it or not. By the way, if it does I would rush in and buy it at that point.

It's not the end of the world. America had huge setbacks in the twentieth century. We were a debtor nation in 1899 and we had huge difficulties on our way to becoming the richest, most powerful country in the world. In 1907 the whole country fell apart; it went broke in 1923, and then in the early 1930s the whole thing fell apart again.

The other day in Washington someone asked the Premier of China if he was going to devalue the currency. He replied, "No, we're not going to devalue the currency, but if you think we're going to devalue the currency then you should buy puts," which I thought was a brilliant answer. The reporter should have said, "OK, will you write me the puts?" — that would have been the real test. "Alright, Mr. Premier, if you mean that, let's do a deal! You write me some puts!"

If I were the Chinese I would just say, "Look, we want to join the WTO, we want to be a major world power, so we're going to float the currency." That would be a backdoor way of letting the whole market take care of it. For some reason, somebody has got it into their head that it's an act of weakness if they let the currency float or if it goes down, so they're standing there fighting this losing battle. When it happens, I want to buy as much of China as I can. I'll probably buy it through overseas Chinese companies in Singapore, Thailand, Malaysia, San Francisco, and Vancouver.

If the Chinese don't make the currency convertible and let it float, there will be turmoil of some other kind — social, political, something. Either way, that's when to buy.

LG: Not Hong Kong?

Jim Rogers: Probably not Hong Kong, just because … I mean, who knows? I think the opportunities will be bigger elsewhere.

It's going to be the Chinese who make a lot of money in China, and the overseas Chinese are considered Chinese. I mean, they're all the same as far as China is concerned, so get involved with overseas Chinese companies because they understand the rule of law, they understand dividends, they understand accounting, they understand shareholders, and the mainland Chinese don't. They love it when Merrill Lynch comes in and gives them a cheque for $300 million because they had a public offering — these guys bought them Rolexes or Mercedes, all kinds of wonderful things. Now when they come back three years later and say, "Where's the factory?" they reply, "We didn't build a factory. We decided we had better uses for the money."

When I get to Shanghai I'm probably going to open an account in China, which I've never bothered to do before. A real account. The country is even more astonishing than I realized and I've been wildly bullish about it for a long time.

Japan

LG: What about Japan?

Jim Rogers: I don't have any investments there at the moment. I'm going to Japan and I think I'm going to buy some things. Japan is the richest country in the world right now, but it's still a very expensive place in which to do business. The stock market is still high for the most part. It's still very expensive by my traditional measurements anyway — low dividends, high P/Es. Some companies are becoming cheap. Interest rates are unbelievably low right now in Japan — they can only go higher, but that doesn't necessarily mean the market can't go up.

Japan may be the richest country in the world and getting richer, but the Japanese do have serious problems. They live longer than we do, for a lot of reasons. As the population is ageing, they've got a very serious demographic problem. I don't mean thirty years from now, but right now. That's one of the reasons the political structure in Japan is fracturing. There was a period between 1940 and 1960 when the birth rate dropped right off, so you've got all these old people and all these young people, with entirely different interests. The old people want high interest rates so that they can live off their savings. The young people want low interest rates and a flowing economy.

The point is, the wind's not at your back any more in Japan; it's at your face. But I fully expect there to be some interesting secular changes taking place there. The Japanese movie industry, for instance, used to be a great industry, but now it's at the stage where it's either going to disappear or have a revival. I'm going there to have a look. Even if it's going to disappear, there might be a lot of money to be made on a short-term revival.

One of the great things about stock market investing is you don't have to do something all the time. In fact, most of the time the best thing that you can do is do nothing. You know, look out of the window, go to the movies, drink beer. Most of the time, people think they've got to jump around and do something and that's when they make mistakes. Just wait; it's going to happen. If you saw some money lying in a corner, you'd go over and pick it up, wouldn't you? Well, just wait, and when you see something like that in the investment world, when you know there's money lying over there in the corner, run over and pick it up. *That's* when you do something.

The U.S. economy

LG: Can we talk about the United States? Everybody is saying, or at least the media are telling us, what great shape the U.S. economy is in. In your book *Investment Biker* you didn't think so. What do you think now?

Jim Rogers: In my book I made the point that we were a debtor nation; we were living off borrowed capital and it was getting worse. It's only gotten worse since then: we're living on more and more borrowed capital, gigantic amounts of borrowed capital right now, even though the recorded numbers of the budget deficit are now positive. If you and I kept books the way the U.S. government keeps books, we'd be in jail.

The government deficit has continued to build, so we're much more of a debtor nation now than we were when I wrote that book. I'm even more worried about it now because the magnitude has gotten greater and the bubble has gotten bigger. There wasn't really that much of a bubble in the stock market when I wrote that book. I was really talking about the big picture of the country and the macroeconomic trends of a major international debtor nation, major internal government debt, all of which have gotten worse, not better.

The tax structure is wacky and hasn't gotten better. If we had attacked the problems in 1994, that would have been one thing — we would have had some pain, but not too many people would have suffered. When the problems erupt in 1999 or 2000, or whenever they do so, it's going to hurt a lot of people because there are a lot of people now investing in the stock market who don't have a clue.

The market is going to go down some day. This isn't necessarily the top; it *might* be, but the top may have been made a year ago. Most stocks have been going down for a year. In 1986 a lot of smart guys, not me, sold out of Japan because the Nikkei Dow was 20,000 — much, much too expensive. Then it went to 40,000 over the next three years, so those guys looked like damn fools. Now it's 1999 and the Nikkei Dow is 16,000, down 20% from 1986 — thirteen years later — so who's the damn fool? The guy who sold out in 1986 and said this is madness, or the guy who stayed in and stayed in and said, "You don't know what you're talking about. This is a new era. We don't put on our trousers one leg at a time"?

So, these things always go on, on the upside more than anybody expects and likewise on the downside. If you had said to anybody in 1986, even to the smart guys who sold out, that in 1999 the Nikkei Dow would be at 16,000, that would have been the end of you.

We're at a stage in America where, the next time the economy gets worse, the budget deficit is going to reappear in spades because a lot of the so-called budget balancing is from capital gains taxes, which won't be there if the economy slows down. When you stop having capital gains taxes, you have a reinforcing process where taxes go down, welfare benefits go up, and the deficit gets much, much worse.

Internet stocks

LG: Would you like to say something about Internet stocks?

Jim Rogers: The Internet is going to change the world, more than any of us know. A kid who is under five years old today will probably never go to a post office, never go to a bank, never need a life insurance agent. He'll never meet his lawyer. Never meet his accountant. His accountant could be somebody in India at the other end of a computer. Everything is going to change. A lot of the shopping that we do will change. The automobile is going to have to be reinvented, too.

The Internet is going to do as much to change the world as did the telephone or electricity or the radio — there's no question about that. It will change the world perhaps even more dramatically than some of those things did. Take the railroad; I would remind you that anybody who bought railroad stocks in the middle of the wild booms of the nineteenth century never made much, even though railroads became a huge business.

If you bought some of those great technological breakthroughs that have occurred at various times — such as Sperry Rand, which invented the computer — you probably never really made any money. IBM made all the money in computers, so you picked the wrong company. Just because an industry changes the world, it doesn't mean you're going to make any money if you buy that industry at the wrong time in the frenzy. Most such companies don't survive, so you've got to buy the three that survive and not buy the sixty-three that are going to disappear.

LG: Would you like to suggest which ones are going to survive?

Jim Rogers: I don't have a clue. The automobile changed America and changed the world, but there were a hundred automobile companies in the U.S. seventy years ago, so if you had bought them, you wouldn't necessarily have made any money. Likewise, the railroad industry. Hundreds of railroads existed. In the 1960s there were computer companies and computer leasing companies, but you wouldn't have made any money unless you happened to buy the one or two that survived, and even then you might not have made any money because you probably paid too much for them.

I don't have a clue which ones are going to survive. I haven't bothered to find out about the managements to see who is smart and who isn't. Everybody is smart right now. They're too expensive for me to buy; it's too much madness for me to sell them short. Even if I were in the States I wouldn't sell them short, because I've learnt that just because something is too expensive, it doesn't mean it won't get even more expensive. Too many times in my life I've been assured that something is at its absolute top, then watched it double. There is more madness coming to the fore, and you've really got to find the catalyst. When a mania is going on, it's not just a matter of finding the catalyst that's going to be the negative change; you've got to find the thing that's going to make the perception of the negative change. Since I'm out here on the road, there's no way I'm going to be shorting Internet stocks.

On life after Wall Street

LG: You decided to retire at thirty-seven, I think. But what did that really mean?

Jim Rogers: Well, I didn't know — it's like a lot of those things I've said in my life: that this is something I wanted to do. I set out to do it, and I did it, and I didn't quite know what it meant to do it. Since I was sixteen, I've wanted to have more than one kind of life, more than one career. By the time I was thirty-seven, I'd made a little bit of money, more than I knew existed in the world when I was growing up in Alabama, which doesn't mean it's a lot of money. In Alabama, if somebody had come into town with an extra $200 in his pocket, the whole town would have gone through rapid inflation.

I knew that one of the things I wanted to do was to go around the world on a motorcycle — that had long been a dream. I set out to try to do that, and I pulled it off. It took me longer than I thought it would, because it was impossible to do, I know now. But I persisted, and just by being persistent I was able to do it. Finally, after years of trying, the Chinese said yes; finally, the Russians said yes. I stumbled into a little bit of a career as a professor, which I thoroughly enjoyed. Never in a million years would I have put that on the list of things I was going to do, but I did a lot more than I ever thought I would. I stumbled by chance into TV and broadcasting. I had a lot of fun doing that, but I would hardly call these careers; they were just diversions along the way. These things took time and energy and I had a lot of fun doing them, but they're not things where you make a lot of money.

I have a lot of friends on Wall Street who are content just to pile up money. There's nothing wrong with that if it's what they want to do. But I wanted to do more than one thing, and to have the great fun I've had doing public speaking, and going around the world, and writing articles, and being a professor. I could have used that time and made a lot more money, but I still make money in the market. I can pay my bills and still go around the world for three years.

I didn't want to wake up when I was seventy-five and have somebody say of me, "Rogers, one of the greatest investors who ever lived." I wanted to do more than that. Don't misunderstand me, the financial markets are the single most exciting way I know of to make a living. More exciting than anything else, because the whole world is your oyster — it's always changing, it's a four-dimensional puzzle. The fourth dimension is time — you come in at 10 o'clock and you know the puzzle and at 10.08 somebody changes all the pieces, so the puzzle is wildly exciting and there is no other profession in the world that's that exciting.

One of the great joys of going around the world is that out here I have no idea what's going to happen to me five minutes, or five kilometers, from now. I don't know if I'm going to be in jail, in the hospital, rich — I have no concept. I don't know what I'm going to see, or who I'm going to meet, so going around the world is a little bit like the market, only more exhilarating in its own way.

Africa

LG: So, Africa is a place to invest. You mentioned Ghana, but where else would you suggest?

Jim Rogers: I'm not sure I'd invest in Ghana at the moment. I invested in Ghana a long time ago. I'm optimistic about the future of Africa, much more so than many parts of the world. More so than Central Europe, for instance, or Russia. The Africans have been through their euphoric period. They went through all sorts of euphoria in the 1950s and 1960s when the liberators came.

Africa has been a disaster for decades, but the reason is that in the 1950s and 1960s they had the liberation movement. All the liberators became dictators; they started stripping or confiscating assets, buying votes, and passing laws and regulations — "Oh, don't worry," they said. "This is a short-term thing" — and it ruined Africa. Then the CIA and the KGB got involved in Africa, so there were wars. Africa doesn't have to be a catastrophe. In the 1950s Ghana was the richest country in the British Empire — in fact, Ghana alone was richer than most of the British Empire. Ghana was richer than Thailand, a reasonably comparable country. Nigeria was richer than Indonesia — both oil countries.

The Asian miracle we all know about, but in the 1950s there was an African miracle. A lot of those African countries did well. When the Berlin Wall fell in 1989 there were three open economies in Africa and now there are ten times that many. Nothing goes straight up and nothing goes straight down, but I submit to you that Africa is changing for the better. The wars are winding down. They did away with the KGB. There are lots of entrepreneurs. There are 800 million people in Africa, and they are opening those economies. Africa is the land of great natural resources and we're seeing the bottom. You are going to see great fortunes come out of Africa in the next ten to twenty years because all of Africa is cheap and there is positive change.

Where to invest? Zimbabwe, at the moment. The guy who runs Zimbabwe, Mugabe, periodically goes mad and he's gone mad again. The country is a disaster. I find Zimbabwe attractive at the moment to buy because no matter how bad Mugabe messes things up in the next year or two, he's not going to ruin Zimbabwe. They have a lot of resources. It is essentially one ethnic group. It's a time to buy. Ghana's up a lot, so I wouldn't buy Ghana at the moment. South Africa I don't include. Now that Mandela has gone, we're probably going to see a period of turmoil in South Africa.

I would love to get involved with Mozambique. There is no stock market in Mozambique, which is a problem. Uganda is high on my list, as is Ethiopia. There's a little war going on there right now, but it's coming to an end and it's going to be a very, very exciting place. I plan to visit Ethiopia next year and see it for myself, war or no war. Eritrea is also high on my list. Zambia is a place that I was involved in, but I'm not involved at the moment. Zambia and Angola are places that one should be aware of. If there was a way to get involved in Angola right now, I would, despite the fact that the war is still simmering. Egypt is a good chance to buy next year.

LG: What would be your preconditions for investing in Egypt?

Jim Rogers: Egypt has discovered a lot of hydrocarbons in the last few years and will soon be an exporter of hydrocarbons, which is pretty remarkable given that ten years ago it was a net importer in a big way. They've got a huge population, which is good because you need a big market. If the macro picture continues to improve, I may have to invest in Egypt.

LG: What about the rest of the Maghreb: Algeria, Morocco …?

Jim Rogers: Not Algeria, unless something pretty dramatic happens soon. There's too much internal conflict right now. Morocco had a boom earlier in the 1990s, but maybe by the time I get there in 2000 it will be time for another boom. Likewise Tunisia.

Pick the stock or the country?

LG: Do you think that finding the places that are going to boom is much more important than finding the right company?

Jim Rogers: Well, both is best. Most great companies aren't going to go up a lot unless the stock market goes up. In the 1970s there were a lot of American companies that were doing wonderful things but really didn't do anything in the stock market because the stock market wasn't doing anything. No matter how much people talk about internationalization and globalization, the main market for a company stock is its home country. Some break out and become more international, but they are very few in number and they usually don't last long because if their own market collapses they get hurt no matter how much the international community loves them.

You've got to find the right stock market, and you've got to find the right company as well. It's rare that the right company will do well unless the stock market does well too. It's more likely that if you get the right stock market a lot of companies will go up, than vice versa. In a stock market that's going down, you may have five great companies, but chances are they won't do so well. If the German market is going down, those five great companies aren't necessarily going to do well. If the German stock market's going up, even the five worst companies are going to go up and the five great companies are going to go up a lot. So, I'd say the market is usually more important than the company.

If an investor is really looking at the long term, he'll probably be looking for the right company. But if you look at the number of companies that have been great investments for even twenty years, there are very, very few of them. It's much more likely to be the case that a country's stock market has done well for thirty years than that a company has done well for that long. It would have been a lot smarter in 1965 to invest in Japan than to buy the best ten companies in America. If you still owned Japan, you would be better off now than if you still owned those ten best American companies. You're not likely to be able to leave them to your kids unless you happened to find those ten or so rare companies that are just going to go on and on forever. Most people don't find those ten long-term winners; they may find three, but the others sort of flop around and do nothing.

LG: Could we talk a bit about risk? I take it that the idea with your method is to get high returns — very, very high returns, if you make the right call.

Jim Rogers: I don't particularly like taking risks. I don't ever go to the casino, for instance, other than just to look around and say, "Isn't this amusing." I know that if I go to the casino I'm going to lose money, and I don't like taking that sort of risk.

LG: What I was going to suggest was that you will make such high returns if you get it right, that it's actually quite a low risk because what you stand to lose isn't very much.

Jim Rogers: Exactly. If you do it right and the things are cheap, you're probably not risking more than stagnant money, or maybe a loss in the order of 10%. But don't misunderstand the risk of stagnant money — it can be very painful, especially in inflationary times. Anybody who bought gold in 1981 or even in 1986, when gold was making a low, had pretty painful stagnant money for eleven years. I don't like risk. I try to find things that I think are ignored or unnoticed, but where, even if I'm wrong, I'm not going to lose a lot of money and if I'm right, I'm going to make an enormous amount of money.

If you bought Japan in 1955, which I didn't, you'd be rich. Forget trading, because you've got it right. The time to get out is when you see that some major negative secular changes are taking place. That kind of investing I love. I'm too lazy, especially now in my retirement — I love that kind of investing, because I can forget about it and not bother with it.

LG: How long do you like to hold for? Or expect to hold for?

Jim Rogers: I don't ever want to have to sell. If I sell, first of all I've got to make another decision. I've got to do more work to decide it's time to sell and then I've got to find something else to do with the money.

Remember, you've got to get the social, political, and economic situation right. Some countries are pretty dependent on a few industries or products. You may think Chile is a great place to invest, but if you don't understand copper, you can forget how great Chile is if copper is going down the tubes. Chile could be the greatest country in the world and be making the greatest changes in the world, but not a whole lot is going to happen there with copper going down the tubes.

I have some countries that I've owned a long time and it grieves me to have to sell them. Argentina, which I thought I would never sell, I sold back in 1997 because I could see too many things going wrong in the world and I knew this would affect Argentina. I owned some

Asian stock and was short Hong Kong in 1997 because I thought that Hong Kong was the place where Asia would start to fall apart. That shows how much I know — I should have been short Thailand and Malaysia. It was a nice experience, don't get me wrong, because I made a whole lot of money, but if I had been short Thailand or Malaysia, I'd have made more.

I've since bought back Thailand and some of Singapore. I don't own them yet in a big way, because I'm still waiting for something to go wrong with China and Indonesia, as I mentioned earlier. When I buy Asia again, I think I'll probably own it for the rest of my life. I don't know yet which companies or which countries I'll buy, because I don't know how it's going to unfold. I'm sure I'll buy the wrong thing. I'm sure that if I buy Thailand, Malaysia will go up thirty times and Thailand only twenty times, but that'll be enough. I can still pay the heating bills if it goes up only twenty times.

LG: Do you think a lot of people do too much because they're trying to make money very quickly?

Jim Rogers: If you get out the compound interest tables you can see that if you just compound steadily, you'll make a whole lot more money than if you go up 40% a year for three years in a row and then lose 40%. For the most part, you haven't really done a whole lot. But if you just clip along there at 12% or 14% a year for five or six years in a row, you might not have as much fun as if you had gone up 40% and then down 40%, but you'll sure make a lot more money and I guess that's the key.

This is how I make my living. I pay the rent from my investments; I don't have a job, and so I have to get it right. From my point of view, it's a whole lot more important to get it right than it is to have the fun of jumping around and being able to brag about soaring profits. The reverse side of that is always sudden massive losses, which no-one brags about. It's better just to make money consistently. Find the things that you're pretty sure are going to work and then invest in them — and always have something on the short side to make sure that you're covered if, out of the blue, something does go really wrong.

LG: A lot of people were surprised that interest rates have come down as far as they have. Was that a shock to you?

Jim Rogers: I'm astonished that the rates have come down as much as they have. It turns out it was because of the Long-Term Capital Management jiggle (see page 136).

LG: Isn't it a great time to borrow money long term?

Jim Rogers: Yes. If you're thinking about taking out a mortgage and you're in Europe, Japan, or the U.S., I would strongly urge you to stop reading this book right now and rush out and take out the mortgage. By the time this book is published it may be too late. I would strongly urge you to borrow as much long-term money as you can right now.

I don't think we're going to see these days again. Even if we do, if there is an economic setback in the next few years, which I expect, it's going to be hard to borrow money. The bankers don't like to lend money when things are bad. But right now, when interest rates are very low, they love to lend money. Just the fact that you have it will be useful in a few years' time when it will be much harder to borrow money.

Latin America

LG: What are your views on Latin America?

Jim Rogers: I'm very optimistic about Latin America. I'm optimistic about Central America, but not particularly about Mexico because the Mexicans haven't learnt their lesson. The Americans have bailed out Mexico four or five times in the last few decades. Every time Mexico gets in trouble, the Americans step in and write them a check. The rest of Latin America have learnt their lessons. We all know about Latin America — the banana republics, the military coups, the hyperinflation — but that's all changing. I'm convinced that a fundamental change has occurred in the psyche of Latin America.

I sold out of Argentina when it looked like trouble was brewing, but I still own Peru, Chile, and Ecuador, which isn't helping me right now. I sold out of Brazil and Venezuela, but I still own El Salvador.

LG: Why did you sell Brazil?

Jim Rogers: The problem with Brazil is it's the next great country in the world. It always has been, and always will be, say the Brazilians. God created the most wonderful country in the world and called it Brazil, and then he put the Brazilians in it. They say this of themselves. I would be much more confident about Brazil if the country were split in two, which I suspect will happen some day. Perhaps I'll buy Brazil again — let's see. If the market goes down 80%, then sure. If the market goes down 18%, no.

Again, one doesn't have to make these decisions today. I don't have a board of directors howling at me. I don't have a bunch of mutual fund shareholders calling me up and saying, "What are you doing? Why aren't you jumping into something new?" I don't have to bother with all that kind of stuff.

Diversification kills?

LG: Warren Buffett only owns a handful of shares. It sounds like you own a lot — isn't that over-diversifying?

Jim Rogers: It may sound that way, but it depends on how you look at it. If I own Peru, I may own fifteen companies in Peru, but for the most part I consider that just one position. Or if I own the tea industry — which I don't at this point — I may own fifteen companies in the tea industry but, again, I consider that to be one position. So, yes and no. I'd have a lot of companies in, say, the tea industry if I were very bullish on tea. I don't consider that a lot of positions, because it's one phone call to sell them all.

I own the European defense industry, but that's not twenty positions for me, that's one. The non-U.S. hydrocarbons are one position, within limits. I don't particularly like a lot of diversification either, because diversification can kill you. It's wonderful having seven out of ten stocks that go up, but if the other three go down, that's bad. It's better to have six stocks that go up, period, and a couple of shorts that go down — that's the ideal as far as I'm concerned. So no, I don't really like diversification. I like to buy things that I'm confident about.

One difference between me and Warren is that I'll get very optimistic about the European defense industry and I'll buy them all, while he might find a great company in Europe in the defense industry and buy a lot of it. I just buy all of them, because invariably if I got bullish on the European defense industry and only bought one company, it would be the worst one. I was short Hong Kong and that was the worst country to short in Asia.

LG: It's not possible to short some foreign exchanges directly. How do you short?

Jim Rogers: You can actually short ADRs [American Depository Receipts] all over the world, just about. These days there are usually some mutual funds you can sell short somewhere. There are more and more indexes that you can short. You can short the index or the options, so even if England doesn't let you sell short, you can short the FTSE index. There are ways to do it: you can sell options; you can sell calls.

LG: Do you use warrants?

Jim Rogers: Not on the long side. I usually only use options and warrants to sell. Warrants are long-term options — long-term calls. You're always having to pay a premium, and time is going against you. There was a study done, I think by the Securities and Exchange Commission, which discovered that 90% of people who buy options lose money, because they've got time going against them, and they've got the premium to pay. So, I figured that that means 90% of people who *sell* options make money. So it's been years since I've bought an option. If I'm bullish on a company, I might very well sell a put. If I'm bearish on a company, I might very well sell calls. If you sell the call short, you've got time on your side and you've got the premium on your side. You can sell an option short and be wrong on the stock and make money. For instance, let's say IBM is at 110. If you sell 135 calls short, the stock can go to 134 and you can make 100% on your money. You can be dead wrong on the stock and still make 100% on your money, as long as it happens by August. That's one of the reasons I adore selling options, and I do a lot of it because you can sit around and be dead wrong and still make money. Let's say that IBM goes to 137 — if you sold it at 4, you'll still make 50% on your money by maturity. It's a wonderful thing.

Oil

LG: Can we talk about oil? I'm very intrigued that you're bullish when everybody is saying it'll never go back up.

Jim Rogers: You just made my case, partly. There was a lot of learned analysis in 1981 about how oil couldn't help but go to $100 a barrel. Before the 1960s, when oil was about $3 a barrel, it was technologically impossible to drill more than 1500 meters for oil. Then there were enormous, incredible technological breakthroughs in the oil industry, so that you could drill down to 10,000 meters. You could drill out in the North Sea. There was the Hughes diamond drill bit, which could just drill and drill and drill, while the old drill bits would wear out after 5 meters. Despite these great technological changes, the price of oil went up fifteen times.

I've heard this story before about how oil can't go up, because of technological breakthroughs and because the world is different now. The number of drilling rigs has declined over the last few years, and not much money has gone into oilfield productive capacity. Very few people have built offshore drilling rigs, much less boats to go out and service them — those boats have all been converted to stockbrokers' yachts to take out mutual fund customers!

Inventories have been whittled down, but I'm optimistic that the use of oil will continue to rise. Look at China. When I was last in China, there were virtually no cars, virtually no motor scooters. Right now there are more taxis alone in this town than there were cars the last time I was here. Hydrocarbon consumption has continued to grow and the world hasn't added a lot to its reserves in the last few years.

The other reason I'm optimistic about oil is because Saudi Arabia is essentially bankrupt right now.

LG: Can you expand on that?

Jim Rogers: If you look at the IMF [International Monetary Fund] and World Bank numbers you'll see that in 1981 Saudi Arabia was one of the five largest foreign reserve currency owners in the world. Now Saudi Arabia is a gigantic debtor nation. They have huge overheads in Saudi Arabia: they've got all those princes and all those social services where everything is free. The princes have got all their mistresses and cars and everything else, so Saudi Arabia is now a very, very large debtor nation.

LG: But isn't all the money hidden elsewhere?

Jim Rogers: It may be hidden elsewhere, but it's in private accounts and they're not going to bring it back into Saudi Arabia to bail out the country. The point I'm making is that if the price of oil stays down, Saudi Arabia is going to go bankrupt and the price of oil is going to go higher. Or the price of oil will increase and bail out Saudi Arabia. So, either way, the price of oil is going to go higher.

A couple of other countries are in a similar situation: they kept spending even though they had run out of money. There are lots of reasons to be bullish on hydrocarbons. I know the technological arguments, I know the bit about Iraq. But even if Iraq comes back on, it's going to take them a while to do so. Don't buy oil in the United States. Buy international hydrocarbons.

I don't really think that the price of oil is going to go to $150 a barrel in the next ten years. It could, it could very well do so, if you have a couple of wars or something. I'll settle for a triple. Right now, if the price of oil triples I'll make more money than I deserve. I'll be able to pay the light bill.

Interpreting accounts

LG: Company accounts in many countries either don't follow the same standards as the U.S. or don't come up to the same standards as U.S. companies, which themselves must be taken with a pinch of salt. As an investor, what can you do about it?

Jim Rogers: I know we in America like to hold ourselves out as having great standards and everything, but I've been an investor for a little over thirty years and I'll tell you that at the end of the 1960s, for instance, when I started, American accounting was hopeless. Somehow, people were able to invest in the stock market and make a living. In the 1930s it was even worse.

As long as everybody has got the same playing field, it can be done. People were able to do a lot of good research and make a lot of good money in American stocks in the 1960s, appalling as our accounting standards were, just as they were before that.

If I look at country X, maybe their accounting standards are only where America was in the 1950s, say; but if I'm looking at all the companies, I can at least make a comparison. And it's not just accounting. When you invest in anything, you need to understand the country, you need to understand the currency, you need to understand the industry, you need to understand the companies — you need to understand a lot of stuff, including the numbers.

The numbers are wildly important. Most people don't know how important they are. You've just got to do your homework. Even in America, every year there are accounting scams which come to the fore.

Nobody ever says it's easy to get rich. Certainly, nobody ever says it's easy to get rich in the stock market. I guess plenty of people think it's easy to get rich in the stock market right now. But it *isn't* easy. This isn't an easy way to make a living; it just looks that way. You have to work.

LG: If you get a balance sheet from, say, Ghana, how do you know that anything on it is real?

Jim Rogers: We will presume, if it's a company in which you're going to invest, that you would have learnt a bit about the industry. I try to do statistical analysis and if I see that the inventories are increasing for some reason, I like to figure out why. It's not just your company; you have to do it for the whole industry.

If you're looking at the plumbing industry, say, you need to look at all the companies in the plumbing industry to see if something strange is going on. As long as all the plumbing companies in Ghana use more or less the same standards, an anomaly might stand out. Now, there are not that many companies in the plumbing industry in Ghana, so I'm being a little simplistic, but if you do those numbers and ask the questions and call around, you might or might not find out that something is going wrong.

You've got to read the annual reports, you've got to read the numbers, you've got to look at the numbers on a historic basis going back ten or fifteen years to see where there may be a change.

LG: That's not always easy to do, is it, getting the historic figures?

Jim Rogers: Listen, if you know of an easy way to make a living, please tell me! I want to take that pill, I want to take that course, I want to learn it!

You've just got to go back and get the annual reports for company X, as far back as you can get them. And if you don't have enough information, don't invest. There's no rule that says you've got to invest in this company in Ghana, or that industry in Ghana. It's better to do nothing most of the time than do something that you can't get enough information about.

On being too smart

LG: Is it possible to be too smart for your own good as an investor?

Jim Rogers: Sometimes you're so smart you don't make any money. I know plenty of times I've been too smart, which in the end means I was really dumb. Harley Davidson motorcycles is a perfect example. I've been riding motorcycles for a long time, been around the world on one, been in the *Guinness Book of Records* and all that. Harley Davidson went public and I wouldn't have bought it even with *your* money!

I knew that it was a hopeless motorcycle and a hopeless company. Then the stock went up twenty times or something, despite it still being a hopeless motorcycle. I have to admit they've done a brilliant job. I know a lot about motorcycles — I know it's the last motorcycle in the world you'd want to go around the world on, the last motorcycle you'd want to do most things on. But none of that matters if everybody in the world is dying to have one! If you get yourself a Harley Davidson and take it down to your local bar, everyone will stand around outside and check it out. It's one of the great investing stories of the last fifteen years, and I missed every bit of it. I knew too much — I was too smart for my own good.

LG: It does seem to me that however closely you analyse companies and compare industries, it isn't the way to make good decisions. Is it possible to overdo that kind of analysis?

Jim Rogers: Absolutely. I can't tell you how many times I've been too early on something because I figured everybody else knew what I knew. I now realize that not everybody knows what I know when I know it, and that I have to factor that in.

The future of agriculture

LG: What are your views on food in the future?

Jim Rogers: The world has always somehow found enough food. When there's not enough food around, the price goes through the roof. I'm optimistic about agriculture. If you look at the past thirty years, we had huge increases in food prices in the 1970s because there was a shortage of food, but by the mid-1980s the world had its highest ever inventories of foodstuffs.

Since then we've worked off those inventories. At the moment, food prices are low because Asia stopped buying last year, but we now have the lowest inventories we've had in a long time. You're going to see a big boom in food over the next five to fifteen years. This has happened every three decades or so throughout history. Supply and demand are getting out of whack again. Most of the arable land that people can bring on has already been brought on, and most of the marginal land has been brought back into production.

Asia will have to start buying again soon, because their inventories are down. If we have bad weather, the story gets even better.

In the last ten or fifteen years, lots of people have gotten an MBA. Ten years ago most parts of the world didn't even have MBA programs, but now they're everywhere. What they should be doing is starting programs in universities called A&M — agricultural and mechanical — where you go to study engineering or agriculture. People should be taking mining courses or agricultural courses, instead of doing an MBA.

If you look at the figures, you'll see that most commodities made their lows in 1992 or 1993. The Asian crisis hit again in 1997–98 and most commodities went down — but I don't think you'll find more than one or two that made new lows. So, in my view we're having a period here in the 1990s where agriculture and raw material prices are making their lows in preparation for the next big bull market in raw materials.

We've had a long bull market in shares, but that's coming to an end, and we're now going to have a long bull market in raw materials. There's nothing magical about any of this.

LG: Because of your bearishness on Central Europe, you wouldn't go buying agricultural companies in, say, Hungary?

Jim Rogers: Absolutely not. Hungary is going to be at war with at least one of its neighbors some time in the next few years. All the borders in Central Europe are artificial borders; they were drawn up in 1945 by the victorious armies who were rewarding their friends and punishing their enemies. Actually, you could say they were drawn in 1918 and then Stalin saw them and said, "These are the ones we want to keep; these are the ones we're going to change." There have been problems in that part of the world for centuries — ethnic problems, religious problems, linguistic problems, national problems — and they're going to come back. If you think those borders are stable now, then you must think that Stalin was a great statesman, and I for one don't think that.

That part of the world is going to experience economic disillusionment. When the Berlin Wall came down in 1989, everybody was euphoric. "Now we've got democracy," they said, "which means we're going to have prosperity." They'd all seen "Dallas" on TV — in America they have democracy, America is like "Dallas," so let's be rich. But they don't have anything to sell to the world. Under the communists the manufacturing was hopeless; they just sold to each other. There was no quality, no competitiveness, no manufacturing skills — or virtually none. More and more economic disillusionment is setting in and that's bringing up those age-old animosities. You're going to see what's happening in Yugoslavia happen in other parts of Central Europe.

I'm not optimistic about Central Europe. It's a little like after Africa got its independence: there was huge euphoria, everybody rushed in to invest a lot of money, and then it got worse and worse until Africa spiraled down for forty years. I see no reason to get involved in Central Europe. There are other places where the wind can be at your back. This is a hard business we're in; despite appearances to the contrary, it's a hard way to make an easy living.

Why go to a place like Central Europe where you're going to have the wind hard in your face? There'll be rallies, and if you get it right you can get in and make a few dollars, but you've got to be nimble, you've got to be a trader. I'm a horrible trader. First of all, I'm no good at trading; and second, I don't like it because it's work.

Traders — born or made?

LG: A lot of people who are attracted to trading are perhaps fairly naïve. Do you think it takes a certain personality type to make it as a trader?

Jim Rogers: Yes. I've worked with some great traders in my day and I don't know if you're born with it, or you learn it, or how it happens, but the good ones who've got it are really very good at it. I never really had that ability or skill or whatever it is and never even wanted to develop it.

With some of those guys, it's just astonishing. Thirty years ago I worked with a guy named Roy Neuberger, who is now in his nineties. Roy would sit and read the newspaper. The market opened at 10 a.m. and he started working at 5 minutes to 10. He would sit there reading the newspaper and then pick up the phone and say, "There's a big block of IBM for sale on the floor. I want to buy x million shares at such and such a price, two points below the market." I would ask him, "How did you know that?" I mean, I never even saw him looking at the tape, but he must have watched it occasionally and he could tell by the way the stock market was acting that something was going on in IBM. Lo and behold, nine times out of ten it happened. It was the damndest thing I ever saw in my life.

He'd been sitting there doing this for forty years. He told me stories about how he went to work for Wall Street in 1929 at the top. He left the retail business because everybody knew that was a bad business. Everybody knew that the great place to make money was Wall Street, so he went to work on Wall Street and by 1932 he was wiped out. He didn't have enough sense to leave because he loved it so much. He learnt to trade, he told me, and it was just like the retail business. You buy them and you sell them. You mark them up and you sell them. In the era in which he went into Wall Street, the only way you could survive was by trading. In those days, long-term investment was for madmen because stocks always went down.

He also learnt how to short. That's the way it was; everybody knew that stocks always went down, so he would trade them. He couldn't care less about the whole concept of long-term investing, or doing research, or digging out big macro trends. He was a fantastic trader and still is. He still goes to work every day and trades. There are about 200 companies that he's been trading for fifty or sixty years now. He doesn't see Yahoo! go by on the tape, even though Yahoo! may be the most active stock on the whole stock market, but when IBM goes by he knows every tick.

So, the ones who are great at it are *really* great at it. But I think they would tell you this isn't an easy business. Day traders are multiplying by the millions in America, because "stocks always go up." I don't know how it will end up when the margin calls start coming.

LG: Are all these day traders doing it on margin?

Jim Rogers: I would presume they are. They probably started out doing it in cash accounts, but by now it's like hedge funds. Everybody has learnt that the way to make a lot of money is not just to buy stocks, but to buy them on margin, buy the options, buy the futures. Why sit around and buy stocks at 100%? Buy them on margin, buy their calls, get the leverage.

Whenever an industry gets hot, everybody tries to figure out how to get to be the richest. If it's real estate, they figure out a way to leverage themselves to the full. If shipping is hot, they go and buy tankers, but they don't put up any money at all; they figure out a way to do a deal. They leverage themselves to the hilt; that's the way to get the richest the fastest. It's also the sign of the top in shipping, or real estate, or wheat, or whatever it happens to be. I'm sure that the day traders probably started out without margin, but by now they've all figured out a way to do it, even if it's just to borrow money on their credit card and stick it in the market.

LG: Have you ever used leverage in a big way, and if so, in what circumstances?

Jim Rogers: Yes. Back when we had the fund [with George Soros] we always leveraged to the hilt. In my own account back then I didn't have any money, so of course I would use as much leverage as I possibly could. Since then, not usually, because I'm not trying to lead the league any more; I'm just trying to pay the rent and see a bit of the world. Back in 1987 I had a lot of shorts, and you have to have leverage to sell short. When I was short the ruble, I had to have a lot of leverage to make it worth my while.

How to deal on foreign exchanges

LG: Although it's getting easier for smaller private investors to purchase stocks directly on foreign exchanges, it's still quite tough. Take an African country, for example. How are you going to find an honest broker over there, or are you going to pay a lot of extra charges for using a U.S. broker?

Jim Rogers: Using a U.S. broker isn't at all wise. I've heard some real horror stories about how much people have had to pay when investing abroad. A guy once told me he invested in an Australian company that I own — he told me that he bought the company when he read that I liked it. Incidentally, never do something because someone says in the press to do so. That's madness. Do it only because you know a lot about it yourself. He said he bought the stock and he lost 50%. I said, "How can you lose 50%?" The stock has never been below the price it was at when I mentioned it in the press; in fact, it's been going up. His American broker had charged him so much that the guy lost 50% of his money.

If I'm in a country where I'm not known and don't have any reputation, I don't ever say, "Oh, by the way, I'm ..." I just go in and say I want to open an account. I never tell them anything or ask any special favors. You can open an account just about anywhere in the world. I always go to the largest bank in a country, because you don't have to worry then about the brokers going bankrupt. If the largest bank in the country does go bankrupt they're going to be nationalized, they're going to be forced into a merger with somebody, and they'll nearly always have an office in the States, so it helps communication. So, anybody can do that. If you're living in Kansas City, you can do that. I've never been to Ghana, but I've been investing in Ghana since the day the Ghana stock market opened six years ago.

LG: So, you don't take physical possession of stock certificates; you let your broker hold the certificates. Do you deposit money with them so that there isn't a problem with settlement and so on?

Jim Rogers: First of all, I never take delivery. Some countries try to send you the shares whether you want them or not. I've gotten my shares from Ghana two or three times. I've even had dividend checks from Ghana. I have to send them back. That's why you should choose the largest bank — they're not going to go broke. They'll keep your certificates, you hope. They'll collect your dividends, you hope, which you reinvest as fast as you can because you know that the currency is collapsing in many countries. These days, this is less necessary because more and more exchanges are becoming electronic and they have central deposits. Paper shares are really an anachronism.

LG: Does it ever worry you that a big bank that you are using as a broker in a small country might suddenly just forget about you, or not send you statements or your money?

Jim Rogers: I'm terrified of everything in the world, but the only thing I know to do is to get involved with the largest bank, and then to watch things to make sure it's OK. I know things will go wrong. When I was going around the world last time, I went to invest in Bolivia. The banks didn't do it and I had to go to a broker. I went to a broker who I was told was large. (In those days you didn't have large brokers; you barely had brokers at all.) A year or two later I called and said that I wasn't getting any statements. After first saying they couldn't find the broker, they changed their story and said he had died of AIDS. It seemed to me very unlikely that the broker could have contracted and died of AIDS so quickly. I don't know what happened to the money. I never saw a penny of it. It wasn't a whole lot of money, so I never bothered to pursue it. It would have taken more time than it was worth to collect it. When you're the first one in — or one of the first ones — don't rush in and make a big splash until you know that the infrastructure is sound. I always start out small, just in case.

There aren't many markets anymore where you can be the first. There are probably 10,000 people on planes flying around the world right now looking for markets in which to invest.

LG: You said in your book that John Templeton will invest before

currencies are freely convertible, but that *you* won't. Do you have any
more to say about that?

Jim Rogers: Well, it's still an accurate statement, I think. I've been
thinking of investing directly in China only because I believe it's going
to have to be opened before too much longer. I have always wanted to
make sure it was convertible. If, when a country opens up, the big
names are going in there, missing the first 10% or 20% isn't going to
be the end of the world. You're going to make a lot of money in the
end anyway. I'd just as soon wait to make sure it has really happened.

The best thing to do is to go to a foreign country. People take
vacations. If you're interested in Australia, or Malaysia, go there instead
of going to Denver on your next holiday. Open an account. You can do
your homework before you go, then open an account when you
arrive. These days, many brokerages have offices in the States, and if
not, you can open one by phone, fax, and email.

I've opened accounts in several countries that I've never been to. I
don't go in and say I'm some big dog in America, an international
investor and all that. I just call them and say I'm Joe Blow and I want
to open an account. You'd be astonished at how easy it is to open an
account these days. As long as you can send them legitimate
identification and your check clears, you can do it. People think it's
some kind of magic. Don't be afraid to do it. But you must do your
homework first. You must know what you're doing before you get
involved with a country.

LG: If you had a choice between an American-owned brokerage in
that country or a local broker, which would you choose?

Jim Rogers: I would usually choose the local broker, only because, as I
said before, if something happens to, say, Merrill Lynch in that country,
I'm not saying that Merrill Lynch wouldn't stand behind their local
office, but I know that the largest bank in the country will have to
stand behind their office one way or another. You also usually find that
the U.S.-owned foreign offices have bigger requirements and they
charge more.

I want to be with a local guy who doesn't try to do anything fancy with me, who'll just do what I tell him to do.

I don't take advice from brokers anywhere. One of my characteristics — whether it's a weakness or a strength, I'm not sure — is that I insist on making my own judgments and decisions. I don't want input from anybody else. I'm confused enough by myself! Other input just makes me more confused, so I avoid it.

LG: Isn't that true of anyone that's any good?

Jim Rogers: I can't speak for other people, but it's certainly true of me.

ADRS — a great American scam?

LG: What do you think about ADRs?

Jim Rogers: ADRs are a great scam, a great rip-off of the American public. ADRs were invented in 1927 by J. P. Morgan, and it was a fantastic thing at the time because in those days, if you wanted to buy shares in Germany, say, or England, you put your order on the boat and you shipped it over. Then you had to get your money there, and then wait for them to send the shares back to you by boat. All in all, it was a very time-consuming affair. So, J. P Morgan came up with this idea: "Look," he said. "We've got offices in Germany and Europe, so why don't we just buy the shares there? We'll keep them in the vault and our office in New York will give you a receipt saying the shares are on deposit in Germany." Brilliant. That was 1927. The world has changed since then. Nobody has paper shares anywhere much anymore, and you can wire money around the world instantly.

The American brokerage and banking community has done a great job of persuading Americans that ADRs are safer because it says right there, "American Depository Receipt." It's a form of protectionism because the American banks and brokers have bought into this. But they don't want to tell Americans that. Because it makes it very hard for a foreign investment banker to come to the United States and sell Deutsche Bank to the American public, the American brokers have convinced Americans they've got to buy ADRs. Leading banks say it's better, the brokers say it's better; it keeps the foreigners out as far as underwriting shares in America is concerned, or at least it makes it that much harder.

The banks love it because they get a little money every time a trade takes place. You go into some of the big banks in New York and there are hundreds of people working in the ADR department. I don't know what more evidence you need to indicate that, yes, somebody's making a whole lot of money, somebody's paying all those guys in there. But it's you, the investor, who is ultimately paying all those guys, and it's a very, very profitable business. I only use ADRs for selling short because of that little extra expense. It's not much, but in this business every little bit helps.

The other problem with ADRs is that they're not as liquid as shares because, by definition, they're only the ones in trade in America. By definition, it's much more liquid to trade in the original country.

LG: What about Global Depository Receipts (GDRs) and International Depository Receipts (IDRs)?

Jim Rogers: GDRs and IDRs are a recent development. The brokers and the bankers have figured it out; they get a little piece of everything. They try to convince investors that they're necessary, but for decades I and other people have been able to invest around the world without IDRs and GDRs. Brokers and bankers have somehow done a great marketing job of telling people they need to buy these things — they don't. It's nuts as far as I'm concerned. Again, I think all the evidence one needs is the fact that somebody is making a lot of money off these things and it's the investor who is paying for it.

Mutual funds

LG: Can we talk about funds in general and their true value?

Jim Rogers: First of all, no-one should invest in anything unless they know a lot about it. It's like everything else in life: don't do it unless you know a lot about it. That's something that people just don't want to hear; no matter how many times you try to explain it to them or demonstrate it, they don't want to hear. They think it's easy, they think they know enough. What you should do is find the things that you know a lot about — and everybody knows a whole lot about something, even if it's hairdressing, or the latest line of cosmetics, or the best football team. That's the best way to invest: stay with what you know, and don't invest in anything else. The best advice I can give most people is: do nothing until you find the right thing to do.

Most people shouldn't be investing. If they do invest, they should only do so if they've done a lot of homework and they stay just with things they know — they'll get very rich if they do that.

Right now there are 9000 mutual funds in America. Surely, we don't have that many smart twenty-nine-year-olds? At the moment it's like all of them are geniuses. Suppose I came to your door and said, "Look, my name is Joe Smith. I want you to write me a check for your life savings and give it to me and I'll take it to Boston and invest it. But I'm not going to tell you what I'm going to invest it in." You'd probably slam the door in my face and call the police.

Yet, every day, people sit down and write out checks for their life savings, send them off to Boston, New York, Chicago, or Philadelphia, to people they don't know anything about. To me it's mind-boggling. I wouldn't give that to anybody. Even if someone like Mother Theresa knocked on my door I wouldn't give her my money to invest for the rest of my life, especially if she refused to tell me what she was going to do with it.

People should really stay away from funds unless they do a lot of homework and find out who's investing the money, how they're going to invest it, what their record has been in the past, and how much they're going to charge you. Most people don't ask these questions, and the funds realize this. They tack on more and more charges, they raise their fees, they have hidden fees — the number of fees that they've come up with now is amazing. It has gotten to be a lucrative business, and since everybody now knows that investing in mutual funds is going to make them rich, they don't care how much it costs.

That's another reason you should invest yourself, because you don't have to pay that extra 2% or 4% or whatever. That compounds into a big, big rate over ten or twenty years; it makes a huge difference when you start paying all those extra fees.

The mutual fund industry has done a brilliant job of marketing. I know many people who say, "I don't want to invest in stocks because that's dangerous. I want to invest in funds because that's safe." They'll say, "I'm getting out of the stock market. I'll put my money in funds because the market has gotten too high."

I once did a show for TV in the States about mutual funds and we would have mutual fund managers on the show. One night in a restaurant a guy said to me, "Your show isn't about mutual funds. It's about the stock market," as though they were two different kinds of animal. People just don't understand; they think that a mutual fund is something different. This guy seemed to think that if he put mutual funds in his 401K, that was different from the stock market — he wouldn't have to worry, because everybody knows that mutual funds go up 15-18% a year!

My only worry about all of this is that when the day of reckoning comes, a lot of people are going to get badly hurt and there'll be a lot of repercussions that will make it that much more difficult to make a living in the stock market. You'll be up against a bunch of smart guys, instead of watching dumb guys. At least now there are 9000 mutual funds, which makes it a little easier.

There is an enormous amount of leverage in the system which we don't know about. The margin requirements are 50% in the States and have been 50% for decades now, but people can get around that with derivatives in a big, big way. In the 1920s, margin requirements were very low and that led to catastrophe. Now one of the supposed safeguards is that the margin requirements are 50%, but there's so much more leverage out there that it's getting around that rule. That's why when the collapse comes, everyone will blame it on derivatives, just as they blamed options or margins back in the 1920s.

Will the United States change its borders?

LG: You were talking about the next century being the century of

China, and I think you were suggesting that the U.S. won't be as rich in a hundred years' time as it is now.

Jim Rogers: The U.S. as we know it won't exist then. The borders will have changed — how, I don't know. Looking back a hundred years from now, you won't recognize the United States. The U.S. is now the world's largest debtor nation by a factor of many times, and this has been a period of prosperity. Can you imagine what a period of lack of prosperity will do in the U.S.?

No giant debtor nation has ever, thirty years later, gotten itself out of debt and become the rich and prosperous leader of the world. Countries that have built up gigantic debts have continued to lose their relative position, so certainly a hundred years from now, even if the U.S. isn't a debtor nation, it won't be anywhere near what it was. Portugal was once the richest country in the world, and the Netherlands was also once very rich, yet they've long since lost their position.

I can't think of a single country in the history of the world whose borders and government have lasted as long as 200 years. If you know of one, prove me wrong.

LG: What about Britain? Although admittedly its borders have constantly changed within those two islands, it has been around for well, shall we say, a few hundred years.

Jim Rogers: Yes, but I didn't say that Britain hasn't been there as a geographical entity. Remember, Ireland was part of the U.K. eighty years ago.

America, for historical reasons, has never been exposed to much of the rest of the world. First, it was virtually impossible because we were thousands of miles away from anything and we were always focusing on expanding our own interests, whether they were geographic, economic, political, or whatever. For most of its history, America didn't have to be, and wasn't, exposed to other histories, other cultures, other economies. I think that's one reason why there have never been many international investors in America. In America it's a new thing. Even twelve years ago I can remember people at

Morgan Stanley saying to me, "Isn't Australia a member of the Common Market?" and these were people in the international research department. I'm not making this up.

If you were to say to Americans that, in a hundred years, there's a very good chance that the country as we know it will no longer exist, you would be met with cries of disbelief and outrage. Americans are convinced that we're better than any nation, any group, any political entity that has ever been. Maybe we are, but I for one am skeptical about it.

LG: Could you delineate a few scenarios? I mean, are we talking about a sort of Hispanic nation in the southern states, something like that?

Jim Rogers: In much of the southern part of the United States the second language is certainly Spanish — the newspapers are in Spanish. It was part of Mexico historically, and was definitely stolen from Mexico. It's conceivable that you would have a large part of the southern United States essentially saying, "Well, wait a minute. We don't speak your language, we don't like what's going on there, you're going bankrupt, and you stole us in the first place." People can always revert to history when they need an excuse.

There are people in the northwest right now who think that the whole of the northwestern part of the U.S. and southwestern Canada are different from the rest of the States and Canada. They're very similar to each other, they're prosperous, they have a different attitude toward life. Already people out there are saying, hey, why don't we have our own country?

They are not taken too seriously right now, but nobody is ever taken too seriously when they first come up with an idea. Most new ideas are initially ignored; then they're hooted at, then vehemently fought against, before everybody comes around to believing that they're great.

Combining business with pleasure has to be the best way to live, and Jim Rogers is doing it. You can follow his "Millennium Adventure" on his website at www.jimrogers.com/, which logs video footage and text comments as he travels. The idea is to document as much of the world as possible during the three years 1999–2001 as a form of global cultural snapshot at the beginning of the third millennium.

2

Paul Melton: The Equal Asset Allocator

Many of the world's best investors choose to locate themselves far away from the frantic pace of Wall Street and London — Warren Buffett in Omaha and Sir John Templeton in the Caribbean being the most famous examples. It seems that for them, it's just not necessary to be immersed in the white heat of the financial furnace in order to perform well.

So it is with Paul Melton, who moved from New York to the picturesque European city of Amsterdam in the 1970s to pursue a career in the arts before becoming a portfolio manager and, subsequently, a popular speaker at investment seminars throughout the world. He has been quoted repeatedly in Forbes, *the* International Herald Tribune, Investors Chronicle, Portfolio International, Economia Internazionale, La Vie Française, *and a host of other financial publications both in the U.S. and Europe.*

Like most of the other investors in this book, Paul Melton is convinced of the advantages of investing widely across the world. His approach is conservative; it doesn't require an encyclopedic knowledge of obscure foreign economies or the ability to make split-second decisions. As he explains, his method is based on a model of his devising — he calls it the Melton Equal Global Asset Allocation index, or MEGA — which divides a portfolio across some twenty-two major world markets (totaling 70%) and assigns the remaining 30% to emerging markets.

It's not totally mechanical, however. You must choose your investments as you normally would within each market, periodically adjusting your holdings as they change in value to keep the overall balance in line with the MEGA index.

Sounds complicated? It isn't really, and you don't need a huge grubstake to put it into practice. Melton says that if you only invest in funds, you can start with as little as US$50,000 to make the method cost-effective, while if you are investing directly in equities you'll need at least US$350,000.

"There are three kinds of people in the world," goes an old joke. "People who can count and people who can't." Paul Melton is definitely one of the ones who can; the beauties of statistical arguments are overriding for him. He's not out for the huge hit, or the thrill of proving himself right in a series of stock picks or market plays. He's looking for steady — but superior — returns (a compound annual return of more than 26% on average capital invested since 1995 at end-September 1999), year in, year out.

Obviously, such an approach is a matter of temperament. If you are a super-aggressive speculator, or if you are under an inner compulsion to trade stocks every day, it's not going to appeal. But most of us don't have the time for hyperactive investment even if we'd like to; and even if you are *the active type, Melton's arguments are worth listening to — they could save you from some egregious mistakes.*

The rationale of Paul Melton's investment method is explained in detail in his book Going Global with Equities *(Financial Times, Pitman Publishing), which has become recommended reading for students at the Securities Institute in London and has been described as "the bible on global investing."*

Investors who want to adopt his approach for themselves can subscribe to his monthly newsletter, The Outside Analyst, *which, he says, is the only periodical that actually compares stocks worldwide. Since its inception in 1986, it has earned a reputation for sound research and informed analysis, based on Melton's constant search for the world's bargain equities, screening earnings estimates each month for more than 15,000 companies in over forty countries.*

The address of The Outside Analyst *is:*

P.O. Box 70322-TW
1007 KH Amsterdam
The Netherlands
Tel: +31 23 544 0501
Fax: +31 23 544 0502
Website: www.global-investment.com

I caught up with Paul among the tranquil canals of Amsterdam, and started by asking him why diversification abroad is so important to him.

Why global diversification?

Paul Melton: Simple. According to Benjamin Graham, father of us all, swings and roundabouts in fifteen stocks will balance each other up within their market. By swings and roundabouts, I mean the unsystematic risk of each stock.

Let's say Bill Gates and some of his chieftains were to die in a plane crash. Microsoft's stock would plummet and that would be called the unsystematic risk of the stock — it's the risk inherent in one particular company and these tend to cancel each other out as you diversify within a single market.

But there is another kind of risk most people ignore, and that's what we call systematic or market risk — the tendency of shares in any particular market to yo-yo up and down together.

A market drop is like a vice raid. When the cops come along, the good girls and the bad girls are picked up together. The same is true of shares. When a market plummets, the good and the bad shares take the fall together and a portfolio that rises in value is almost impossible to find. But using the same theory, the same approach, for diversifying risk within a single market, one can decide to diversify among markets and the swings and roundabouts of markets will also tend to cancel each other out and you will get a more stable portfolio because there is less market risk.

LG: So, are you saying that global diversification is the only proper diversification?

Paul Melton: That is exactly what I am saying.

LG: Why?

Paul Melton: Because although markets have tended to move more in tandem in recent years, they are by no means anywhere near synchronous. You can see that particularly in the less efficient markets and the emerging markets. In the last year or so, South Korea was hugely up, and so were Finland and Greece, but other emerging markets, such as Russia, were absolute disasters. Nevertheless, regardless of what happens to the world in general, there is always a bull market somewhere. Diversifying widely enables you to profit from the bull markets.

LG: It also inevitably puts you in the less rewarding markets. So, how do you deal with that? Why should you be in the less rewarding markets? What's the advantage of that?

Paul Melton: The advantage is that, over time, markets or shares tend to grow and a market which is down this year may well be up next year or the year after. It's the world index that you should be using as your benchmark and you should be trying to outperform what the world market is doing.

LG: Why should you bother to invest abroad? Most people don't.

Paul Melton: Most don't and most get burnt. That's because no single market is immune to a shakeout. Your home market is in fact riskier than you may think. The U.S., for instance, has had returns ranging all over the lot. In one year the Dow was down 53% and in another it was up 82%.

You can smooth out those frightening swings and roundabouts simply by diversifying into other countries. That's why you should bother to invest abroad. Not only that; if your home market is doing poorly, and of course the U.S. has been doing astoundingly well for the last five years or longer — it's haunting Greenspan, because he doesn't quite know how to deal with it — you will be protected. It's inevitable that it won't perform well at some point. Trees don't grow to the sky. Markets have their season in the sun and their season in hell — that's true of all markets and that's the logical reason for diversifying.

LG: So, why don't more people do it?

Paul Melton: Because people in general, including you and me, tend to look no further than their home market. I live in Holland where people talk about nothing but Dutch shares. And Holland is much more international than the U.S. If I travel a couple of hours in any direction from here, I'll be confronted with another language and another currency, and that's certainly not true of the United States. Here we are, sitting in Amsterdam, and if you can visualize the distance between Amsterdam and Vladivostok, that's roughly the same distance as between New York and San Francisco.

If you are American and living in the United States, you tend to think your horizon is the limit of the world. You don't generally learn another language, you don't generally get exposure to another culture, and you certainly don't generally think about investing in other currencies or other countries.

LG: But that's also true of other nations as well. In England, private investors are strongly discouraged by brokers and institutions, and also perhaps the state, from investing abroad directly. Would you say that countries in general don't really want their investors to invest much abroad?

Paul Melton: What would be the logic of that?

LG: To keep the money inside.

Paul Melton: Could be. But governments can't resist progress forever.

Globalization is an idea whose time has come. In any case, I'm not looking for a villain in the piece. I'm just suggesting the safest approach for the individual investor.

LG: And brokers don't particularly want the trouble of purchasing foreign stocks for their clients.

Paul Melton: That's certainly true and I think there is another factor involved, which is that the SEC, the Securities and Exchange Commission, in the United States places the onus on brokers to recommend only shares which can jump through certain hoops put up by the SEC. Foreign shares don't often follow their Generally Accepted Accounting Standards. Now that, of course, is a contradiction in terms, like "Army Intelligence." There are no generally accepted accounting standards even though we're moving in that direction.

Companies that want to list in the United States — German companies are increasingly doing so — have got to jump through the SEC hoops, but a firm which has its shares listed only on a foreign stock market — a non-U.S. stock market — will have had its own accounting standards or lack thereof. And that's why brokers are quite leery, I suspect, about dealing or recommending such shares.

LG: You wouldn't be scared, for example, of investing in a Russian company even though you might think that their accounts are pretty doubtful?

Paul Melton: If you say would I invest in a company whose accounts are doubtful, the answer is "no." Why should I? On the other hand, if you're asking would I invest in emerging markets, I would say, "yes." And you might say, but information on their shares is generally less available and it's a darker wood than that of the United States — that's certainly true, but when this subject comes up I almost always think of the Chinese ideogram for danger, which is the same as the ideogram for opportunity — actually it means both things.

Of course, if a market is less transparent, if information is less readily available, that's where the opportunities may be. Investing in ignorance can be an intelligent course.

I think of the time when Sir John Templeton went into Japan. People thought he was a fool because you couldn't expatriate the funds out of Japan. Nevertheless, he went into Japan and it turned out to be prescient — it was absolutely the right time and the right place. And that's really what Sir John Templeton had always said. The right question is not, "Where is the sun shining?" The right question is, "Where is it dark and gloomy?"

Should you buy ADRs?

LG: A lot of private investors purchase ADRs in the belief that they're somehow safer than purchasing directly on foreign markets. What would you say to that? Or about ADRs in general?

Paul Melton: Well, I could only encourage anyone to diversify outside their home market, and an American who purchases ADRs is at least doing that. But buying a serendipity of foreign shares with no overall framework isn't a good idea. There must be an underlying strategy.

As to ADRs, they have two slight disadvantages. First, they are sometimes more expensive than purchasing the underlying share on its home market, even allowing for the extra charges of purchasing direct with double commission. You can get a better price sometimes, in fact often, by purchasing shares on the home market. Either way, you've got the same currency risk.

Second, I notice that ADRs tend to reflect the U.S. market and the movements of the U.S. market more than the movements of their home markets. So you lose some of the advantages of diversification when you go into ADRs. Another couple of points: the ADRs are generally the most widely known shares, the large cap shares, and they are not always the best investments. Often they just lie there in a soggy mass — that's called low volatility, but it's not true safety.

You should be looking, if you are going to use my equal asset allocation model, for the best investments in each market — what John Templeton calls the "bargains." The point of going global is to seek out the bargains in a way that guarantees you a certain basic safety, and bargains almost by definition will be more volatile than stocks which are not bargains. Your high cap stocks, your so-called blue chips — which my friend Charles Allmon refers to as "blue gyps" — are stable, but you're not going to get much bang for your buck. It's better to seek your safety in diversification. You want individual parts of the global portfolio to snap, crackle, and pop, not just to lie there like a warm pudding.

The problems of asset allocation

Paul Melton: That brings us to the subject of asset allocation. Most professionals — and I use that word with hesitation, because I keep remembering that the *Titanic* was built by professionals but that amateurs built the Ark — use a benchmark which weights markets in terms of their capitalization, or something like it — their GNP and so on.

There are fatal flaws in this approach. The purpose of asset allocation is to find a good place on the efficient frontier — a good balance of risk and reward. So, you are diversifying essentially to reduce risk, but if you use a size-weighted index, inevitably you are going to be in the markets that have risen the most. In the 1980s, followers of the capitalization-weighted approach found their non-U.S. portfolios at a given moment 70% in Japan just before it crashed. That's certainly not the purpose of diversification.

LG: Then how should you divide the pie?

Paul Melton: Let me answer that question with another. Suppose you have a trusted advisor who tells you he has got a list of twenty foreign stocks that are guaranteed as a group vastly to outperform whichever index you happen to use — let's say the stocks in your home market. How do you go about buying those stocks?

Barring fund managers, whose confidence in their own investment insights is seldom justified by their results, most people will say, logically enough, that you buy them all — an equal amount of each of them. And that's exactly my approach, an equally weighted benchmark for the world, dividing the world into — in the first instance — developed and undeveloped markets, developed and emerging markets. Some people call them the "submerging markets," but that depends on which year you are looking at their performance.

The Melton model

Paul Melton: Studies by Morgan Stanley Capital International have shown that the most efficient division between developed and emerging markets is 70/30; 70% in the developed markets, and 30% in the emerging markets. So, I use that as a point of departure. And that 70% I then divide into three big blocs, which are the yen, the euro, and the dollar. All currencies relate to one of those three.

In the emerging markets, currencies represent an appreciably smaller part of the portfolio. The currency variations don't matter that much and those currencies will also tend to track one of the big three; but, as I say, I divide that 70% in developed markets into the three major currency blocs. That means about 23% in North America (I'm leaving out the figures after the decimal point), and roughly the same in Europe and in the Far East — three times twenty-three is sixty-nine, and the other 1% is after the decimal point.

Figure 2.1 MEGA* Benchmark

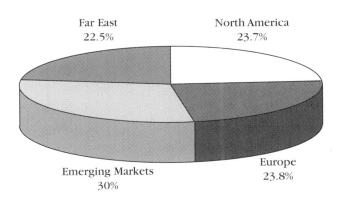

Far East
22.5%

North America
23.7%

Europe
23.8%

Emerging Markets
30%

Source: The Outside Analyst

Now, the U.S. is of course the largest and most diversified market, so it's almost inevitable that it will be heavily weighted even in an equal asset allocation model. Therefore, I've got a 20% weighting in the benchmark for the U.S. — that's the heaviest. And Canada, of course, also North America, that's 3.7%, so you've got a total there of 23.7%. In Europe there are fourteen major countries, eleven of which are in the euro bloc and the others are linked, and those fourteen then each get 1.7% which comes out to the requisite 23.8%. In the Far East, with Hong Kong, Malaysia, Singapore, Japan, Australia, and New Zealand, you've got six countries with 3.75% each and again you come to the requisite 22.5%. That's your 70% in developed markets.

Table 2.1 Melton's Equal Global Index (MEG)

Country	Weight as percentage (%)
Canada	3.70
United States	20.00
Austria	1.70
Belgium	1.70
Denmark	1.70
Finland	1.70
France	1.70
Germany	1.70
Ireland	1.70
Italy	1.70
Netherlands	1.70
Norway	1.70
Spain	1.70
Sweden	1.70
Switzerland	1.70
United Kingdom	1.70
Australia	3.75
Hong Kong	3.75
Japan	3.75
Malaysia	3.75
New Zealand	3.75
Singapore	3.75
Emerging Markets	30.00
	100.00

Source: The Outside Analyst

As far as the emerging markets are concerned, I don't enumerate them specifically. I simply suggest that you diversify equally among no fewer than ten emerging markets — and I use the IMF investable index as the emerging market benchmark. Since the inauguration of the euro I have modified the current allocation, cutting the emerging markets back to 15% and putting the other 15% in sectors, for the reason that some sectors are more global in nature than national. I'm thinking particularly of commodities and oil — those kinds of sectors — but it's true also to a certain extent of such sectors as IT and telecommunications, to a lesser degree, but it's becoming increasingly so.

Real estate, on the other hand, would be more local in nature. So, if you were to invest as an asset class in a fund, for example, that reflects German real estate, that fund would be more linked to its locale than a fund in the German telecom sector.

The power of asset allocation

Paul Melton: Logically, the first step in the global equity investment is to decide just how much you want to invest and in which countries. That's a vital decision and it's going to shape most of the performance and risk of your global equity portfolio. There was a study recently that showed that an average of roughly 90% of the monthly variation in returns on a large sample of U.S. mutual funds was explained by asset allocation and only 10% by security selection. So, it's no surprise then that country selection turns out to be the dominant factor in global equity returns. The fundamental facts of an industry remain important, but most of the time the choice of the country is what matters most. Country selection, however, is confused by lack of conformity and this is what you are talking about. Every country has its own accounting methods, so the term "Generally Accepted Accounting Standards" is an oxymoron. Moreover, you need some valid and reliable standard against which to compare the performance of your global portfolio. So, that's why I say that picking or building a benchmark is essential. Any stock market is a moving target. At any given moment, some markets seem to be priced at roughly twice what they should be and others at about half. Markets constantly swing from periods of being overvalued to periods of being undervalued.

Index tracking — a sound principle or fool's gold?

Paul Melton: Many professionals appear to doubt their own ability to recognize the right countries or to control trading costs. Some pension fund managers assemble an international portfolio in a way that is about as simple as it can get. They buy all the shares of a particular index and weight the fund so that it effectively becomes a mini version of the index itself. In theory, this means the fund should never do worse than its benchmark index and in practice, of course, they allow for a small percentage of tracking error upside and down.

Index tracking is mostly done by highly conservative institutions and pension funds who seek long-term growth. You won't do much worse than the index but, alas, you won't do much better. And a more serious handicap of index tracking is that not all indexes across the world are easily replicated. Certain stocks are restricted to local investors and are simply not available in the quantities needed.

To get around this, some index trackers only mimic their benchmark index in part, and that's not only more complicated but can lead to a higher tracking error. Despite all this, index tracking is on the march. It's been more popular in recent years for two structural reasons: some investors, believing that stock markets are efficient in pricing assets, conclude that it is virtually impossible to achieve consistently superior returns; while others believe — rightly, I think — that many managers generally lag the market due to high transaction costs.

If you believe a market return is the best you can hope for, then your best approach to global asset allocation is indeed a passive investment program replicating market indexes. But for most global investors, especially individuals, the index imitation approach is hampered by the fact that no investment fund yet truly mirrors a global index. If, despite its pitfalls, you take the index imitation route to global investing, there are several ways you can surmount this. For example, the Charles Schwab discount brokerage has set up its own index of the world's 350 largest firms and a fund that tracks it. Although, alas, it is tilted toward the heavyweights, this is currently just about the only way an individual investor with limited assets can imitate a global index, and that's just as well because individual investors who imitate an index are surrendering their edge over the institutions.

Why track?

The very notion of index imitation arises from the various constraints faced by institutional investors which don't apply to individuals.

LG: What sort of constraints?

Paul Melton: Above all, the fact that institutions need more liquidity. So, like giraffes, institutional investors have to browse upon the tall and familiar trees. Individual investors, on the other hand, like gerbils, can scurry around below: an area where small investors have the edge.

While the giraffes are nibbling on, say, Philip Morris, we gerbils can often find better nourishment in the underbrush, where many a choice morsel is ignored by the herd. Morgan Stanley put it this way in a 1986 report: "The performance of institutionally overowned stocks relative to institutionally underowned issues is embarrassing. You would make money if you simply bought every stock the learned institutions sold."

Not that the giraffes are stupid. They just have their own needs, logic, and priorities. If you're nevertheless determined to surrender your edge as an individual and try imitating a global index, there are funds to track, such as Morgan Stanley's EAFE (Europe, Asia, Far East) index and its emerging markets index.

There are also many funds that track a single country index, enabling investors to place high-risk bets on individual markets. There were two such instruments set up in 1996: World Equity Benchmark shares, or WEBs, developed by Morgan Stanley; and Country Baskets, developed by Germany's Deutsche Bank. Each is a listed security based on an ordinary mutual fund owning equities in a particular country.

These are relatively low-cost ways to invest in equities that mirror a country index. Normal mutual funds are priced once a day, but country baskets, in the same way as closed-end country funds, are repriced continuously over the course of the day. Unlike closed-end funds, these new tools generally trade at prices close to the net asset value of their underlying equities. To invest $1000 or $100,000 in a country basket, a single-country index fund, you simply call your broker.

Apart from imitating an index, there are three ways in which investors normally determine country allocation. As I've mentioned, one method weights countries to reflect the size or capitalization of their equity markets. The second approach allocates assets to reflect each country's contribution to the world's total gross national product, and the third approach simply weights major markets equally — that's my approach. So, let's examine the attractions and the drawbacks of these three allocation techniques. The most striking thing initially is that, over the long run, they seem to differ very little in risk and return. In an article entitled "The Portfolio Management Process," published in the *Financial Analysts Journal*, David Umstead reports that the risk and return profiles of these three techniques were virtually identical from 1970 through 1989, but I'm going to get to that year 1989 — that fateful year — in a minute.

Weighting by market capitalization

Paul Melton: Let's talk about allocation by market capitalization — in other words, size. Investors who confine themselves to the U.S. renounce approximately half of the global equity market, and non-U.S. investors who stay at home are spurning even more of the world. That's part of my argument for going global.

Since that is part of my argument for going global, you might expect me to favor weighting countries to reflect the size of their stock markets, but allocation in ratio to the size of stock markets has a number of serious drawbacks. For one thing, it hands you a rubber yardstick because the size of each country's capitalization relative to the whole expands or shrinks as that particular market rises or falls. You can see that clearly reflected in a capitalization-weighted index, such as Morgan Stanley's EAFE index, which covers Europe, Australia, and the Far East — all major markets outside the United States. Japan's weight within the EAFE capitalization-weighted index was less than 15% in 1969 when EAFE was created and it swelled to almost 70% by 1989. The big jump in Japan's weighting in the EAFE index came at the expense of virtually all the other EAFE stock markets.

Such instability in your country allocations is an inevitable and unwelcome by-product of splitting your assets among countries, based purely on the size of their stock markets. It makes you scramble just to stay in the one place, rebalancing your portfolio every few months as capital ratios shift and that's both impractical and expensive.

Capitalization-weighted asset allocation also creates severe distortions. Some countries have thinner public stock markets than one might expect from the size of their economy. Germany, for instance, has a big economy, but with most equities privately held, its various exchanges add up to a relatively tiny public stock market. So, allocating assets by stock market size inevitably under-weights Germany in a global equity portfolio.

Conversely, most Japanese companies are publicly listed and they trade at steeper earnings multiples than the rest of the world, so Japan's relative stock market capitalization looms far larger than its economic production. This distortion is further compounded by the cross-holdings of Japanese companies, by which I mean ownership by one listed company of shares in another listed company.

Sony, for instance, owns large blocks of stock in Matsushita, so allocation of investment funds in proportion to the value of Sony and Matsushita stock outstanding involves counting some of the Matsushita shares twice. This effect artificially inflates reported market capitalization. Cross-holdings and the resulting double-counting do exist in other markets but to nowhere near the extent in Japan. Japan's market capitalization is roughly 50% higher than its underlying economic value.

So, what I am saying is that allocating assets by stock market capitalization inevitably tilts a global equity portfolio far too heavily toward Japan, and this can lead to crazy imbalances as it did in that fateful year of 1989 when firm followers of the capitalization-weighted approach had allocated no less than a mind-boggling 70% of their non-U.S. assets to Japan. These supposedly prudent institutional investors were just in time to participate almost fully in that market's giddy rollercoaster ride over the next three years — a 36% plunge in 1990, followed by a 9% rise in 1991 and a drop of 22% in 1992. On average — even ignoring the rebalancing and associated expenses — these three years wiped out more than 45% of the heavy asset allocation to Japan.

By allocating assets to mirror the size of stock markets, these unreflecting organizations had put nearly all their eggs in the wrong basket at the wrong time, exactly the blunder asset allocation is meant to avoid. Investors clutch at the notion of a capitalization-weighted index only when global diversification comes up. No sensible investor holds domestic equities in proportion to capitalization weights. So, why then should we impose such silly ratios on foreign equities?

LG: We do, though. Or at least the institutions do. Why is size-weighting so widespread?

Paul Melton: Once again, liquidity. The giraffes can't invest easily in firms or stock markets with small capitalizations. That's because, first of all, an institution almost always has more money to invest than an individual. Heavy investment in a security with low capitalization, which is thinly traded, can affect not only its price but also its liquidity. It is far easier to find a buyer for a thousand shares at $50 than for a hundred thousand.

Second, investment in a low-cap stock can often result in more than 5% ownership, which in several countries — the U.S. and the Netherlands, for instance — requires an insider's report to comply with security regulations.

And finally, such an institutional holding can easily loom large enough to require a voice in the company's affairs, which may fall outside an institution's interest and expertise.

LG: Apart from these three structural reasons, isn't there also the matter of preferences?

Paul Melton: Sure. Institutional fund managers sometimes wish to avoid the greater risk they think is associated with small firms and small markets. The megabuck men are expected to follow a prudent investment policy, which, alas, often translates into lemming behavior: doing just what everybody else does.

The key point is that splitting your assets among countries based on the size of their stock markets creates distortion and instability in your country allocations.

GNP weighting

LG: How about allocating assets to reflect each country's contribution to the world's total gross national product? Morgan Stanley, for instance, has its GDP-weighted EAFE index alongside its capitalization-weighted index.

Paul Melton: It's true that the GDP weights better reflect the underlying economic relationships of major markets, but this approach too has severe drawbacks.

LG: For instance?

Paul Melton: For one thing, governments sometimes own huge chunks of an industry. Banks and utilities are part of the French GDP, but until recently you couldn't buy shares in French banks and utilities for love or money because they were government-owned. Big slices of Argentina's largest privatizations are still in government hands. Asset allocation reflecting GDP weights is subject to distortion by government-owned firms whose shares aren't traded on any stock exchange.

And then there are the multinationals. Like a 400-pound gorilla, a huge multinational sits where it likes. But how does that affect the GDP of, say, Hong Kong or Singapore? Many of their firms operate globally with little or no relation to where the corporate headquarters are located. Nestlé earns more than 95% of its cash flow outside Switzerland. So, should companies that just happen to be located in a particular country but do most of their business elsewhere be counted in that country's GDP? Weighting by GDP obviously tilts a portfolio toward markets dominated by multinationals or national firms.

And on this score, weighting by market size is no better because it automatically emphasizes big companies as well. The ten largest quoted firms make up over half the total stock market capitalization in Switzerland, Holland, Singapore, Sweden, Italy, and Spain. The top ten in Switzerland account for a hefty 68% of the total, slightly more than the 67% in Holland. No single firm accounts for a bigger slice of its national stock market than Royal Dutch Petroleum, which has a whopping 25%; its capitalization exceeds that of several European countries: Austria, Finland, Denmark, Norway, and Luxembourg.

LG: Just as an aside, I notice that Shell is mainly owned by U.K. investors while Royal Dutch is mainly owned by Dutch people, despite the fact that they are basically the same firm.

Paul Melton: Yes. Again, people are afraid to try the foreign waters. Anyway, here again is a moral: whether you weight by GDP or by capitalization, you're going to have a portfolio that's badly tilted by uninvited 400-pound gorillas. Of course, you can say, well, what's wrong with big company bias? Why *not* invest in big companies? There are two things wrong with big companies. First, as I've mentioned, assuming equal risk, shares in big concerns tend to produce smaller returns than shares in small concerns. The second and more basic disadvantage is that your country allocations can become lopsided even if you substitute, say, smaller Swiss companies for Nestlé and Roche or smaller Italian companies for Assicurazioni Generali.

Despite such tinkering, your global portfolio will still be badly tilted toward Switzerland or Italy at the expense of possibly more promising markets. You've placed bigger bets on those markets simply because that's where the gorillas chose to sit. So again, you get a moral: both GDP weightings and weightings by market size are biased toward markets dominated by big multinationals.

The equal asset solution

Paul Melton: And now we come to my area, to what I see as the answer to these unconsidered problems. As an investor, whether institutional or private, you are unlikely to be able to forecast returns in large markets any better than returns in small markets. So, it makes no sense to let yourself be forced to bet more heavily on a market simply because it's large. What's needed is a safe plan for country allocation that is easily used in the marketplace as a long-term, low-cost, passive strategy, and by this yardstick equal allocation is the ultimate in country diversification. This seemingly haphazard and also arbitrary method emphasizes no country at the expense of others. Any allocation other than equal weights calls for a forecast.

Any other set of weights makes sense only if you had further information about the expected returns or about the relative price movements of the stocks. But neither allocation by market size nor by GDP embodies a particularly good forecast of these elements. The aim is to assemble a global portfolio offering the most promise of profit with the least threat of loss. To this end, you have to remember you are selecting countries to be combined — that's the key word. Careful construction of your total portfolio is far more important than the accuracy of individual countries and the country choices and weightings. Allowing for your own ignorance is intelligent.

LG: And your own errors?

Paul Melton: Absolutely. A number of rather inaccurate estimates for securities can be made to combine to form an exceptionally accurate estimate for a portfolio. The estimate for one security may be too high, another too low, with the result that the average is just right. The more equal your company weightings, the less impact any one security has on the whole; and similarly, the more equal your country weightings, the less impact any single country is likely to have on your total portfolio and your global portfolio's overall performance.

Equally weighting countries builds a global equity allocation that is widely diversified and stable over time. It's not an all-purpose elixir, but it's clearly your most practical point of departure for global asset allocation. It offers the best protection against the unknown, and avoids big firm bias.

Investing in funds the Melton way

LG: Can we talk more in detail now about the funds method of global investing? How much money do you need to get started?

Paul Melton: I would say that you could get started quite comfortably with somewhere around US$50,000. You can get a good spread. I know that the Robeco funds, for example, have what they call self-select funds. There is one for Poland, there's one for Brazil, and so on.

For the United States, they've got two such funds. There's a fund simply for Europe, there's one for Europe based on the euro, a small cap fund, and another one for European mid cap funds. I think that low cap and mid cap funds are going to be coming into their own in Europe, because they are selling at a P/E of around fourteen at this point as against P/Es of above twenty for the European blue chips.

LG: OK. So, taking it step by step; I've got my US$50,000. Where do I start?

Paul Melton: You start by taking a pencil and determining just how you want to modify the equal asset allocation model. You don't want to follow it blindly.

You say, OK, I've got a 20% benchmark for the United States, but I'm still quite sanguine about its chances, so I'd like to up that a little bit — say to 22%. I see that Canada is largely a raw material and commodities economy and perhaps I want to shave that 3.7% a little bit to put more into the United States.

You might have similar ideas about Europe. As I said, there are fourteen countries each getting 1.7%, but with the inauguration of the euro, the common European currency, European countries are tending to converge more in terms of their market movements. Your choice of country now becomes less significant, less critical, within

Europe than it was, let's say, a year or two ago before the introduction of the euro. So you might say, well I don't particularly believe in the U.K. — it seems to me a market that I might even like to avoid or cut down to a minimum. I like, oh let's say, Spain, because Spain just managed to get into the euro bloc by the skin of its teeth and it's clear that the country is going to thrive. It's going to have more markets, and it's going to be able to export more. France also looks appealing to me, as does Italy, but less so than Spain. Considering all these factors, Scandinavian countries look strong, Finland and the Netherlands look very strong. Germany I've got some questions about. And you might say, well OK, I'll modify that 1.7% accordingly with each of these countries.

LG: I've done this on paper. I've decided on what percentage I'm going to put into each of these categories. What do I do next?

Paul Melton: Well, with $50,000 you want to use funds, so you have to make appropriate fund choices. I would say the first place to look is in "no load funds." A very good source for no load funds is a newsletter edited by Janet Brown called *NoLoad Fund**X (see page 99). The subscription isn't too expensive and it gives you a list of no load funds, country funds, and sector funds, and their relevant performance. It's the best source I know for analyzing the performance and relative performance of no load funds.

LG: Does it also cover funds that U.S. nationals aren't able to buy?

Paul Melton: No. They are all funds that a U.S. national can purchase. I would suggest the next place to look would be the closed-end funds that are traded globally, some in the U.S., some in Europe, some in Hong Kong and other places. Again, there is a newsletter which is very good: the *Lipper International Closed-End Funds Service* (see page 99). It analyzes the relative performance of closed-end funds, both sector and country funds, over the entire world. It gives you a very clear insight into where you get the most bang for the buck. Of course, you could go the index route by buying WEBs, which are listed on the American Stock Exchange and reflect country indexes, or the NYSE-listed country baskets put out by Deutsche Bank which do the same thing. But again, your aim is not to track an index; your aim is to outperform an index, so I would suggest that the investor who wants to use my system's equal asset allocation model shouldn't concentrate on indexes and on tracking indexes, but should focus on finding funds which tend to outperform the indexes.

LG: And which indexes should I be using as a benchmark?

Paul Melton: It doesn't really much matter which one you choose, because they don't diverge that much. You could use the Morgan Stanley Capital International index, or the FTSE indexes.

The key index you want to watch is for the world as a whole. Morgan Stanley again has a global index, as does Dow Jones; they don't diverge by much more than two or three percentage points. Naturally, I prefer my own MEGA index, because it is equally weighted.

Are indexes truly representative of their markets?

LG: Just a general question on indexes. It's sometimes said that some of them are not truly representative of the markets they are supposed to represent. For example, the Dow Jones Industrial Average with only thirty stocks — what is it really representing other than its actual constituents, and why should it be quoted as an indication of how the U.S. is doing as a whole?

Paul Melton: For no good reason other than habit. Indexes are also constantly being changed and shifted. Indexes are simply an agreed fiction.

Finding the best funds

LG: Now, returning to the global investor on his first day with his $50,000. He has spent a few hours deciding on the proportions he is going to invest in the different categories, and he has got hold of his fund directories and is now choosing which funds to actually purchase. How does he or she do that?

Paul Melton: Having determined your country allocation, the question is how to go about finding the best funds. I have already mentioned two sources of comparison among funds — one for no load funds and the other for closed-end funds. At a pinch, if there are no good choices within one of those two categories, then you might turn to open-end funds, which are listed in *The International* and *Resident Abroad*, both published by the Financial Times in London.

But at the risk of blowing my own horn — perhaps I should, because if I don't, who will? — I would say a subscription to my newsletter, *The Outside Analyst* (see pages 50–51), offers you a very easy solution. It has a model global portfolio based on funds, as well as one based on shares. It gives you funds which have been successful over the last year, and that's a more valid period of measurement than five years, according to the studies. I break it all down in terms of my asset allocation model. So, I've done the research for you, and if anyone wants to subscribe I'd be delighted to welcome you aboard. *The Outside Analyst* is US$390 a year and new subscribers receive a copy of my book *Going Global with Equities* at no additional charge. There is also the option of a quarterly rate, which is $85, so you get a $50 discount on an annual subscription.

LG: To go back to our hypothetical investor; I'm starting on day one. Let's say I've chosen not to subscribe to your newsletter right away. What work do I actually have to do? What criteria am I going to use to pick my fund?

Paul Melton: As I said, the criterion that seems to work is how well they have done over the last twelve months. If they've done well over five years that doesn't seem to matter much.

LG: So I've allocated my fund, I've picked the funds that I'm going to invest in, and it looks to me like I'm going to buy a bunch of funds and put only $1500 into most of them. Should I be worrying about cost and minimum charges and all that stuff?

Paul Melton: You have been thinking about that already because your first choices were no load funds. Those are funds which have no charges. They have no charges up front. They are open-end funds with no load and no back-end charges, and no so-called 12B charges, which are essentially back-end charges. There is no charge for entering the fund.

You were talking about cost. You've certainly been aware of cost, because of your emphasis on no load funds and closed-end funds, which can frequently be purchased at a discount to net asset value. You should certainly look at those discounts. The only time you should buy a closed-end fund at a premium to its net asset value is when you cannot enter a market in any other way.

The third and least advisable choice, and I suggest it least often, is the open-end fund with a front-end charge. It's sometimes 3% or even more, so you're starting with a handicap if you take that route. But in some cases you will be obliged to, because you can't find anything else.

LG: It sounds to me as if it is only going to take me two days maximum to invest my $50,000 at the beginning.

Paul Melton: Well, if you want to be really careful, take a week.

LG: So, once I've done that work, what do I do then?

Effective portfolio rebalancing

Paul Melton: After you've done that, you should go out and have a good dinner and celebrate that you've done something wise. In six months you should look at your portfolio and see if it needs rebalancing. If it doesn't need radical rebalancing at that time, wait another six months. You should rebalance your fund portfolio certainly no more frequently than every six months and preferably every twelve months. Do you know what I mean by rebalance?

LG: Yes. After six months I look at the performance of my investments and adjust them.

Paul Melton: Right. Did you ever see the movie *Being There?* Peter Sellers plays Chance, a mentally retarded gardener who has lived his whole life on a millionaire's estate. When the man dies, the household is disbanded. Chance, impeccably dressed in his employer's custom-tailored wardrobe, stumbles into Washington's political and social upper crust, where his innocent truisms from the garden are taken as audaciously simple economic metaphors. For example, he says, "As long as the roots are not severed, all is well, and all will be well in the garden."

It's very useful to use gardening metaphors to understand the real importance of rebalancing your portfolio. No gardener in his right mind expects to plant, then walk away. Without sensible maintenance, even the best garden slowly turns to weeds, or is overrun by bugs and critters. Likewise, your global portfolio needs periodic tending to realize its maximum potential. Such maintenance need not be tedious to be effective, but you must do it regularly.

LG: Could you talk a little about how to keep the "back office" work — the paperwork — to a minimum?

Paul Melton: A few simple tools will make it easy to manage your global equity portfolio as you go along. First, build a simple spreadsheet that assigns a percentage to each asset class (that is, region or sector) and each holding in your allocation plan. You want to be able to plug in the total value of the account and have the spreadsheet calculate the values of each desired asset class and individual holding.

Incidentally, always check and save all confirmations and monthly statements from funds and brokers. Once a year, you should get a consolidated tax statement. Keep it! Otherwise, you may face the disorganized people penalty. Suppose you decide to sell a fund bought ten years ago. If you live in the U.S. or another country that taxes capital gains, you have to know the price of the shares when you bought them. So, you need account statements for every year you've owned those shares, assuming you reinvested the dividends. If you can't find those records, you'll have to ask the fund company to provide you with duplicates. This can be costly. Many mutual funds will provide copies of last year's records at no cost, but will charge US$2.50 to $15 for older records.

LG: Once my paperwork is in order, how do I approach my portfolio reviews?

Paul Melton: Now you have to rely on the market forces to do what they have always done. Unless history abruptly reverses itself, your superior portfolio will deliver very satisfying results over the long haul. Resist the temptation to tinker endlessly, second-guessing yourself. Turn off "Wall Street Week," cancel your subscriptions to tip sheets, and refuse to be sucked into any predictions of interest rates or market corrections. You're better off spending your time at the beach with someone you love or reading a great book.

Not more than once a quarter, but not less than once a year, you should take time to evaluate your progress. The review doesn't have to be complicated or difficult, but it will involve several distinct steps.

Being human, you will zero right in on the bottom line. You would be very unusual indeed if you were not interested in whether you made or lost money. But this isn't really important information. We know in advance that in about 30–40% of the quarters or years we evaluate, an equity portfolio might have lost money. The success or failure of the overall plan doesn't depend on any particular year or quarter. But by all means allow yourself a brief distracting moment to feel either good or bad, depending on the bottom line, before you move on to the important part.

LG: What's that?

Paul Melton: As a first step, pull out the spreadsheet you constructed and plug in your new capital value. See if your assets are still close to the asset allocation goal. If not, it may be time to reallocate. Call it spraying for bugs. Reallocation gives you three benefits. First, it maintains your original risk profile. Over a long period of time, some of our holdings will grow faster than others. If we did nothing, then the mix of assets would shift after a while. When the mix changes, the risk changes. The resulting portfolio will be neither optimum, nor within our risk tolerance.

The second major benefit is that you end up buying low and selling high. While we're not going to attempt to time markets, it makes intuitive sense that last year's fastest growing market segment isn't likely to be next year's. And the Japanese cherry tree that has long failed to bloom will not be a disappointment forever. So, the discipline of reallocation generally adds value to a portfolio.

Reallocation's third benefit is that it helps you to remain disciplined and to resist "knee-jerk" reactions. Nothing will work every year, but this tactic has proven itself consistently over the long haul. Naturally, there are tradeoffs. Reallocation may involve a transaction cost and/or a tax cost. But if you're using no-transaction fee funds at a discount brokerage house, or trading within a single family of funds, you can easily avoid transaction costs. And if your account is an IRA, or other "qualified" plan, you have no need to be concerned with taxes.

How often should you rebalance? Roughly once a year is optimum. Or you may prefer rebalancing when asset allocation gets off by a predetermined amount, say 2–5%.

The next step in performance monitoring is to build your global asset allocation plan portfolio using only indexes. This is your real base line for comparison. It helps you to put the portfolio's total performance in perspective. It's not enough simply to know whether you made or lost money, or even how much you made or lost, to evaluate your performance relative to your strategy.

The final step in monitoring your performance is to compare each holding with its appropriate index to see if it is performing as expected. If not, there may be valid reasons. International funds that overweighted Japan, for instance, lagged the Morgan Stanley EAFE index for the last several years. Like me, you may consider heavier Japan weighting a valid position going forward, and not be too concerned about past performance relative to the index.

Given what we know about the efficiency of markets, the burden of proof on fund managers that they can actually add value is becoming very heavy. You may not wish to subsidize poor fund performance for very long in the hope that its manager can pull a rabbit out of the hat. Nevertheless, during these performance reviews you must doggedly resist the temptation to replace a disappointing fund (or share) with last quarter's hero. Endless pruning of so-called weeds is unlikely to improve performance, and chasing last period's stellar achiever is a proven way to become a loser.

LG: How often should you evaluate your strategy?

Paul Melton: You may need to re-examine your plans if some major event — divorce, illness, job promotion, or such like — alters your financial situation, objectives, time horizon, or risk tolerance. Barring such basic change, only a new approach or a new market should cause you to alter the asset allocation plan. Every once in a while, new, fundamental research shows us a way to build better portfolios. Just a few years ago, for instance, a study by Eugene Fama and Kenneth French pointed out that superior results could be obtained by pursuing a small company and value strategy. This information was fundamental and important enough to justify a total shakeup of existing portfolios.

But insights like this don't come along every week. You don't want to react to every half-baked theory that appears. As a rule of thumb, I expect to encounter at least two half-baked, brain-dead theories each week. *Money Magazine* has no trouble generating four or more per issue. So it's important to try to discriminate between proven, tested, fundamental, academic, or industry research, and mindless page-filling. None of us needs to be first to try out a new idea. Let others blaze the trail. Remember, it takes a long time to make up for a dumb mistake.

Discipline is the key to success for long-term investors. So, don't fall into the trap of managing your holdings according to newspaper headlines, sound bites, mindless predictions, gut feelings, or last time-period results! Think of your periodic reviews of share and fund performance as an opportunity for fine-tuning and occasional modest course corrections, not radical revision and second-guessing.

LG: OK, for now we are just talking about the fund method. Let's say that, overall, I've done reasonably well and I have to rebalance. I'm going to sell a proportion of my big winners in order to rebalance, but let's say I've had one fund in Russia that's gone down by 98%; I'm just going to leave it, am I?

Paul Melton: It depends on your view on Russia. Your brain is still working. The equal asset allocation model isn't a substitute for thinking, it's a guide for thinking. What is your opinion on Russia? Is it going to recover? Is Yeltsin going to die of a heart attack? What will that do to stocks in Russia? Have you had the worst hit that you are going to have?

The portfolio as a whole has taken maybe a 1% or 2% hit due to Russia. Do you want to liquidate the Russian fund? Can you do something with that small amount of money? Those are considerations which you have to make and the answers must be *your* answers, not my answers.

LG: But what do I know about Russia? What I read in the papers and the magazines. What I know six months down the line is probably not much more than I knew when I invested in the first place.

Paul Melton: And the equal asset allocation model has protected you from your ignorance. What is more, you've been following the emerging markets, you know; you've been sleeping well at night but you've been watching how the emerging markets have done in the last month, two months, three months, six months. You've been following them probably on a monthly basis. You can say — hey, South Korea is rather strong. I might be able to get a nice ride from South Korea. You can say, hey, Finland, an emerging market — well, actually we might be able to class that more as a European market because it has entered the euro — but you might find an emerging market that you are more sanguine about than Russia and in that case you would switch your fund, take your hit, take your loss. If, on the other hand, you feel Russia has gone down too much and now will recover, if it's rational, and based on good fundamentals, then you follow your instincts. You follow the knowledge that you've been able to acquire.

Of course you have to read the newspapers, of course you do your own research. But you don't need to do it in depth; a certain amount of ignorance is permissible with this method. The model will tend to offset your errors.

LG: What do you think I should be reading on a weekly basis?

Paul Melton: *The Economist.* Your local newspaper if it's as good as the *Financial Times* in London; the *Herald Tribune* if you are more internationally based. Perhaps the *New York Times* if you are based in America. Any reputable newspaper will inform you.

LG: What about business magazines? Should I be reading *Barrons* and *Forbes*, and so on?

Paul Melton: Why not? It's your own choice. Any information you can gather is of use. But one of the most interesting things you can do in terms of country asset allocation in the emerging markets is to see exactly what the countries have done.

It's not the analysis that concerns you in this case, so much as the performance that the market has shown over the last six months. Based on that, you can say — hey, it seems to make sense to shift in or out of the Scandinavian countries, for example, or it seems to make sense now to shift into more of the Asian emerging markets than it did six months ago.

You will see that in the figures. Figures are much more valid and reliable than somebody's opinion. I used to be a theatrical director and I always remember what Molière said about critics: "Le journal, c'est un monsieur," which means the newspaper, or the reviewer, is simply one man.

LG: Say I have a job, and I don't have time to read all the papers all the time. Would you say, am I understanding you correctly, that the basic minimum I need to do each month is to look at the changes in the various indexes and the performance of my investments?

Paul Melton: That's what I'm saying. Put much more simply than I could! There's a phrase, it's an acronym actually — KISS — keep it simple, stupid. I consider myself as stupid as the next guy, so I try to keep it simple.

Surviving the Apocalypse

LG: I'd like to talk a little bit about doom scenarios. I mean, they sell papers, don't they? They sell books, and as a private individual one can develop a lot of rather nameless fears about possible crashes. I increasingly feel that the equity markets will outlive me and that I shouldn't worry about the end of the world too much. Is that your feeling? You're not worried about a recession or a 1930s-type depression? Supposing one were to happen — what would you do? Do you stay in the market at all times?

Paul Melton: Let's talk about a fire or an auto accident. What's an appropriate response? People say, "Don't just stand there, *do* something." With a bear market or a panic, frequently a wiser response is just the opposite: *don't* do something, just stand there. And the calm approach is especially warranted when you are globally diversified.

In the long term, stocks always outperform bonds. The equity markets will outlive us all and doom scenarios are a waste of time. Markets may fall in unison for days, or weeks, even months, but each inevitably resumes its own personal and unique pattern of movement within the economic cycle. Unlike fires or accidents, market drops, even when severe, are simply part of that cycle.

What is a recession, after all? Merely a temporary falling off of business activity during a period when such activity has been generally increasing. It doesn't mean the sky is falling or there will be bread-lines throughout the world, simply that growth will slow. Now, even if we're entering a period of global recession, as many gurus

Figure 2.2 Investing Globally through Funds — a Sample Portfolio

In this portfolio Paul added equal amounts of cash each year between 1995 and 1998 for purchases. At end 1997 he had achieved a return of 86.5% on average invested capital, representing a compound annual return of 23.1%.

All prices in Dutch guilders

Current holdings at February 13, 1999

Date	Name	Price purchased	Price purchased at Feb 13, 1999	% Gain/loss	Portfolio weight %
20 Jan 95	Latin American Equity Fund	73.30	66.11	−11.09	1.74
22 Dec 95	Latin American Equity Fund	63.50	66.11	2.29	3.09
11 May 95	RG Emerging Markets Fund	82.10	76.36	−8.25	2.23
26 Mar 96	Fortis Obam	94.63	200.76	109.24	3.66
2 Feb 96	AEX Index Fund	522.00	1,195.95	125.88	2.62
27 May 97	Orange Midcap Fund	28.80	35.48	21.46	2.85
27 May 97	RG Europe Fund	228.30	316.23	36.61	5.07
16 July 97	ING Bank IT Fund	68.30	116.58	68.37	4.25
16 July 97	RG America Fund	291.60	418.70	42.57	4.58
1 Sep 97	Van Lanschot Global Equity	68.80	88.59	27.48	3.88
15 Sep 97	Postbank IT Fund	50.00	76.69	53.38	3.91
13 Oct 97	Orange European Small Cap	20.00	23.14	15.69	3.80
5 Jan 98	ING Emerging Eastern Europe	60.50	36.58	−40.27	2.67
6 Jun 98	RG Zelfselect Health Care Fund	100.00	120.87	20.87	4.41
6 Jun 98	RG Zelfselect Financials Fund	100.00	90.46	−9.54	3.30
6 Jul 98	RG Zelfselect IT Fund	123.30	177.95	42.60	6.49
5 Aug 98	RG Zelfselect IT Fund	119.50	177.95	47.73	12.98
8 Jan 99	RG Zelfselect Media Fund	122.31	131.12	6.05	5.64
8 Jan 99	RG Zelfselect Spanje Fund	143.35	130.02	−10.29	4.74
8 Jan 99	RG Zelfselect Telecom Fund	128.92	136.85	5.01	5.59
26 Jan 99	Trans Europe Fund	274.58	262.24	−5.56	4.78
1 Feb 99	RG Zelfselect VS Fund	217.40	216.18	−1.40	7.88

Realized gains/losses

The following table shows details of funds which Paul purchased for the portfolio and subsequently sold.

Date purchased	Name	Price purchased	Date sold	Price sold
7 Feb 95	Stork	45.80	22 Dec 95	37.80
7 Apr 95	Stork	41.30	22 Dec 95	37.80
7 Jul 95	KNP BT	48.50	26 Mar 96	43.60
7 Apr 95	Philips Electronics	52.90	17 Jan 97	65.00
17 Jun 96	ASM Lithography Hldg	79.00	21 Jan 97	104.20
20 Jan 95	Asian Tigers Fund	93.40	22 May 97	129.40
2 Feb 96	Asian Tigers Fund	113.50	22 May 97	129.40
24 Dec 96	Holland Europe Fund	87.80	1 Sep 97	113.00
28 Nov 96	ING Bank Global Fund	77.90	1 Sep 97	101.50
16 Jul 97	RG Zelfselect Zwitserland	157.40	13 Oct 97	148.00
15 Apr 96	ABN AMRO Aandelenfd.	118.70	13 Oct 97	194.30
27 May 97	ING Bank IT Fund	58.50	5 Jan 98	73.00
16 July 97	RG America Fund	291.60	11 May 98	358.50
1 Sep 97	RG Europe Fund	241.50	11 May 98	322.50
25 Jul 97	ING Bank Mid-Dutch Fd.	33.40	8 Jul 98	42.50
2 Feb 96	AEX Index Fund	522.00	14 Jul 98	1325.00
27 May 97	Orange Midcap Fund	28.80	14 Jul 98	45.00
26 Mar 96	OBAM	94.63	5 Aug 98	195.20
16 Jul 97	ING Bank IT Fund	68.30	5 Aug 98	91.60
15 Sep 97	Postbank IT Fund	50.00	5 Aug 98	63.00
22 May 97	Fortis Azie	122.90	8 Jan 99	63.91
14 Jul 98	Orange Deelnemingen	130.00	8 Jan 99	99.17
16 Jul 97	Global Emerging Mkts	103.50	8 Jan 99	55.97
13 Oct 97	Global Emerging Mkts	97.00	8 Jan 99	55.97
20 Jan 97	RG Zelfselect Canada "B"	110.00	8 Jan 99	118.23
11 May 98	RG Euro Midcap	101.10	8 Jan 99	88.26
11 May 98	ABN AMRO Europe	222.80	26 Jan 99	226.98
13 Oct 97	Orange Europe Small Cap	20.00	1 Feb 99	22.48
1 Sep 97	Van Lanschot Global	68.80	1 Feb 99	92.23

claim, some economies will still outperform others. In adjusting your global weightings for value, awareness of these various regional economic cycles will help tilt your portfolio toward the world's most promising markets, thus adding to your bottom line.

Moreover, it's advisable to diversify into countries in another phase of the economic cycle, especially if your home country is in recession. Spotting overvalued and undervalued markets is a rewarding exercise. Literally hundreds of profit opportunities occur every year around the world. Although as a global player you are no longer compelled to peg market cycles, you do have the option. I remember Jim Tyrone in Eugene O'Neill's play, *A Moon for the Misbegotten* saying, "There's no present or future, only past happening over and over again. You can't get away from it." Well, the economic and investment cycle is equally inexorable. You can use this probability to create steady profits. Over the long term there are many reliable signs of roughly when to enter and when to leave a specific market. And, following our global context, when to over-weight a country and when not.

LG: How do you decide that?

Paul Melton: By its point in the economic cycle. Bear markets have always been temporary. Share prices turn up from one to twelve months before the bottom of the business cycle. Here are some other events that are likely to take place in the buy area: the mood of popular magazine covers is bleak; the money supply, or the amount of money in circulation, shrinks in the wake of the central bank's policy of restraint; bankruptcies are at a high level; bank write-offs are high; bank loans are shrinking; and union negotiations concentrate on job security.

Conversely, here are some factors likely to be present in the sell area — when you should be selling: the prime rate is up sharply from its lows; corporate capital expansion improvement projects are started; volume is up in the commercial bond market; and there are substantial reports of poor vendor performance. Not all these events will always be visible, but a recognizable pattern should be evident. In the world's equity markets, the time of maximum pessimism is the best time to buy, and the time of maximum optimism is the best time to sell, and the only way to get a bargain is to buy what most investors are selling. And that again, I believe, is a fair representation of the philosophy of Sir John Templeton.

Some readers may not have heard of John Templeton. Born poor in Tennessee, he worked his way through college during the Depression and won a Rhodes scholarship to Oxford. When war broke out in 1939, he became convinced that stocks would boom, borrowed $10,000, and bought 100 low-priced U.S. stocks with the same dollar amount in each (about $100). A perfect example of equal weighting! Four years later he had quadrupled his money.

After running a successful investment firm for many years, including managing eight mutual funds, Templeton sold out and moved to Nassau in the Bahamas. In his mid-fifties, he started over with one fund, the Templeton Growth Fund, which has now mushroomed into a large family of offshore funds. Perhaps the first truly global investor, he is famous for his method, which is essentially to search all over the world for extremely undervalued stocks. (See Chapter 4.)

Does technical analysis work?

Technical analysis (TA) is an investment method that relies on the study of price movements to predict future moves. TA describes a host of patterns in price charts that are thought to recur; according to TA, if you observe such a pattern developing, you may be able to make accurate price forecasts.

LG: What are your views on technical analysis as an investment method?

Paul Melton: It reminds me of a poem by Ogden Nash, "Candy is dandy, but liquor is quicker." The "technician" tries to predict stock movements through the shapes on a stock's price chart, without reference to value. Technical analysis does seem to me one of the most interesting ways of committing suicide.

LG: Yet there are departments in banks that do it.

Paul Melton: Of course, there's a demand for the product. People want to be told where the security is, where the safety is. They want to be told absolutely what to do. They want not to think. They want to feel that a guru can give them the answers.

When you appear at investment seminars in the role of guru, which I frequently do, people are expecting answers from you. I give them questions, I give them suggestions about how to approach the thing, how to survive uncertainty and live with it. But I don't give them certainties in the sense of knowing what the future is going to bring. I can say. "Here's a structure; it will help you regardless of what the future brings," but I'm not going to tell you what the future holds. I don't know.

LG: Nor does anyone else?

Paul Melton: Nor does anyone else.

What is professional advice really worth?

LG: Could you talk about the pressures on professionals — when they have to seem to know even when they don't?

Paul Melton: There are enormous pressures. Investors frequently want hand-holding from their brokers and advisors. And the brokers and advisors are pushed into it. I've spoken to brokers about this problem. I won't name any names, but I've said, "Look, people are asking you to take a position on this; you know that it's not feasible" — and brokers have said to me quite honestly, "Yes, we realize that it's not feasible, but we can phrase it in a kind of weasel way" — they don't use those terms, but that's really what they mean — "to give people a feeling of security so that they will remain invested with us." I'm sorry, but that's not for me. I cannot and will not play that game.

LG: With brokers increasingly being bought up by large institutions, do you think their advice is becoming even less useful? Does anyone really need their advice?

Paul Melton: Some brokers are highly qualified and some aren't. Unqualified advice is worthless, or sometimes worse than worthless — dangerous. Somebody who tells you that the market is going up can cost you an arm and a leg. And somebody who tells you the market is going down — if he keeps saying it for a number of years — will be right. Just as a stopped clock tells the right time twice in any twenty-four-hour period.

LG: George Soros's approach, according to his own books, is all about making judgments about the future, using a lot of leverage, and so on. Do you think that he's just lucky? How does he do it?

Paul Melton: I think it's skill. I think it's enormous intelligence and skill and discipline and dedication, thinking about it twenty-four hours a day. And I trust his intuition and his instincts much more than my own in that regard, because he's a trader and I'm an investor — there's an enormous difference. I couldn't trade to save my life, and I know it.

LG: In what circumstances should/could a private investor trade?

Paul Melton: Well, a private investor could go to Las Vegas and play the slot machines. I've been to Las Vegas and the gesture that one uses — the arm motion that you use to pull the slot machines — is the same one you use to flush a toilet. If you want to spend a vacation flushing toilets, fine. I'm not a trader and I don't want to talk about trading.

LG: Why not?

Paul Melton: I think it was Peter Lynch who said, invest in what you understand. I don't understand trading.

Investing in equities directly — the Melton way

For reasons that he explains below, Paul Melton believes that you should diversify much more widely when you buy equities globally than you would in your home market — a minimum of fifty stocks, compared with ten or fifteen domestically.

LG: We've talked about how to use your model, starting with a fairly small lump sum and investing only in funds across the world. But this model also applies to investing in equities, although you say that you need between US$350,000 and $500,000 minimum in order for it to be effective.

Paul Melton: The model applies particularly to investing in equities. It was developed to invest in equities.

LG: Let's suppose that I have US$500,000 and I want to use your system — what do I do on day one? What's the first step that I take?

Paul Melton: It's exactly the same as you did with only $50,000. You take a pencil and a pencil sharpener, and you sit down and figure out in which countries you want to invest for the 85% of your portfolio that's going to be in countries. Then you resharpen your pencil and figure out which sectors you want to invest in for the 15% of your portfolio that's going to be in sectors.

LG: Supposing one of my sector choices is also one of my country choices. Should I worry about that or not?

Paul Melton: Yes, you should worry about it and that's OK. What you're asking me is which is more important — country or sector. Let me go back a step to answer that.

The first question is how widely should you diversify. Expanding the global portfolio beyond fifteen stocks — which is optimal for a domestic portfolio — brings you far more risk reduction than going beyond fifteen stocks in a domestic portfolio. Even a mutual fund with fifty different foreign stocks could benefit from additional holdings. But you certainly don't want to expand a portfolio beyond your capacity for tracking it.

So, the question is what rule of thumb you should use to diversify your equity portfolio globally while still limiting your number of holdings. The simple selection approach would be to assure good geographical diversification by picking stocks across countries. The more conventional way is to select stocks across industries. Stocks from all countries can be classified by industry, so choice by industry automatically provides some international diversification.

A third selection method combines the first two by selecting stocks across both countries and industries. A guy by the name of Bruno Solnik was one of the first to publish on this subject, back in the 1970s. Using weekly price data for 1966 to 1971, he put together share portfolios of various sizes from the United States, the United Kingdom, France, the former West Germany, Belgium, Italy, the Netherlands, and Switzerland, and this was his conclusion: a well-diversified global equity portfolio is one-tenth as risky as a typical stock and half as risky as a well-diversified portfolio holding the same number of purely U.S. stocks.

To put it another way, you get a higher level of return for the same level of risk. More bang for your buck. And there have been other studies. I won't cite them all, but that was the germinal study. It also tested the three ways of combining countries and industries — namely, selecting stocks across industries, selecting stocks across countries, or combining the two. Solnik found that diversifying across countries generally brings you better investment results than merely diversifying across industries, and that's because stock price movements usually correlate more with the market in which the company exists than with its industry.

Swiss stock market trends, for instance, largely determine the price of Nestlé shares even though, as I mentioned, more than 95% of Nestlé's cash flow comes from abroad. So, for this reason, a portfolio diversified across countries is normally less risky than one that is internationally diversified across industries and, as you might expect, combining industrial and geographic diversification gives you slightly better investment results than pure country diversification alone. Other studies confirm this.

The introduction of the euro has dramatically altered the playing field for every global investor. While individual European investors still largely confine themselves to their own markets, there's a new market — the euro. From now on, every listed stock in each of the eleven member countries is a potential investment object.

To profit from the situation, investors have to think about asset allocation in a different way. At present, global investors usually decide which countries they want to invest in, then which sector, and only then in which company. That will have to change. Country borders are no longer wholly paramount in asset allocation. In many cases it will be better to choose a sector in which to invest and then pick a suitable company in the whole euro grab-bag. Financial institutions have been tailoring investment funds for this new European situation for quite some time.

Remember, we are seeking a rule of thumb here to help you diversify globally while limiting your number of holdings. You can approach this problem in a highly useful way simply by posing the following question: Which will have more impact on your investment return, the country in which your stock trades — Japan, Germany, or what have you — or the industry to which it belongs — oil, say, or pharmaceuticals?

Studies over the last two decades show that some industries — such as oil — are global in nature, whereas others — such as healthcare and retailing — are local. When U.S.-listed Amoco and London-listed British Petroleum announced their merger early in August 1998, for instance, other international oil companies such as Royal Dutch Petroleum, based in the Netherlands and listed on the Amsterdam Exchange, saw their stock prices plummet.

The return to investors holding shares in any international oil company is heavily impacted by global oil production, product pricing, and distribution. In fact, for almost all publicly traded oil companies, the country of domicile plays a lesser role in share price movements than industry classification. The same is true of most auto and natural resource companies.

The very nature of these businesses provides a certain degree of insulation, but as global capital markets become more integrated, and in certain regions of the world this is already taking place, industrial classification will play a growing role in the return investors receive.

OK, you want to get simple and direct answers. What are the implications of these findings for your global investment program? Simple, when a country effect tends to dominate the industry effect, focus on country asset allocation; but where a sector is decidedly global in nature and the industry effect dwarfs any country effect, it's wiser to focus on a given stock's industrial classification. This handy rule of thumb will help you build a global equity portfolio while limiting your holdings.

In Europe, if you're going to have 1.7% of your portfolio in each country you could conceivably have 100% of that 1.7% in one stock. If it's a good one and you have faith in it, why not? Or you might, say, split it and have half in one and half in another. If you looked at Finland, you might say, "Nokia, that's suitable." Or you may say, "No, I'd like a small cap stock." It depends. It depends on your own individual insight. There's no hard and fast rule — you must decide what suits you best.

You've got fourteen European countries at 1.7% each, so that's a minimum of fourteen companies. Let's go out from those minimums. You've got six countries in the Far East at 3.75% each, but do you really want 3.75% of your portfolio in one stock? I should think not. You might want to have two companies in each country. So you have fourteen companies in Europe, and in the Far East you've got six multiplied by two, which is twelve, twelve and fourteen is twenty-six. You've got Canada — you want at least two stocks in Canada if you're going to go there. So you're now up to twenty-eight. And you've got 20% of your portfolio in the widely diversified United States. You're certainly not going to put that 20% into one company. Again, you're going to cut it up into small pieces. If you decide 1% in each company, you've immediately got twenty more stocks. If you say 2% in every company, you've got ten more stocks because twenty-eight plus ten is thirty-eight.

In emerging markets we say OK, let's have a minimum of ten uncorrelated stocks. If it's 1% in each of them, that would be an

additional ten, so we are now up to forty-eight. And now you've got
your 15% in sector funds and here's where it gets interesting. You can
make heavier bets. You might say just three or four stocks in sectors
— Nokia, for example.

You may say that's where I'm going to put my telecommunications
bet and that might even be 3% of your portfolio. In the context of
country asset allocation, you wouldn't put 3% in Nokia, but in the
context of sector allocation, you might well do that. So we're talking
about fifty stocks, a minimum of fifty stocks for a prudent global asset
allocation, using stocks — individual stocks, rather than funds.

LG: It sounds like quite a lot of work to keep track of them.

Paul Melton: Yes, it would be. But you don't have to track them on a
daily basis. What you have to do is select them. Then look at them
again in six months and see what happened. Did you make any
terrible blunders? You need six months to see if you've done that and
rebalance if necessary. And if you don't need to rebalance in six
months, look at them again at twelve months.

LG: Is six months really long enough to know if you've made a
blunder?

Paul Melton: In some cases it could be. If the earnings of the company
plummet and management hasn't foreseen it and comes out with
weak excuses or changes its accounting methods, or if you suddenly
lose faith in the company because management has been replaced —
there are many things — that's what we call the unsystematic risk and
that's what you'd be looking at during that six-month period.

Valuing companies

Paul Melton: What is a company worth? This question, which to most
investors is the all-important one, keeps hordes of analysts all over the
world in full-time employment. In New York, Paris, London,
Amsterdam, Frankfurt, Zurich, and Hong Kong, these investment

professionals — and you remember my point about professionals — are tracking which shares they expect to show the most powerful earnings growth well into the next century. The number crunching involved in sifting all the earnings forecasts for all quoted companies is staggering.

Take the London market alone; roughly 1100 London-listed companies are researched by analysts. Multiply that by the number of brokers who follow each stock, let's say six. Multiply the result by two, because every company reports results twice a year when forecasts usually change, and then factor in another small multiple, say 1.3, to take account of forecasts being revised up or down between results announcements, and the answer is 17,160 — a very approximate figure for the number of analysts' forecasts swimming around the London market each year.

So, monitoring such vast numbers is an impossible, formidable task for the private investor. But fortunately a major industry has arisen around gathering, logging, and combining earnings forecasts in all the major markets and then disseminating the information.

Earnings expectations are the most important determinant of stock prices. The stock price of any company is determined by the market's view of that company's future earnings. The best way to approximate this market view is to pool the maximum number of qualified analysts of that security and take the average of consensus of their forecasts. As share prices move to reflect the current level of analysts' earnings forecasts, this consensus becomes embedded in the current price of stock.

So, a stock's price is largely determined by what professionals now think it will earn in the future. I'm not saying they're right; I'm saying that their opinions move markets.

Some investors believe that extrapolation of the past is a much more reliable guide to future prices than analysts' guesstimates of future earnings, but simply extrapolating from the past can mean gazing into the rear-view mirror as you drive into a wall. Naturally, a company's past history is important, but any decent analyst has already factored it into the earnings estimate.

The U.S. analysts have an even bigger universe. They follow some

4200 listed firms which report four times, rather than twice, a year, so if we apply the same formula as I did for the U.K., there are roughly 131,000 different annual U.S. earnings forecasts. There is an eighty-page earnings outlook from Nelson Publications that carries earnings estimates each month on about 3800 U.S. stocks.

Coverage of earnings estimates by all 185 U.S. brokerage firms is available from Zacks Investment Research, which provides performance ratings on some 4000 U.S. stocks. Then there's First Call, which is a unit of Thompson Financial Services, that reports earnings estimates from about 150 brokerage firms worldwide and some 15,000 equities, 10,000 of them outside the United States and 5000 in the States, including about 1000 ADRs. First Call will give you estimates in various forms, including printouts, electronic feeds, and via the Internet, and it's got a world equities Windows database updated weekly by CD-ROM which covers some 7000 companies in about thirty countries which I use, among other things.

What I also use, and this is really just about the best, is the Institutional Brokers Estimate System (IBES) (see page 99). This is a veteran global tracker of monthly changes in earnings estimates. Subscribers pay an average of US$15,000 a year — they are mainly brokers who want to know what their competitors are doing and, more importantly, what institutional investors are doing. Before IBES set up shop in 1971 as the first database of analysts' earnings estimates, there was no way to prove the relationship between stock prices and earnings expectations. Since then, over a couple of hundred studies have confirmed that this relationship exists worldwide.

More and more evidence supports the hypothesis that earnings expectation works in similar ways everywhere from the U.S. to the U.K. and on to Hong Kong and Sri Lanka. The IBES database is a superb treasury of statistics on earnings estimates comprising detailed profit forecasts updated monthly from over 7000 top financial analysts around the world.

And now let me plug my own newsletter, *The Outside Analyst*, again, because not everybody can afford to spend $15,000 a year for IBES. *The Outside Analyst* is the only newsletter that compares stocks globally and it gives subscribers the benefit of such forecasts. I read the First Call estimates, I read the IBES estimates, I have them in print, I have them on CD-ROM, and each month I sift all major analysts' earnings estimates for over 15,000 firms in more than forty countries.

My newsletter reports on which stocks professionals now consider the most attractive, and I supply fundamental research on each. In theory, a share's quoted price should reflect its future value, but fortunately that's not always the case and, for this reason, a disciplined coverage of brokers' forecasts can pinpoint the world's bargain equities.

LG: And how can I do it by myself?

Paul Melton: Subscribe to one of these databases. Subscribe to First Call, subscribe to IBES — or subscribe at a lesser price to *The Outside Analyst* — and you'll find which shares have the highest expected earnings growth combined with the lowest P/E ratio for the coming year. That's what I do, among other things.

LG: Is your model a relative strength system?

Paul Melton: Sometimes. In the case of the developed markets, the benchmark mentions specific countries and gives a weighting for each. You can depart from that weighting somewhat. In fact, I'd encourage you to. So, it has little to do with momentum. In the case of the emerging markets, I simply say diversify equally into no less than ten emerging markets, and there momentum might have some significance. We talked about rebalancing every six or twelve months. I said look back over the last six months and see what the emerging markets have done. See which of them seem to have risen over the last month or two.

Sector investment

Paul Melton: Momentum certainly comes into play in sector allocation. At present, I recommend a 15% allocation to sectors, but I don't advocate equal asset allocation in sectors. There are forty to fifty sectors, depending on which models you are following or which benchmarks you are looking at — Morgan Stanley has close to fifty, Fidelity has forty-four, as I recall. I'm certainly not suggesting that you should diversify at forty or fifty sectors on an equal asset allocation basis. I'm saying that you should abandon equal asset allocation when it comes to sectors.

Instead, by using what I call the polar bear strategy — and I'll get to that in a minute — you can profit from the hot sectors. If you followed this strategy during 1998 you could have appreciably increased the returns from this sector slice of your global portfolio. The benchmark — what I call the MEGA benchmark, Melton's Equal Global Allocation Benchmark — isn't written in stone. Its principle of equal weighting may be a practical and prudent point of departure for country allocation, but that by no means rules out adjustments — quite the contrary. What's more, when allocating the roughly 15% of your global portfolio set aside for sector investment, the principle of equal asset allocation should be abandoned to ensure that some portion of your portfolio is always in the top-performing sector. You don't have to buy a wide range of sectors as my model suggests you do with countries. Why? Because the hot sectors are easier to identify, and hot sectors remain hot longer.

When it comes to sectors, you no longer have to assume that no-one knows which area will perform best, and that frees you from the rigid asset allocation that would inevitably put you in the worst-performing sectors as well as in the best-performing ones. Investors who apply fixed sector allocations and ignore, for instance, the fact that commodity-based stocks have badly underperformed other sectors for at least five years, will suffer. Their allocation calls for a fixed natural resources position and they have it. But you can use a more profitable strategy. When an ice floe melts, the polar bear springs to another floe. Similarly, if a sector's relative performance has dwindled badly over a year or two, you simply step to a leader. You stay with the winning sectors until they are no longer winners, then move on to the new leaders. And this polar bear strategy of upgrading sticks to the sectors currently doing well. When market leadership rotates, your sector allocation also shifts into whichever area is showing strength. But it's wise to avoid upgrading until a recognizable trend appears.

Risk and volatility

LG: Getting back to your model, how do you deal with risk?

Paul Melton: Some people believe that risk is volatility — that a stock that has large swings up and down is intrinsically more risky than a stock which doesn't. There is a flaw in that thinking, because you actually want volatility on the up side. It's not the volatility which is the risk, but the fact that some of the swings are on the down side. A stock which steadily lost 5% annually would be regarded as riskless by the theorists, because the volatility is low. On the other hand, they would regard a share which shot up 30% year after year as highly risky, because the volatility is high.

Obviously, market volatility isn't quite the same thing as risk. In a rising market, volatility is highly advantageous. For the serious investor, volatility actually provides opportunity. So, strange as it may seem, in a global portfolio you are likely to achieve the highest return for any given level of risk by maximizing the volatility of each individual market. For the biggest bang for your buck, each part of your global portfolio has to contribute as much as possible to the bottom line. So, your aim in each individual market should be to ensure that your stock selections exaggerate that market's movements as much as possible.

Therefore, in choosing individual holdings for a global portfolio, it is wiser to seek market risk than to avoid it. Maximum risk reduction — that is, reducing the volatility of returns — is already inherent in the fact that you are investing worldwide. The volatility of a global portfolio will be far less than that of its typical holding. Though market risk cannot be totally eliminated, going global does reduce it sharply. In fact, going global is the key to lowering market risk. Over time a consistently undervalued global portfolio will not only outperform a world stock market index, but also tend to be far more stable than individual stock markets.

An American in Amsterdam

I asked Paul how he came to give up his show business career for a life in finance, and why he made the move to Europe.

Paul Melton: Where shall I begin? I began as an actor, appearing with Jason Robards Jr. and Don Murray. I played Simon Stimpson in *Our Town*, and Dr. Bradley in *Blithe Spirit*. And then, before I finished university, I was in the U.S. Air Force Intelligence. I did finish university, actually. I interrupted university to go into the Air Force and on graduation my first job was as production manager of "Candid Camera." Shortly thereafter I got a job at CBS as a researcher and within less than a year I was a producer there, one of the youngest then.

I used to do a show called "New York Forum" in which three lawyers cross-examined a political celebrity from a partisan point of view, and I did "Face the Nation" and "Face New York." While I was at CBS I was also studying and working at the Actors Studio in the directors unit with Lee Strasberg. I left CBS and went to ABC, and I worked for an educational television station as well. I did a program called "Strategy of Truth" which dealt with the function of the press in a free society and the guests were Dr. Arnold Toynbee, a historian, very good at generalization, A. J. Liebling, a press gadfly, and James Reston, a columnist with the *New York Times*. The moderator was Charles Collingwood.

Then I became a theatrical director, directed Tippi Hedren in *Black Comedy* after she was in Hitchcock's movie *The Birds*, and I directed Bob Newhart in *Harvey* and, I don't know, a whole lot of other plays — I don't remember them all.

Then I got a telephone call inviting me to direct a Dutch cabaret artist in Holland. I flew over and worked with him for a while, learnt Dutch, directed in Dutch and in French in Europe and Rotterdam, Amsterdam, Liege, Brussels … I founded a theatrical company. I was artistic director of one of Amsterdam's four municipal theaters, then founded a theatrical collective.

The Europeans kept making me offers that I couldn't refuse. I was over here, I met my wife here, who is Dutch, and we went back to

New York where we were married with the full intention of remaining there. The telephone rang and there was something else and then something else again, and I maintained my apartment in New York City for five years on a sub-let while I lived in Europe. I had no intention of relocating; I didn't consider myself an expatriate in any sense. But after five years I suddenly realized, "Hey, this is where I live. I don't live in New York City anymore." I sort of made the commitment to remain, or I had made the commitment to remain and suddenly realized it.

LG: You have lived in Amsterdam ever since?

Paul Melton: I've lived in the Netherlands ever since. I've lived in Amsterdam, and in Maastricht. I'm now living in a suburb of Amsterdam which is very laidback, very pleasant. The quality of life is superb.

LG: What made you make the switch to a financial career?

Paul Melton: I'd been directing in Holland, working with Dutch actors and trying to imbue them with the method that I had learnt at the Actors Studio. And there is an enormous dichotomy between the American and the Dutch approach. There's a sort of unspoken agreement between a director and an actor in the U.S. The director defines the events of the piece and the underlying relationships, and the actor or actors are free to inhabit those events and underlying relationships in a way that reflects their own truth. In Holland, and it took me years to discover this, the unspoken agreement is just the reverse.

I'm sure that Dutch theater has grown and improved somewhat, but in the 1970s the way a scene might be built would be that one actor might say to another, "Look, I'll do it as if I'm angry and you pretend to be afraid." We call that "indicating acting" — indicating an emotion or an event that isn't really taking place — and, of course, it's empty; it's dead at its core.

I finally decided I didn't want to direct such actors anymore. So I wrote seven one-hour dramas for television based on the fourteenth-century writings of Geoffrey Chaucer, Giovanni Boccaccio, and others.

But then I had the problem of watching what a Dutch director did to my work and I decided I didn't want to work with Dutch directors either as a writer.

I had always played around with investments. I knew quite a bit about options, more than most other people, because options were new, and I thought, "Well, what can I do?" There was an advertisement in the paper for an option specialist put there by a London firm and I got the job, to my amazement — I think nobody else applied. So, I was now an option specialist in their Rotterdam office and within a few weeks I was a portfolio manager for the company. I did that for about a year. Then I combined my background in journalism with my experience as a portfolio manager and started *The Outside Analyst*. This was in 1986. In that period I also advised several institutional investors. Since then I haven't changed my profession.

LG: At what point did you develop your model?

Paul Melton: I had read everything that John Templeton had written; I was one of the founding members of the International Society of Financial Analysts, which was later merged into the Association for Investment Management & Research; and I received the *Financial Analysts Journal* every month and read it religiously. I really began to educate myself in how to combine risk and reward in the most profitable way. The idea, the seeds, I am sure were acquired from John Templeton because he always emphasized global diversification, and much of what I say today is a quote from John Templeton, sometimes conscious and more often not.

Useful addresses

Paul Melton has kindly provided the following list of useful books and information sources:

*   *Dow Jones Irwin published* Global Investing the Templeton Way *in 1988. Although an "as told to" book, it is the best source in print for an insight into Sir John's thinking on this subject. More*

philosophical in tone, but a good guideline for living life, is The Templeton Plan: 21 Steps to Personal Success and Real Happiness. *The title sounds like hype, but the book is anything but.*

- NoLoad Fund*X, *which I consider the best guide to no load funds for the U.S. investor, is published by DAL Investment Company, 235 Montgomery Street, Suite 662, San Francisco, CA 94104, United States; tel: +1 415 986 7979; fax: +1 415 986 1595; email: fundx@fundx.com. The toll-free number is (800) 763 8639.*

- Lipper International Closed-End Funds Service, *distributed by fax each month, is published by Lipper Analytical Services, 47 Maple Street, Summit, NJ 07901, United States; tel: +1 908 273 2772; fax: +1 908 273 6184. This publication ranks the monthly performance of closed-end funds traded across the world and also tracks their discount or premium to net asset value.*

Paul uses two main sources of global earnings estimates:

- *Published on CD-ROM,* Estimates Direct, *incorporating World Equities, supplies earnings estimates from some 140 brokerage firms worldwide. It covers some 8500 equities: 3000 in Europe, 1800 in Asia, and about 4700 in North America. It is published by First Call Quantitative Services, 22 Pittsburgh Street, Boston, MA 02210, United States.*

- *IBES International Inc. supplies earnings estimates in print and electronic form for approximately 15,000 stocks worldwide, including 5780 U.S. and Canadian stocks. Their home office is at One World Trade Center, 18th Floor, New York, NY 10048-1818, United States.*

3

Peter Everington: In Pursuit of Growth

The 1980s saw a revolution in the psyches of many countries around the world; socialism began to give ground to capitalism, and many of the ideological givens that were beloved of the postwar era seemed to evaporate. In Britain, Thatcherism gave hope to a new generation of investors and business people who had only ever known the "British disease" of stagnant, over-regulated industries and a surly workforce. The yuppification of the U.K. gave rise to many excesses, and the 1987 crash served as a useful reminder that extraordinary performance rarely lasts for long.

Star fund manager Peter Everington is the exception to the rule. The coiner of the term "Tiger fund," he made fortunes in Asia for his investors throughout the 1980s and 1990s, neatly sidestepping the worst of the crashes. Now back in the Isle of Man as a director of the Regent Pacific Group, he continues to outperform the majority of his fellow professionals — if you had stayed with him in the eighteen-year period between 1981 and 1998, for instance, you would have made over thirteen times your initial investment.

Peter is a "top-down" investor who seeks out countries that are heading for rapid growth. At forty-one, he is the youngest investor interviewed in this book. Now that Asia is, for the time being at least, slowing down, he has moved on to new pastures. I met with him in London to discover how he achieved his remarkable record and what he sees as the most fruitful places to invest in the coming decades.

LG: You started out as an aircraft engineer?

Peter Everington: Yes, I studied engineering at Cambridge and while I was doing that I also flew with the Air Force Reserve. I then went on to do aerobatic flying with them. When I finished at university, my original intention was to take my engineering and try to set up a business. I needed some business training, and back in those days — it sounds like I'm old — but twenty years ago there weren't many places where you could get business training in the U.K. There was nothing of the caliber that you've got over in Switzerland or in America. The idea that I came up with was to take a kind of self-designed business course by getting into research on companies in the investment field.

I joined a company called GT Management — which actually stood for Griffin Thornton and not "Good Times" as a lot of people used to say — and my intention was to spend a couple of years working on stock market research, visiting companies and analyzing them, and to combine that with my engineering expertise to set up my own business. What's happened since then is that I ended up enjoying myself so much in financial services that I just stayed. I worked four years for GT, initially two years in the U.K. and then I was transferred to the U.S.

I worked in San Francisco for two years and that's when I started working with Jim Mellon, who is still my partner today. I've been working with Jim now for nineteen years. The reason I went to the U.S. was that in April 1982 Jim had forecast that the U.S. was going to go into the biggest bull market in its history. He came up with this strange idea that the Dow would go up from 1000 to 10,000 over a twenty-year period and that it would be driven by the demographics of the postwar baby boom. It would be initiated by the tax cuts that Ronald Reagan had instituted in October 1981 which had the effect of transferring US$200 billion of cash flow from the government sector to the corporate sector, thereby doubling corporate cash flow in America overnight.

In April 1982, he made this call and the Dow at that stage was about 855. In June 1982 I was drafted out to help, and during all this period we were taking the American funds to higher levels of investment — to become more and more fully invested. We were just running around the country visiting companies and doing research. Everything seemed incredibly cheap, and I must admit that I liked Jim's argument — of course, I was only two years into the business, so I was easily convinced. We were supremely confident that this was all correct; it never entered our minds that we might be wrong, which was rather rash. I remember that when I arrived the Dow was falling, but we weren't fazed by that and we went around buying all these companies. The market kept on going down, but we kept on persuading our colleagues to give us more and more money.

GT was a company that was built on its Asian focus, and once we ran out of money we then had to go to our Asian colleagues in GT and say, "We need you to cut your allocations to Japan and increase your allocations to America, because we still think you should buy more." That was sacrilege in the context of GT, but we managed to persuade them and so we upped the investment levels, not just on the American funds but also on the international funds. We carried on buying and buying, the market kept on going down and down, and finally on August 12, 1982 — it's only a two-month time-span I'm talking about — the Dow Jones index hit 780.

There was a fellow around in those days called Jo Granville, who was a sort of Dr. Doom type, and he had predicted that if the Dow fell below 780 then the next technical support level was basically zero — in other words, real black hole stuff. So, on August 12, 1982 it hit 780 and it bounced, and I wiped the sweat from my brow and went back to my desk. Half an hour later the market came back down again and it hit 780 for a second time. The screen that we were looking at was one of those old Quotron machines where you put up your fifty favorite stocks with their ticker symbols. Every time they traded, the symbol would flash three or four times. When the Dow hit 780 for the second time, the screen lit up like a fireworks display as all the stock started trading. What was actually happening was that program selling had started to kick in. The market plunged through 780 and within fifteen minutes it was down another five points.

To put it in context, in those days the Dow never moved more than three-and-a-half points a day — three-and-a-half points was a big movement. Five points in fifteen minutes was absolutely out of this world. It had gone through the technical support level and things had gone super active. I was as white as a ghost, and turned to Jim and said, "What do we do now?" "There's only one thing left to do," he said. "We're going to get on our knees and pray."

We got on our knees with our elbows on the desks and we prayed — and the market turned around. Within three days the Dow was up 100 points, and by the end of the year we had the best performing fund in the world, making 127% for 1982 as a whole. Of course, at the same time this fellow Henry Kaufman, who was the strategist for Salomons, came out and said that perhaps interest rates of 18% weren't going to go up; perhaps they might come down after all. He thinks he turned the market, but I know that really the great fund manager in the sky had a long position to protect and our appeal worked, so I've been working with Jim ever since. We use that praying trick on occasions, but it hasn't seemed to work so successfully subsequently!

In 1984 GT went through an internal shake-up, and Richard Thornton, who was one of the founders, then left. Jim and I decided that GT would probably go through a dull patch for four or five years as it digested those changes, and so we decided to go off and set up our own business. We flew down to Australia one weekend from San Francisco to negotiate all that, and when we came back we decided we would quit GT and work out the details of our new business in due course. Then, out of the blue, Richard Thornton surfaced and said, "Why don't you consider joining me again and we'll set something up together?" Richard was in London, and Jim and I then went off to set up the Asian side of what became Thornton & Company. We moved to Hong Kong in June 1984 and focused solely on the Asian side of things, so it was a big change for us.

In 1985 we came up with this idea that the Southeast Asian countries, the NICs — the Newly Industrialized Countries — were going to go into a spectacular economic boom, bigger than anything they'd seen in forty years. The argument was very simple — it was based on the G5 Plaza Accord which occurred in September 1985. G5 Plaza basically dropped the value of the U.S. dollar significantly; the dollar halved against the yen. For the Southeast Asian NICs, the biggest competitor was Japan, and the Japanese economy in those days was twelve times bigger than Hong Kong, Singapore, Korea, and Taiwan combined. It was quite clear that a doubling of Japan's prices would blow it out of the water competitively, so Southeast Asia would get a huge competitive advantage and would obviously have an export boom as a result.

We postulated that Japan would respond to that by relocating her manufacturing facilities offshore into Southeast Asia, thereby creating a capital spending boom in Southeast Asia at the same time. That's unusual — capital normally picks up at the trailing edge of an economic cycle, not at the leading edge — and we were postulating that these things would happen simultaneously so you would get a double-sided boom, an export-led boom and a capital spending boom simultaneously. That's why we were arguing that it would be so spectacular.

We decided to launch a Southeast Asian NICs fund on the back of that, and in looking around for a name for that fund, I happened to read a *Business Week* article in September 1985 that described the Asian NICs as being like tigers prowling the jungle of Asia. I thought that was a good name, "tiger," so we took that name and we called our fund the Thornton Tiger Fund. We claim as a result that we invented the "tiger" name as far as funds are concerned.

LG: Did you coin the name "Little Dragons" too?

While the original "Tiger" economies were Hong Kong, Singapore, Korea, and Taiwan, the "Little Dragons" were the newer arrivals on the rapid growth scene — Indonesia, Thailand, Malaysia, and the Philippines.

Peter Everington: Yes, that name followed after. We budgeted for our original fund to raise US$5 million within six months and $10 million after a year. What actually happened was that after a year we had $100 million and after three years it was a $1.5 billion business. By that time we had sixteen different funds. We diversified from Tigers to Little Dragons and cut it all sorts of different ways. In essence, that became Thornton's entire business; everything else became irrelevant.

LG: Was it mainly institutional money that was coming in?

Peter Everington: No, it was actually money coming through independent financial advisors — a lot in the U.K., but also many internationally. It was much more retail-oriented, but we weren't dealing with the retail ourselves, we were going through the advisory network. Asia was booming at that time, so performance came relatively easily; from start-up to mid-1987, the original fund basically tripled.

The 1987 crash, I'm afraid, is something that I didn't foresee at all, because at that stage I wasn't really focusing much on Wall Street and I just figured that some of the Southeast Asian markets were perhaps going a bit too far, too fast. Everything that I was saying about them — that they had been discovered by the mainstream — was truly happening and, indeed, it *was* the case that they were going too far, too fast. Wall Street, of course, had elevated itself into a significant excess and then it crashed. That was very damaging to Southeast Asia; the Hong Kong market was closed for four days and the chairman of the stock exchange ended up going to jail subsequently, so the whole thing was a mess. Our Tiger Fund actually halved in that period in unit price terms, which was quite a shock, and it took me eighteen months to restore it to its high, which I achieved by the middle of 1989 or thereabouts.

In fact, 1988 was a spectacular year for us. Having failed to foresee the crash, the one decision I did take, which proved to be fortunate, was that I worked out, within a couple of days, that the markets would bounce and that the appropriate strategy was to stay fully invested and only raise money to the extent that clients were redeeming. We tried to persuade them not to.

Throughout 1989 we had constant redemptions, but we kept the fund fully invested all the way through and that decision meant that by the end of 1989 we were the best performing fund by a long way. That really laid the foundations for the recovery of the business.

Eventually, Thornton was sold to Dresdner Bank, who bought it out at about 550 times the equity price for Thornton at its inception. It's nice to make 550 times your money, but it was 550 times a small figure. We set up Thornton with just £25,000 of equity, but basically the original shareholders made 550 times their money. That was on the back of Southeast Asia, which proved to be a tremendous bonus for us.

Jim Mellon left Thornton and I stayed on, believing that once the company was sold to Dresdner Bank it would lead to a new direction and I could make that work — but obviously in a more corporate environment. It worked OK for a while, but the bureaucracy became a bit too much for me and I realized that I belong in a small set-up and not in a big set-up. By that stage Jim had gone through another situation and eventually, in late 1990, he set up Regent so I then rejoined him at Regent in 1992. It had already been going for a year by then and, like an old dog, you go back to your old tricks, so we focused Regent initially on the Southeast Asian Tiger markets again.

By then we were worried that the valuations had got much higher and so we were looking around for new approaches. Jim came up with this great idea of buying closed-end funds selling at discounts, and breaking them open and extracting the discount. Some of these funds were selling on really very substantial discounts and it proved to be a very, very profitable strategy. Almost by accident we had hit upon another aspect of it which turned out to be very important: over the last ten to fifteen years the financial services industry has become increasingly vertically integrated, as the banks have bought the fund managers, who've bought the securities companies, who've formed relationships with the insurance companies, and so on. That vertical integration in the industry has actually created a tremendous conflict of interest.

Indirectly we were exploiting that conflict of interest with what we call an undervalued asset strategy, but it's really a fund raiding strategy. To put that into perspective, if my old company Thornton, now owned by Dresdner Bank, were to try and raid, say, a Barings fund and break it open, what would happen is that Barings would go and complain to their new parent ING. ING, using its banking relationship, would go to

Dresdner Bank; and Dresdner Bank would drop down to Thornton and say, this isn't acceptable. You can see how, because of that vertical integration, those two companies can't do the fund raiding business. The industry is now overwhelmingly vertically integrated, particularly in the English sphere, and as a result the closed-end fund raiding strategy is unusually profitable as it can only be pursued by the relatively few independent managers that now exist.

We have been exploiting it ever since. We've taken that strategy and made it more sophisticated. We've systematized it and introduced various risk controls, but we've also introduced hedging techniques which have turned an aggressive strategy into a very mechanical, consistently profitable strategy. For example, the other day we bought a big stake in a fund called the Israel Fund run by Barclays, and it was selling at an 18% discount to NAV [net asset value]. We don't know anything about the Israel market at all and so we didn't particularly want the market risk. It's an indexing tracking fund and, while we normally like to work at higher discounts than 18%, you can go out and hedge an index tracking fund.

We bought a swap on the Israel index — I say "bought," but we were paid a 2% premium for the swap itself. From that point onwards, whether Israel went up or down made no difference to us whatsoever. That one turned out to be our fastest deal of its kind. As soon as we went to Barclays and told them we had this big stake in their fund, they said: "We know what you're going to do, so don't do it; we'll just do it ourselves." So, they moved to unitize the fund themselves and we made a very respectable and very quick return. The actual IRR [internal rate of return] on that was tremendous and, as I say, the combination of taking the more disciplined approach, applying measures of hedging where we think appropriate, has ended up with a strategy that is just very consistent. It's a beautiful little strategy that has been going on for years now and it's still a core part of Regent.

LG: At what point did you decide that the Asian boom had gone too far?

Peter Everington: I joined Regent in 1992 and we set up these Tiger Funds, as I mentioned. As we went through 1993 we were increasingly concerned about the excesses in the market. Most of the Asian markets doubled in the second half of 1993 and we were just standing there absolutely aghast. Then we did two things: first, in October 1993 we set up an Asian hedge fund — there are numerous hedge funds in the States, but ones for Asia were relatively rare and when we set it up there were only two or three of them operating. Even today there are really only around twenty Asian hedge funds.

We set that up in October 1993 when the markets were booming so as to be able in theory to make money out of falling markets as well as out of rising markets. Jim and I had got into the habit of working over Christmas in Asia, because we had found that while Christmas day is a holiday for most people, it's not for the Japanese markets. If we went into our offices then, we'd be about the only fund managers around, and we'd get all the good deals for that particular day. That was always a profitable strategy.

So, Jim and I were working over the Christmas and New Year period in 1993, and right through that time these Asian markets were just climbing in a parabolic fashion. Jim and I were shoveling out stock as fast as we could and we went short, not just for our hedge fund but also sold all the traditional funds as well. We literally exited Hong Kong completely, just in that few days. We couldn't believe our eyes when the market carried on climbing into 1994. By the end of January things had stuttered, and then you had this minor debacle in the States where a hedge fund went bust and then interest rates began to rise. That triggered a substantial setback in Asia in 1994. We managed to capture that positively for the hedge fund, which was short, while our traditional long funds were saved by being out of the market.

By the end of 1994 the Asian markets were down twenty-something percent. We only had two "long only" funds that were down, and they were down only single digits; almost all of our long funds were up for the year, so 1994 was a spectacular year for us. When you have a spectacular year when it's a bad year for most people, that of course works very, very well for you.

These events had set us in mind that Asia was sort of peaking out, so when it picked up again in 1995 we never really believed it. We made some money out of it, but we weren't prepared to climb back on board in a big way. In 1996 we actually sold off all our Asian mutual funds, believing that prices had become excessive. People were paying stupid prices to get into the industry, salaries were going through the roof, and so you faced the threat of losing people or having to pay ridiculous prices to keep fund managers. The whole economics of the business were being destroyed. Basically, the price of outputs was coming down as fund management fees were being squeezed and input prices were going up, so we could see that the business was rapidly commoditizing, and we sold it. It turns out that we sold the business a year too early, but we were very, very fortunate to be out of the Asian mutual fund business when Asia collapsed in 1997.

The 1997 Asian currency crisis

During 1997 a hurricane of currency devaluations tore through Asia, causing havoc in the economies of the NICs. The IMF was called in to bail out the worst-affected countries, Thailand, Indonesia, and South Korea, amidst a series of banking scandals. In Thailand, for instance, it is estimated that non-performing loans represented a third of the country's GNP in early 1997.

LG: Did you expect that to happen in the way that it did?

Peter Everington: It was much more dramatic than we anticipated. We certainly expected a severe correction, but I think even we were taken by surprise by the way whole countries blew up. After some currencies started crumbling, we concluded that there was going to be fairly widespread currency damage. We actually thought that there was a severe risk that the Hong Kong peg might go at that stage; certainly there was huge pressure on it. That's one of the reasons why Hong Kong actually suffered so badly. The Hong Kong peg is a simple mechanism for exchanging currency pressure for interest rates. If you don't take the pressure through the currency, you're going to take it through the stock market instead and that's why Hong Kong is now such a volatile place to invest. The peg creates huge stock market volatility in exchange for currency stability.

May 15, 1997 was a critical day, if you go back and look at the charts, because that's when the Thai baht began to wobble. It didn't actually devalue until July, but you can quite clearly see that things began to wobble at that stage. Interest rates began to blow out, forward rates blew out, and that was the start of the crisis.

It's quite interesting that in the two weeks prior to that we'd had a very significant move on the yen. I am a great believer that what has been indirectly driving the financial markets over the last five years or so is Japan. Although the Japanese stock market has been highly depressed, what the Japanese have been doing in response to that has had a huge impact on international markets. In particular, in July 1995, Japan made a huge policy shift. Up to that stage they had treated their problems — problems that date from the beginning of the 1990s — as being substantially economic problems.

Certainly there was an economic manifestation — the economy had slowed down and they were facing recession and stuff like that — but I'd always thought the core of the problem wasn't the economy. The real problem was the banking system, which was a monetary phenomenon. In effect, from 1991 to 1995, the Japanese tried to solve what they saw to be an economic problem with fiscal medicine, which was completely inappropriate. In July 1995 they reversed their policy and shifted to monetary stimulation, which I believe to have been the correct policy. Of course, they were starting that five years too late, so they'd lost a lot of ground by then, but from July 1995 the Japanese began printing money like it was going out of style. In their case if they hadn't, it would have gone out of style permanently because the banking system in Japan was completely bust.

The resulting easy money didn't stay in Japan; it was exported and ended up substantially in the U.S. dollar system, via the purchase of $400 billion worth of U.S. Treasuries by Japanese institutions in the 1995-97 period. That, I believe, has acted like a shot of morphine in the arm of the dollar system.

LG: What do you mean by the dollar system?

Peter Everington: It is the U.S. equity market, the U.S. bond market, but also it is most of the world's emerging markets because they are dollar-based. I believe that it has created a huge bubble in that dollar system and that bubble is now bursting. It began with the collapse of Asia in 1997, then Russia in 1998, then South America; and then, when the tidal wave began knocking on America's door, Greenspan acted to prevent it from coming in. That may be an appropriate policy — history will eventually be the judge. I think that Greenspan is strongly motivated by the fact that when he started at the Fed it was in 1987 and more or less as soon as he came in he faced the stock market crash, so he's very keen not to face the same situation again.

I think that what you're looking at today is a situation where the bubble in America still exists, the bubble in the emerging markets world has collapsed, and we're sitting in suspended animation between the two situations. I fully expect Wall Street to face a crash within the next six months.

A bust coming in the U.S.?

LG: How bad a crash?

Peter Everington: It'll start a fall that will eventually take it down to about 6500 to 7000 on the Dow. I don't think it's a 1987-type situation. I don't think it's all going to happen in one day. If I had to guess, I would say the likely prognosis is that it starts with a crash, but people will react by assuming, incorrectly, that 1987 is the model, so they will buy and you'll get a terrific bounce and then the bear market will begin. So, the 1929 situation is more the model for what's coming.

LG: So, a six-year bear market?

Peter Everington: No, no. I think it's getting much quicker — you'll have the crash, followed by a bounce, and then a two-year bear market, something like that. I'm not talking about an economic depression or anything like that, I don't see that, but I see us sitting on a four-year cyclical excess that needs to be excised from the system. Bonds in America have been going down now for nine months.

Equities have carried on sailing through the roof, but the bond market is telling you the true story, so to a certain extent the tidal wave of correction is already whipping through America. You just haven't seen it in the equity market yet. Actually, that's a classic divergence that you see before any crash. You saw that in 1929, you saw it in 1987 — bonds and equities go out of line for an extended period of time and it is unsustainable.

If I had to put markers down, I would say that when the interest rate went above 6% in America on the long bond, that started to put the equity market on amber — it went from green to amber in traffic light terms — so I believe the equity market right now in America is topping out; we are in the equivalent of August 1987. If the long bond yield goes to 6.4% or 6.5%, which I expect will happen sometime in the next three to six months, then that's when you'll have your crash. So, as we talk today, the long bond is 6.06%; it was even as high as 6.18% two weeks ago. The long bond yield has been climbing, and I believe it's indicating that liquidity is drying up in the States. There is a squeeze going on. So far it's just a liquidity squeeze and sentiment in the equity market has been able to counterbalance that liquidity, but it won't be able to do that forever.

LG: Where does the liquidity squeeze come from?

Peter Everington: The Japanese have started to withdraw their money. Although the U.S. economy is itself whipping along at a hell of a pace, the Japanese economy is also picking up and that's very bad for America because the Japanese will bring their money home and that will just absorb a lot of money if it gets the Japanese economy going again. That will bring Wall Street down.

The funny thing about our business is that when markets fall you have to explain it, but when markets rise, that's considered to be the norm. You have long-term secular trends and the secular up-trend in Wall Street began in 1982, the secular disinflation-driven boom, that's absolutely sound. It's probably still got another five or six years to run, and I have always thought that the bull market in America would peak around 2002. Making money in the 1980s and 1990s I never thought to be any problem, but holding on to it after you go past the year 2000 I see as being a problem.

LG: Why?

Peter Everington: Mainly because the demographic trends then start to turn very decisively negative, which is the main factor driving all this. So I am not, at the moment, talking about an end to this secular up-trend. I do believe that there is this cyclical excess that's built up that has to be dealt with. Cyclical excess in stock markets is due to liquidity and it's the same effect, if you like, as excess liquidity in your body. If you drink too much of an evening, then the following morning you have a hangover. The hangover is the painful part, but it's not actually the problem. The problem is the excess drinking the night before.

You have the same phenomenon in the stock markets. The 1987 crash wasn't the problem; it was the resolution of the problem. The problem was the bubble that was built up in 1985 and 1986.

We have a client who is eighty-eight years old who was in our office recently, and he said that in America today — and I'm quoting this because I think it's absolutely correct — every day a million people wake up, log on to the Internet, and buy and sell shares — day trading, in other words — in many cases without any knowledge whatsoever of the value of the underlying assets they're buying. Now, any way you look at it, that is pure speculation, it's gambling. When that stops, you're going to get a tremendous drying up of liquidity within the system. Our client looked me straight in the eye and said — of course, I'm forty-one years old and he's eighty-eight — "You're probably too young to remember the 1929 crash, but I remember it very well. I wasn't investing huge amounts of my own money by that stage, but I do remember the speculative excesses that came beforehand, and in my opinion the speculative excesses in the United States today are worse than they were in 1929."

The other most significant change that people don't dwell on is the change to the bank clearing system that was introduced in 1992. Up to that point, banks in America had to clear with the Fed once a day. At the end of the day they had to satisfy all their capital ratios, so at the end of the day they closed the books and everything had to balance — once a day, at day end. In 1992 the Fed went from a batch processing system to a real time system. If you've got to balance once a day at day end, you don't know until the last minute how close you are to the line, because you've got thousands of transactions coming in, so you have to build in a margin relative to that line. Because of the change in the clearing system, you are able to look into the Fed real time twenty-four hours a day. That means you don't have to build that margin anymore, because you know precisely where the line is at any point in the day. You still have to meet your adequacy ratio once a day, but you can judge your position close to the line.

It's estimated that that has indirectly given rise to the ability to create US$50 billion of intraday credit within the system, credit that arises in the morning and disappears by the evening. If you put that in classic monetary analysis, you would say that, in effect, measuring the money supply today is completely incomparable to measuring it yesterday, because you're not measuring the intraday effects. The true money supply is bigger than what is being measured. You could translate it another way and say that it has increased greatly the velocity of the circulation of money; therefore, monetary conditions in America have been far looser than they would appear to have been — and that also explains the bubble.

How to use charts

LG: You mentioned technical support levels earlier. Could you talk a bit about your views on technical analysis and whether it has any value at all?

Peter Everington: I think technical analysis is like a map. If you can't read a map and you're going on a journey, you're stuck. A map can enable you to find your way when you are lost, but it doesn't guarantee that you don't get lost. When you go on a journey, you have to establish first off where you are at the start and where you want to get to at the end. In stock market terms that's actually very difficult to do. You have to establish where you are right now, what level is the market today — I don't mean the level of the Dow, I mean what is imputed into the market to reach that level. You have to know what economic figures are discounted to achieve that, what earning figures are discounted to achieve that. Charts have this very useful effect as far as I'm concerned, particularly long-term charts: they can help you tell where you are right now. As to technical analysis, the kind where you start drawing head-and-shoulders patterns and you decide to get in or out of markets solely on that basis, I personally find that rubbish.

If you are looking at a stock and you think you've come across some information about a company that isn't discounted, and then you go back to the chart and it says the stock prices just jumped 30% in the market in the last three months, it's pretty obvious that the information that you've got is already known by other people. You may think the stock is still cheap, and you may go on to buy, but it does tell you that something has happened, that some information is already discounted. The same is true of the bond markets and currencies.

Charts are also useful if you have decided that things should be going one way but actually they're not. A chart can give you a very sharp slap in the face by saying, "No, you thought it was going to go this way, but it's actually going the opposite way. You are, by definition, wrong. Go back and work out why you're wrong, which of your assumptions are wrong."

Analyzing the baby boom

Peter Everington: What's happening in China is precisely the same thing as has been happening in the States in the last twenty years. It's a demographic effect. The argument in America at the moment is that the demographic effect of the baby boom is behind the bull market and the simplistic assumption is that, as the postwar baby boomers have moved toward retirement, their children now have pretty much gone through school so they're starting to save more money, and that money is going into the stock market in 401Ks, hence the bull market. That analysis is completely ridiculous, because all that extra saving that may well be taking place is being more than offset by greater levels of consumption by younger people, with the result that the net savings rate in the United States has been falling for fifteen years. The argument that higher savings is driving the stock market up is therefore completely wrong. The baby boom argument in that sense is completely wrong. However, the baby boom *is* a significant driving force in the U.S. for a completely different reason, and that is the sheer economics of the labor force.

Figure 3.1 U.S. Demographics

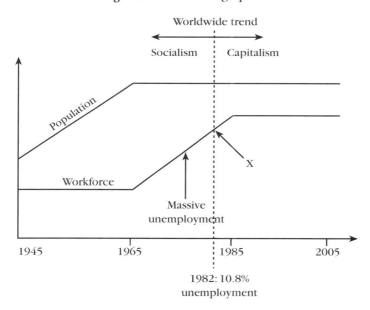

An increased population leads to an increase in the size of the workforce, in turn causing massive unemployment. An excess supply of labor, argues Everington, has weakened its bargaining power and ushered in today's go-go capitalism across the world.

Looking at Figure 3.1, if we put the end of the war at 1945, then from 1945 to 1965 in America the population grew very rapidly. Now, I'm a great bull on babies myself — I've got three so far and I'd love to have six by the time I'm finished — but the main thing about babies is they're economically negative for the first twenty years of their life, and in some cases for a lot longer.

If you look at the equivalent line for the workforce, it goes sideways from 1945 to 1965, then it takes off from 1965 to 1985, and then it goes sideways. So, the workforce chart would be similar to the population chart lagged by twenty years. The consequence of this huge increase in the size of the workforce was that by the late 1970s, you had massive unemployment. For the United States, in 1982 it was 10.8% at its peak (see point X on Figure 3.1). Some people say that's because in the 1970s you had terrible economic management and all that sort of stuff, but that's nonsense. In the United States the rate of job creation has been a rising statistic every year since the Second World War with only minor down ticks at times of recession. The United States has been creating more new jobs every year; therefore, the unemployment didn't result from *insufficient demand for labor*, it was the consequence of an *excess supply of labor* — in other words, the postwar baby boom effect.

If you're an economic chef, you only have three ingredients, which are land, labor, and capital. Of those three, land is a fixed item which doesn't vary except, perhaps, every 200 years with land reform, so take it out, it's not a variable. The two variables are labor and capital. Economics and the stock market are all about the interplay between those two factors. What the postwar baby boom did was to create a position of a huge excess supply of labor which destroyed the bargaining position of labor relative to capital. That is why, since this period, we've moved into a period of great capitalism which you can say followed a period pre the 1980s of great socialism. If you think back to the 1960s and 1970s, across the globe you had rising socialism, great leaps forward, great plans, and all this stuff that was introduced in the postwar period.

Suddenly, since the 1980s, we've found ourselves in this great free enterprise capitalist period and the driving force behind that is the baby boom. If you have massive unemployment, labor has no bargaining position; therefore, your wages will be flat or falling. Capital, on the other hand, is in relatively short supply, so the return on capital will be high and rising. That's what's been happening, and that's the source of the bull market in America.

If you go and look at the future statistics — for example, for the United States — and you compare 2015 to 1985, the ratio of workers to non-workers will have halved. What that means is, assuming everything else stays the same — which in fact will not be the case, but if you take that assumption — you can work out that by the year 2015 the U.S. will be running a cash flow deficit on its Social Security account of US$1500 billion a year, which is clearly unsustainable. And that represents massive dis-saving because the baby boomers will start to spend instead of save once they go into retirement. So, you can postulate that sometime in the future there is going to be a massive decline in the savings rate from the current position of zero.

What does it mean for stock markets when you have net extraction of capital taking place? We've never seen that before; we don't know the model. So, clearly other things will not be equal — most likely by the time you get to 2015, the retirement age in America and most countries will have had to rise to seventy-five.

The other difference is that in earlier periods of the baby boom where you had a lot of non-workers compared to workers, those non-workers were all children. In the future the non-workers will be retired adults, and the big difference between children and adults is that adults vote and children don't. You'll get the emergence of gray parties, and you could end up with a tremendous voting fight between the workers and the non-workers because the non-workers will be wanting their promised retirement benefits which should have come from savings made over the years, but we all know that the Social Security accounts are actually bankrupt. When Maggie Thatcher came to power in Britain at the beginning of the 1980s, England's Social Security system had four months' cash flow and no assets — it was completely bust. If you ran a corporate pension fund on that basis, you'd be sent to jail for fraud. So, for years in the English system, basically, all those savings into national insurance were just raped by politicians who used them on stupid projects that never yielded a return. The retirement savings were all blown years and years ago, but all those people still expect to be looked after in retirement.

LG: And it is even more true in continental Europe.

Peter Everington: Yes. It's a terrible, terrible problem. You could take a slightly more Machiavellian approach. You could argue that this actually represents the seeds of the ending of the great Western boom. The current economic leader of the world is America; the previous economic leader was England. England had the highest per capita GDP at the turn of the century and now we're number eighteen, so we've been going downhill for nearly a hundred years. At the turn of the century the British capital markets represented 75% of the world; they're now 7%.

Before England, the various economic powers were the Spanish, the French, the Italians, the Hapsburgs, not in that in order, but if you go back even further, a thousand years or so, you get back to when Europe was nothing and all the action in the world was taking place in Asia. In the tenth century AD in China they had an iron industry turning out more tons of iron on an annual basis than Britain did at the peak of the Industrial Revolution in the nineteenth century.

So Britain gave up its supremacy to America, and America inevitably gives it up to whom? In my view, clearly it's the Japanese who are destined to be the new economic leaders of the world. That's not necessarily a savory conclusion for a lot of people. The next super-power is clearly going to be an Asian power — I would suggest the Japanese, but I'm not necessarily wedded to that conclusion. That will automatically mean the ending of that period of 500 years of Western dominance.

LG: So, where does it go from here?

Peter Everington: America wasn't the only country that had a baby boom effect. Any country involved in the war had such an effect. In 1978 in China, Deng Xiaoping came along and opened up China to reform. He really tried to decentralize, revive enterprise, and get the economy moving. In 1979, a year later, Margaret Thatcher came to power in the U.K. on a platform of decentralization and revival of enterprise. In 1980 in America, Ronald Reagan came to power and his platform was again the revival of enterprise and the decentralizing of government. In 1981, Mitterand in France came in as a socialist president and within two years he was a born-again capitalist. In 1982, Kohl in Germany and Gonzales in Spain came in, again on similar platforms of decentralization and the revival of enterprise. That's a five-year tiny window of history where I've just shown you six countries apparently all moving in exactly the same direction, but for what reason? I mean, they're doing exactly the same thing at virtually exactly the same time, and it's inconceivable that China conspired with France or that the U.K. conspired with Germany, or whatever, so what you have there is a statistical aberration. These people were all doing the same things at the same time, apparently randomly.

There must be an underlying explanation for it, and the underlying explanation is the postwar baby boom. In China in 1978, Deng Xiaoping woke up and said, "Look, we've got a serious unemployment problem." Officially it's zero in China, but we estimate now, looking back, that it was 25%. And Deng Xiaoping, like any good politician, would say or do whatever is necessary to keep himself in power — it's the nature of politicians. He said, "If we don't get these people into productive employment, we're going to have social unrest, revolution, and that will lead to the end of the Communist Party. So if we want to keep the Communist Party in power, how do we do that? We've got to revive the economy. The Americans have this thing called Capitalism; it seems to work for them, so why don't we try that in China? We've got to give it a new name, of course — we can't just admit that the Americans got it right and we Chinese got it wrong — so we'll call it the Policy of the Four Modernizations." That's what they introduced in 1978 and it's been stunningly successful. The economy has grown 8% compound now for nineteen years, and unemployment has been absorbed. The Communist Party has stayed in power as a result. That's what's going on in China; it's an economic transformation based on the same factors as occurred in the United States. There's no reason for that to reverse, so it's a reasonable assumption that enterprise — rising enterprise — is a real trend in China that will continue.

That doesn't say anything about the political equation. I happen to think that eventually the enterprise and the political equation will clash, and I don't think that point is too far off. I also make the observation that just from a pure investment point of view, even if you've got enterprise, and you've got a booming economy there, it doesn't necessarily mean you can make money out of it. The amazing thing in China is you've had nineteen years of 8% compound growth and yet I've never met a person who's made any money out of it. Foreigners don't make money out of China. The local Chinese do, but the investments that are offered foreigners, the typical rubbish that's put on the exchange, isn't good investment and that's what the poor foreigner is stuck with. So, China remains for me a wonderful theoretical story, but something that you should never invest in.

LG: What about Hong Kong companies?

Peter Everington: I think that's a complete charade. Investment through Hong Kong companies is a joke. There are some good companies, but in the broad general sense two-thirds of the Hong Kong stock market still comprises real estate-related companies. What you are investing in is the real estate value of Hong Kong and, since the Hong Kong stock market is now worth a third of Southeast Asia, in effect you're trying to say that a good quarter of the value of Southeast Asia's stock markets is based on the real estate of Hong Kong itself. I mean, is that really investing in China?

I can see how you can pull yourself into it because that's the only option, but if you think about it, for the last twenty years, people have been chasing the great China dream which goes like this: if we can sell a single matchstick to a billion Chinese, we'll make a fortune. People have been trying to do that for years and years, and the feedback loop doesn't seem to be working. Western companies have been sinking money in there, and it's been going down a hole. Only in the last couple of years have you started to see some boardrooms in America and Europe wake up to the fact that this endless flow of money isn't leading to the great dream that they thought they were aiming at.

I'm not saying it's not possible to make money in China. I'm saying that if you're part of the thundering herd that's chucking money at China willy-nilly, you shouldn't be surprised if the Chinese, as anyone would, turn around and tilt the equation against you. It's not cheating; it's just natural when you have excess demand.

LG: I've heard from overseas Chinese that they too have lost money, which is perhaps a bit more surprising, in mainland China.

Peter Everington: A lot of Hong Kong Chinese hate visiting their relatives in China, because when they go they're expected to bring lots of presents and it's a very expensive experience. There's this image that China is poor and foreigners are rich, and therefore there is an expectation of transfer. It's the same effect — there's no difference between your relatives demanding presents from you when you go and visit, and the country demanding presents from you as an overseas Chinese in business.

I think there are a lot of overseas Chinese who have made money, but equally you hear that there are plenty of overseas Chinese who are latter-day China enthusiasts. They've been caught up in the swirl and don't know China any better than any other foreigner, so naturally they'll get caught.

LG: When would you start investing in Asia again?

Peter Everington: It's tempting for us to rebuild or repurchase a mutual fund operation, but we decided not to do that. I think that the broad portfolio approach to Asia in the next five years isn't the way to go. By a broad portfolio approach I mean, say, buying the index. I don't think that is going to work, because 20% of Asia's companies are now bust — 20% of what's gone down isn't ever coming back again.

In Indonesia, about 70% of companies are bust — these are the walking dead; they're not necessarily declared bankrupt yet, but they are bust, in the old-fashioned sense of liabilities exceeding assets. Some of the greatest excesses in Asia were caused by the biggest companies. I wouldn't be surprised in five years' time to look back and see that the Asian market, broadly speaking, has gone sideways, but with great volatility. But the real opportunity in Asia is actually buying up real businesses and turning them around. If you are a fund manager, it's the stock picker over the market player, so I think Asia is now in a phase when good stock picking will yield great rewards, but more particularly if you can go ahead and buy actual companies entirely. I think there are many opportunities, such as we've been taking advantage of, in buying bankrupt companies and turning them around. We bought a securities company in Korea last year, and our control position was bought on a US$45 million valuation for the company. We didn't buy it all in one go, but having performed some fairly radical surgery on that business, which involved downsizing by 30%, introducing new products, and restructuring the balance sheet, etc., that company will make over US$100 million profit this year. Our original investment was on, as it turns out, less than half a year's earnings.

The Korean market has turned around and business is booming, so obviously in the Wall Street crash everything like this takes a backward step for a while. However, I happen to think that the way to make money always, but particularly in this environment, is to buy what's cheap and sell what's expensive. A lot of those assets in Asia are now incredibly cheap and can be bought. Given my expectation of a severe wobble on Wall Street, which eventually could drop it down to the 7000 level on the Dow, Hong Kong in particular will do very badly. I think you'll see the Hang Seng index down below 6000, which will be pretty severe and Hong Kong will then truly begin to understand the cost of its pegged exchange rate system. Property prices in Hong Kong are down by 40% and some people think that's enough, but the problem is that property prices went up fourteen-fold between 1984 and 1997. The reality is that even at these so-called depressed levels of property prices in Hong Kong, per square foot prices for offices in the center of Hong Kong are 120% above prices in Manhattan. I can't believe that the bottom of the bear market in Hong Kong is 120% above the top of the bull market in America; it doesn't seem right to me.

I don't think the world is in any great trouble here. I think you have this bubble that has been bursting, but the final show, the final act, has to take place in America, which will definitely send some shocks through markets generally. After that, people will get back to real investment as opposed to speculating. In the long run, compound rates of return at 10% per annum are wonderful; but people have started to get used to 30% again and that's always dangerous.

Russia vs China

LG: Why do you think China is getting its act together, while Russia is in a mess?

Peter Everington: The difference is that in 1978, when Deng Xiaoping reformed China, central planning or communism in China was only twenty-nine years old, and it's relatively easy to roll back on that. In 1978, communism in Russia was sixty years old, and there was no-one around who could remember what it was like before — that's why turning Russia was much tougher. After all, Gorbachev tried to turn things around and, indeed, the leaders before Gorbachev. There were early signs of change, but no-one could get the popular mandate.

Russia didn't get the mandate for change until it had completely collapsed. It then embraced free enterprise and is firmly on the path of reform. I'm a great believer that it has genuinely started in Russia and is going to continue. Russia is a tremendous enterprise opportunity, probably better than China in that regard. The question is whether you can make any money out of that — that's a different question. What's going on in Russia is, if anything, overly rapid enterprise. Now let's analyze these points. What is central planning? Central planning is a system that doesn't work. An analogy is that I sit in the center of a room with 400 people and determine when each of those people goes to the toilet; one by one I order them to the toilet. It's highly inefficient. Free enterprise is when each of those 400 people in the room decides individually when they should go to the toilet. That may lead to a crowd at the toilet temporarily, but it does work much better over time. That's the difference between central planning and free enterprise.

Central planning would have collapsed in Russia many years ago, back in the 1940s, if it wasn't for the fact that the Russians themselves enterprisingly got around this rotten system by establishing shadow economies, substructures, black markets, and so on. That took them forty years to build, and when Yeltsin came along and said, "No more central planning. Now we have free enterprise," what do you do with all those substructures? They took years to build and they're going to take years to dismantle. That's the essence of the corruption that you have in Russia. That's what communism basically did, it corrupted people morally and economically because that's how they had to survive. It will take years before you can put that right again, and that's really the hitch as to whether foreigners can make money out of it.

What is free enterprise? Free enterprise is where each of us individually goes and decides what to do based on seeking our own best advantage. Now, that only works when it is surrounded by a system of laws and morals. If you don't have the laws and morals, then free enterprise is a system where I take out a gun and shoot everyone around me and steal their money. That's what you've got in Russia, in essence. You've got the laws, but they're not being properly applied, and you don't have the morals because they were debased by sixty years of communism. On the other hand, what you do also have in Russia is an irreversible economic shift whereby they privatized 127,000 companies, the effect of which was to reduce the government to just 15% of GDP. The American government is 32% of GDP, so the Russian government, by that definition, is already twice as capitalist as America.

In the Russian crisis, their government deficit was 4% of GDP. If that's critical, what about the Japanese with a deficit of 9% of GDP? People talk about Russia's debt problems, but US$140 billion is peanuts in the context of things. Take one Russian company, Gazprom — it's got a third of the world's reserves of natural gas, and is thirteen times bigger than Exxon in hydrocarbon terms. Exxon is worth US$180 billion, so on a hydrocarbon basis you could suggest that Gazprom should be worth US$1 trillion. Perhaps that is excessive, but it's clearly worth a lot of money. Some people say it's not a real company, but it's the same company that's been supplying 25% of Western Europe's demand for natural gas for the last fifty years, so it *is* a real business. Goldman Sachs could do a syndicated sale of the entire business, probably raise US$50 billion, and you could use that to back a currency board, pay off some of the debts, and solve all Russia's problems if you wanted to do it that way. They're not going to do it that way, but you can see how you could easily use the asset base of Russia to deal with the debt problem. Russia's debt problem isn't big, it's peanuts.

LG: Can foreign investors make money there?

Peter Everington: Yes, I think they can, but you have to allow for the risks. Whenever you see huge shocks to the system, you buy. For instance, we've just recapitalized our Russian funds, and anyone who participated in that at the depths is up over 100% in the last three months. You could buy the Russian telephone company, Rostelecom, today on a valuation that is less than the value of NatWest Tower in the City of London. Now, that may mean that NatWest Tower is overvalued, but I happen to think it means the telephone company in Russia is undervalued. So it should be, it should be extremely undervalued, but not by quite that much. I think you can buy something like that today and in five or ten years' time you'll make five times your money.

LG: But is it difficult for a private person to buy Russian shares direct on the Moscow exchange?

Peter Everington: Yes, absolutely. Private individuals should buy ADRs in Russia, that's the way to go. There are plenty of them. You can buy Rostelecom in ADR form. Whether it is still attractively priced at the time people are reading this book, I don't know; they'll have to judge that for themselves. Today the stock has climbed a lot from its low, but I would still recommend it at the current price — about $1.40 in the ordinary stock form — and that is incredibly cheap, in my view, even though it has come up from a low of below 60 cents.

For the average person in the U.S., say, buying stocks on the Russian market is too complicated. You can go to some of the big brokers like Morgan Grenfell or DMG Securities and most of them have got the ability to deal in Russia for you, but once you take transaction costs and all that into account, you're much safer buying the ADRs. Most of the big Russian companies are now available in ADR form. Or you can buy a fund excellently managed by a group like ours, Regent Pacific, or something like that!

Peter Everington is the author of the chapters on convertible bonds in The Financial Times Global Guide to Investing *(Financial Times, Pitman Publishing, 1995). To find out more about his group's views on the latest developments in emerging markets, visit Regent's website at: www.regentpac.com/.*

For reports, contact:

Regent Pacific Fund Management
39 St. James's Street
London SW1A 1JD
United Kingdom
Tel: +44 20 7518 2175
Email: marketing@regentpac.com

4

Mark Mobius:
The Pioneer

At first sight, Mark Mobius Ph.D. looks a fit, energetic forty-something, so it is quite a surprise to realize that he is in his early sixties. Managing more than thirty emerging market funds, worth over US$15 billion, for the Templeton mutual fund group, Mobius spends around 300 days a year visiting companies all over the world, using a Gulfstream jet that he regards as his office. I caught up with him at Templeton's offices in Singapore, following a series of faxes and messages across three continents.

Despite his extraordinary lifestyle, Mark Mobius exudes the qualities you would hope for in one of the world's top emerging market fund managers: calm, objectivity, a profound knowledge of his subject — and charm. Having spent more than three decades in Asia, he is no latecomer to the scene. There can be few, if any, investors who can boast a longer or more intimate on-the-ground knowledge of how the world's newer capital markets are evolving.

His book Mobius on Emerging Markets *(Financial Times, Pitman Publishing, 1995) is a must-read for anyone who is serious about active investment overseas, providing a thorough picture of the hows and whys of emerging market investment. "The world belongs to optimists," he says. Perhaps this is one of those points, like value investing, that you either get or you don't — but, once you have seen for yourself the energy, abundance, and sheer wealth of talent that is flourishing in the developing nations, it's hard not to be optimistic. The future may not lie in the West, but Western investors can still participate in the action.*

LG: Would you tell me a bit about your background? You grew up in the States?

Mark Mobius: I was born in the U.S. of a German father and a Puerto Rican mother. I went to school in Long Island, then I went to Boston University, the University of Wisconsin, Kyoto University in Japan, the University of New Mexico, and finally MIT where I got a Ph.D. in developmental economics. Then I started a career in Asia — in Korea, Thailand, and Hong Kong — so I've been in Asia now for over thirty-five years. About twenty years ago I took up German citizenship, and now I'm traveling most of the time. I'm not based anywhere, really. I spend a month or two here in Singapore, a month or two in Hong Kong, and the rest — well, I'll give you an example: already this month I've been in Brazil, Argentina, South Africa, India, Thailand, and Singapore; on Saturday we go to Korea, then Hong Kong, and then off to Europe.

LG: So, they're very short trips?

Mark Mobius: Usually a few days, sometimes a week. If we're going to a country where we have a lot of investments, then it's for at least a week, but then within the country I may go to a number of cities. Last month I was in South Africa and went to Durban, Cape Town, and Johannesburg.

LG: Are you mainly interviewing company staff?

Mark Mobius: Staff, and also management — talking to the managers, talking to the workers in these companies, looking at the facilities if we can. We try as much as possible to look at what's happening, particularly in manufacturing, and to understand what the problems are, what they are faced with. And then we try to get a feel for the environment in general, just looking around.

We were in Thailand last week; when you see all these unfinished, see-through buildings there, you realize that it's a problem to liquidate these things. You put two and two together and you get some idea of what's happening, and that helps you to make decisions.

Also, the fact that you visit these companies and these places normally gives you more confidence to withstand the shocks when they come. You know when there's a real problem, and you're more likely to say, "OK, let's buy more" if you think that prices have come down enough. So it's really a psychological support that you have when you're traveling in the investment areas, particularly in emerging markets.

LG: Is it because you can visualize what the country is like? It's not just an abstract idea?

Mark Mobius: Right. And it's people. You know you're dealing with people and in most cases you're dealing with honest, good people that you can have faith in. By being on the ground you realize that while headlines in a newspaper will tell you something, they won't give a fully rounded picture of what's actually happening, and that tends to give you more confidence.

Trouble in Turkey?

In his book Mobius on Emerging Markets, *Mark Mobius tells the story of problems he encountered when he invested in Çukurova Elektrik, a Turkish power company. Subsequent to his investment, the family-owned Uzan group obtained an 18% stake in Çukurova from the government, and then built up the stake to become majority shareholders.*

Mobius and his team started to observe a serious worsening of Çukurova's performance in 1993, when profits dropped by 31%. The next year the company showed its first loss (US$18 million) in thirty-four years of trading.

Mobius decided to protest at a shareholders' meeting about what he saw as the board's mismanagement. To do this, he had to specially register ownership of his shares in an awesome rigmarole of bureacratic red tape. He only obtained this registration after a direct appeal to the President of Turkey.

At the shareholders' meeting his objections were noted, but he lost the vote to the Uzan group. In 1995, however, Turkey's Capital Market Board sued the Uzans for numerous serious irregularities. Eventually, the government moved in to remove the Uzan-dominated board, but the dispute continued to widen, involving much of Turkey's financial and political elite. This is exactly the kind of nightmare that keeps smaller investors at home. I asked Mark Mobius what he thought about Turkey now.

Mark Mobius: Well, interestingly, in the case of Çukurova, if we had hung on it would have turned out to be a very good investment because these Uzan people began speculating in the stock and pushed the prices up to remarkably high levels. Even in that terrible case that we had, if we'd hung on long enough we may have come out all right. I don't recommend doing that, but that's the kind of thing that happens in these markets.

Turkey I found to be a very, very good place to invest. Yes, you have some very shrewd business people who can take you for a ride, but there are also some very outstanding and upstanding business people who think of their reputation and try their very best to do well for all shareholders. So, that's one thing. The second thing is that I find that Turks tend to be broadminded, and willing to accept new ideas and new technology and partnerships. A good example of that is the Akbank people, the Sabanci Group. They have joint ventures with a number of major global companies, and that has really helped them a lot. You see that pattern a lot in Turkey. Because they've had an empire, they know what the world is like. And the macroeconomic situation, a very high inflation environment, tends to be good for equities.

We've made money in Turkey over the years. It's been a good market for us, and I find it a fascinating country. It's a wonderful country. I love it.

Political risk

LG: Could you talk about political risk and what to do about it?

Mark Mobius: The thing about political risk is that it can't be predicted very accurately, if at all, because things can change so rapidly. You have political risk everywhere. The potential, at least, for political risk exists everywhere, in every country, whether they are emerging markets or developed markets. The difference in emerging markets generally is that you have a very strong contrast between a stable environment and a very unstable environment, in the sense that in a pluralistic society, which you have in the developed countries like the United States and Europe and now in Japan and Australia, there is continuing chaos but within certain borders, certain rules and regulations. So, the unpredictability is still there, but it's within certain limits.

In the case of emerging markets, you can sometimes have extreme orderliness because of a dictatorship or a hierarchy which has produced very stable conditions, particularly in a benevolent dictatorship or bureaucracy. For example, in Indonesia, Suharto's regime was very stable. He was benevolent to a great degree; even though the oligarchs were making a lot of money, people were eating and things were stable. Another example would be Thailand in the previous era. Now they've become more pluralistic, but previously it was a monarchy with very stable institutions — you know, the monkhood, the military, and so forth. It was very stable, maybe even more stable than the U.S. and the U.K.; personal safety was very good. Hong Kong is another example. Under the benevolent colonial dictatorship, it was very, very stable. In Singapore, essentially one party governs.

So, there are lots of these examples in emerging markets, but then when things get tough, when the environment changes and the oligarchs or the dictators or the single party government aren't able to deliver the kind of food, shelter, and stability that the population wants, there's a problem. You don't know when that's going to happen.

In reality, there's no protection against political instability. The only protection you really have is diversification. Diversification within the country, because different industries will be affected differently. For example, in Indonesia some of the companies we have in Java were in very bad shape because they were surrounded by violence. But one company that we owned on another island, which is the largest tin producer in the world, suffered no effect at all because they were distant from the trouble.

So, diversification within the country is very important, and then also globally. You are always walking that thin line between chaos and stability, and the fact that you have to walk that thin line means that your returns are much better because the risk is there. You're always balancing the risk and reward, and in our business you've got to be willing to take the risk, otherwise you're never going to get the reward.

Investing abroad

LG: Do you think private investors ought to invest outside their own countries?

Mark Mobius: Most definitely. The key to successful investment is to be diversified outside your own country. Ideally, you should have at least 50% outside your own country. And that can be seen in almost every example that you can think of in the developed world. The Japanese should have been diversifying outside their own country; if they had done so, they would have been in much better shape now. And in the U.S. — now, the U.S. market is doing very well, but the reality for Americans is that over the long term, unless you diversify abroad, you're not going to have the kind of returns that you would want.

LG: Yet many professionals do their best to persuade us not to invest abroad. Why do you think that is?

Mark Mobius: Well, I think they don't like the idea of losing a client. A broker or a bank wants to keep all the money at home if they don't have overseas experience or facilities. Nowadays, though, some of these companies are beginning to say, "Look, diversify and buy our global funds." They get a nice commission for that, and they realize that the competition is heating up as well.

This is an interesting point. The whole structure of investments is changing; a whole new world is opening up for the private, and even the institutional, investor. You must remember that most pension funds and most institutions did nothing but buy bonds. Bonds were the way to preserve wealth, and to have a return and so forth. Now there is a whole equity culture as a result of studies done by various consultants and scholars who have said that it *looks* risky, but it really isn't when you diversify — the whole modern portfolio theory and so forth has had a great impact.

That's one thing. The other thing is that, unfortunately, the barriers between financial institutions that were established earlier in order to protect the public are now coming down, so banks are becoming brokers, brokers are becoming banks, insurance companies are becoming investment managers, investment managers are becoming brokers, and so on. All of these so-called Chinese Walls ... ["Chinese Walls" are systems within large financial institutions that are intended to prevent sensitive information leaking from one business within the group to another and being abused.] The term "Chinese Walls" indicates how tenuous these walls are and this affects the whole industry. When you sit down with a banker today, don't be surprised if he says, "I've got this wonderful mutual fund for you to buy and it's a global fund," or "It's a foreign fund and we think you should diversify." Now, he's losing a deposit, but he's gaining an investment customer, and if he doesn't do that then the guy at the bank next door is going to do it because they're all getting on this bandwagon.

LG: But this expansion of the institutions is bad news for the individual client, isn't it?

Mark Mobius: I personally think, and of course I am in the minority, that there's a real danger there of not keeping the separation between the various functions of broker, banker, investment manager, etc. And we got the taste of it with the Long-Term Capital Management situation ...

The trouble with hedge funds

The high-tech world of hedge funds may seem far away from your own investment activities, but they have become a powerful force affecting the world's markets. What is a hedge fund? They are simply private investment pools restricted to a small number of wealthy corporate and private investors. Since they are private pools, they avoid many U.S. securities regulations, which allows them to use an array of complex and often risky investment strategies. Some highly leveraged hedge funds that trade currencies and invest in emerging markets appear to be magnifying the volatility in all markets. Many analysts believe, for example, that hedge fund managers facing margin calls in Russia brought about the steep declines in Latin American markets in 1998 when they sold holdings there to come up with the cash.

Long-Term Capital Management (LTCM), a hedge fund boasting two Nobel Prize winners among its partners, nearly tripled its funds between its inception in March 1994 and the end of 1997. It made this money by making judgments on interest rate spreads and the volatilities of market prices, using vast amounts of leverage and relying on sophisticated mathematical models of behavior to guide its deals.

As long as the data generally mimicked their historical patterns, LTCM's asset pricing models were effective in finding temporary market price anomalies. Then, in August 1998, LTCM's portfolio fell by 44%, giving it a year-to-date decline of 52% — a loss of around US$2 billion.

How could things go so wrong? Commentators say that the problem with the hedge fund's models is that they didn't assign a high enough chance of occurrence to the scenario in which many things go wrong at the same time. It is alleged that LTCM's worst-case scenario was only about 60% as bad as the one that actually occurred in August 1998, when interest rate spreads suddenly widened across the globe.

I asked Mark Mobius for his views on this issue.

Mark Mobius: Money politics, in America particularly, enable hedge funds to gather money all over the country without going through the kind of compliance and due diligence that we have to go through as public mutual fund companies. There's an interesting background to this, by the way. The hedge funds actually contributed to the last U.S.

election, and they got legislation passed which enabled them to get access to money in America which they otherwise would not be allowed near. So, what's happening is that there's a whole lot of investment money that isn't subject to any kind of surveillance globally in these so-called hedge funds. Now there's growing concern about this. That's one thing.

The other thing is the rise of so-called derivatives, which are not fully understood by the participants. This creates all kinds of other dangers that can cause a sort of domino effect in the system and, as I say, the Long-Term Capital Management example is symptomatic of what is happening and can be very dangerous.

LG: But they weren't using private people's funds, were they?

Mark Mobius: No, they had private investors, too. Admittedly, they were high net worth individuals, including some very prominent bankers themselves, but there were a lot of people in on this. Hedge funds have become the buzz word for a lot of people. What happens is that they leverage themselves with the banks, and that's where you now have the danger of a global collapse. People are aware of this. I had a meeting in Basle recently where we were discussing this whole issue. The bankers are very much aware of it, but what are you going to do if you are a banker and someone says to you, "Look, I've got this collateral, shares in IBM. I'll leave it with you and I want to borrow x amount"? It's very difficult for you to refuse if the rates are so good. And they are large amounts, so they're easy loans to make.

We've seen the dangers in the emerging markets. All the hedge funds were piling into Russia and other emerging markets, causing inflated prices on the back of highly leveraged funds. Of course, when the collapse came they tried to get out, but they couldn't so they lost quite a lot of money.

Leverage and derivatives

LG: Do you use leverage?

Mark Mobius: We're not allowed to leverage. The only allowance we have for leverages is when we have redemptions that we can't meet, and then we're allowed to borrow money in order to meet the redemptions. But we can't leverage the investments that we have. We can't say, "OK, as a matter of policy, we will borrow for leverage." In the U.K. you can do some of that in investment trusts, but we try to avoid it; we don't like to do that.

LG: Why is that?

Mark Mobius: Because of the safety problem. You can always run into problems; if interest rates go against you, or the market goes down, you're really in a hole. Or, say you have this extra money and you could borrow more money; if the market goes down, you can really get hurt badly. This is what's happening with futures markets; people hedge and the losses are magnified.

LG: Do you avoid derivatives as well?

Mark Mobius: We try to avoid derivatives. It depends on how you define derivatives. A warrant is really a derivative, and we have warrants. A convertible is a derivative in some ways, and we have those, but we won't buy any kind of derivative that would put a liability on us that could be unexpected — that's what we try to avoid. We don't want any potential liabilities.

LG: Presumably, Barings also thought that they weren't taking undue risks.

In 1995 one of the most illustrious investment banks in Britain, Barings, collapsed unexpectedly. The reason? A young British employee in Singapore, Nick Leeson, had run up staggering losses trading in derivatives, compounding the problem by concealing them and dealing ever more furiously to get out of the hole. His motive was apparently to win higher performance bonuses — a drop in the ocean compared with the huge funds he was risking.

While this kind of misbehavior by young traders has always occurred occasionally, what made the Barings story so staggering was that the system of controls completely failed to detect the problem and, despite the denials, it was evident that senior management in the bank were not fully aware of the nature of the new derivatives or their risks.

Mark Mobius: They knew. They were hedging; they were using derivatives. They thought they had control of it, but Nick Leeson was actually hiding the sales slips. Weeks before this happened the head of Barings said that it's surprising to know how profitable brokerage can be. That's a statement he made because the numbers looked great. It looked like Nick Leeson was making a great deal of money for Barings. But the reality was that the people sitting on the board didn't understand what it was all about.

I don't understand many of these derivatives. I tell them, "You've got to explain this to me in language that I can understand." I have a Ph.D. in economics, and I don't understand what they're saying. They're using jargon; they're making all kinds of assumptions about it which are very tenuous; and the reason why a lot of these "rocket scientists," the engineers and mathematicians, are in this field is because they live in an unreal world. They can create this aura of security and certainty which doesn't really exist.

LG: Is this a case of false precision?

Mark Mobius: Exactly. What they'll do is they'll mistake the difference between causation and correlation. They'll say: "Every time the coffee is hot, the market goes up; therefore, I'll buy a derivative for hot coffee since it's correlated with the market going up." These are the kinds of assumptions they're making, and when they don't work out it's a problem. That's what happened at Long-Term Capital Management. They were saying, "Look, the gap, the yield gap, between the U.S. and the European bonds (I think it was), is much, *much* too wide. We're going to bet that that's going to come down." It went the other way, however, so they were in trouble.

LG: So, who are they fooling?

Mark Mobius: They're really fooling themselves.

LG: And the people who give them the money?

Mark Mobius: Well, they do that because in the past they have been able to have some spectacular successes in bets. You can have spectacular results if you are leveraged to that extent. If you make the right bet, you can do very, very well, because you're spending one dollar and you're getting exposure to $10,000.

If you looked at the records of the hedge fund industry — no-one has really done this, that I know of — and asked what has been the average annualized return, including those that have gone bust completely, you will find that the returns aren't much better than a normal mutual fund. They talk about these spectacular returns, but look at the average number, including those that have gone bust and whose record of being bust is no longer counted.

LG: What do you think of actuaries who say that, in the very long run, you'll only ever get 4% return a year after inflation?

Mark Mobius: In the very long run? Well, it depends on how long is long, but the numbers that we have available to us, done by Ibbotson Associates, show that the equities have done much better than that. We therefore recommend some equities in a portfolio.

LG: But in the case of many emerging markets, they just haven't been around long enough to do such tests?

Mark Mobius: It's no surprise that our best-performing fund is our oldest fund. We've had more time to realize returns. I have no doubt that the other funds that we have will do fine if we stick to our guns. We try our very best to select those stocks that are representing good value. The emphasis now, of course, is not only on good value on paper, but on good value people-wise.

Corporate accounts

In Mobius on Emerging Markets, *Mobius gives a masterly overview of the difficulties in penetrating the mysteries of corporate accounts across the world, given the widely different accounting standards that prevail. "The bottom line," he writes, "... is that all information is useful, none should be discounted, but none should be the sole platform upon which to base an investment decision."*

Mark Mobius: This is another problem that we face and it's interesting how it goes over the head of the powers that be. It's understandable, I guess, because if you stopped most people on the street and asked them about their own finances they wouldn't have a clue. Most people are not really that interested and knowledgeable.

But the fact is that the people on whom we rely for information, independent information about companies, are not really independent. The auditors are hired by management. The auditors have consulting subsidiaries who sell their services to the management. That's a real flaw in the current system as we know it in Western Europe and America, and Japan and the developing countries, which extends to the emerging markets. And until that situation is rectified, we will always have to be suspicious about company accounts. Not that they're falsifying them necessarily — there are enough penalties for falsification that would deter most auditors — but there is a great incentive to hide things.

LG: Are the accounts in emerging markets' companies no worse than ones back home?

Mark Mobius: I would say that's probably the case. Most of the companies that we deal with are larger cap companies in emerging markets. The accountants are the same as in the developed countries — Ernst & Young, Deloitte Touche. All these accounting firms are global and usually will only deal with companies that have an international accounting record.

LG: Could you talk in detail about what you look for in accounts?

Mark Mobius: First of all, we look at who the auditors are. You see if they've got a good reputation — that's important. Then we look at the footnotes first, find out how terms are being defined and what's hidden in the footnotes, because there are things hidden there to make the accounts look simpler. We read a report from back to front; we move into the balance sheet, the profit and loss statement, and look closely at the non-cash items. That's the reason why you'll see a lot of analysts talking about EBITDA calculations, because that will give them some idea of where the cash is going, and so forth. Cash flow is also very, very important. Then we'll look at the balance sheet, the debt, how the debt stands in relation to the equity and how capable they are of paying down their debt from earnings. These are the kinds of things we will focus on when we first look at a company.

LG: That sounds like the normal approach one might use back home.

Mark Mobius: Yes, you would use that approach with any company anywhere in the world, really. At the end of the day, the simple question that we ask is, "What will this company earn in five years?" In asking that question, we then have to ask a whole series of other questions about what's happening today and whether the company will survive.

LG: In your book you describe all kinds of particular problems, like translations of accounting terms from mainland Chinese to Hong Kong Chinese, which don't occur at home. So, isn't there another layer of difficulties which don't occur at home?

Mark Mobius: There's a language layer there, there's no question. Accounting terms may be mistranslated. Most of that is worked through by the auditors, but sometimes archaic terms appear. I remember once in Sri Lanka they had an item in the balance sheet called "Illicit Accounts." We couldn't quite figure out what that could be.

That's the kind of thing that you run into. The lack of detail varies from country to country. Accounting in Japan and Korea, for example, is extremely detailed. You can get right down to the last pencil, so you often get lost in the forest — you've got to try and simplify your numbers. It's surprising that some people are complaining about lack of information; actually, they're often giving us too much information.

LG: It's often quite difficult for private people to get hold of company accounts in emerging markets, isn't it?

Mark Mobius: More and more of these companies are posting their results on the Internet. So, information isn't going to be a problem as far as I can see. Of course, disclosure and transparency is a problem, it's an ongoing problem, but it's being attacked now as a result of the Asian crisis. In fact, we just had a meeting this morning with a Thai bank that said they are going to have a director in charge of transparency and investor relations. So, a lot of these companies are getting the message.

Campaigning for better corporate governance

Even a large fund group like Templeton can suffer as a minority shareholder, and in recent years Mark Mobius has become more determined to improve the corporate governance of firms across the world. Templeton is prepared to go to the press, complain to the authorities, speak up at shareholders' meetings, and even go to court in its efforts to prevent abuse by insiders. This is an interesting development — perhaps the time really is right for a major cleaning-up process in markets across the world.

Mark Mobius: The whole area of corporate governance, which we could talk about for hours, is very underdeveloped. Not only in emerging markets, but in the developed markets as well. The minority investor tends not to be protected as much as he should be.

Basically, the minority investor in emerging markets isn't protected at all, and is even taken advantage of by majority investors.

You have the things I talked about: self dealing, associated company dealing, shareholding problems, outright theft, the dilution of shares ... There are many of these problems that aren't being dealt with by the authorities. They're a real problem, and we're working on that now, trying to get some changes. The OECD, by the way, is working on this. Corporate governance has become very much the buzz word in the multilateral institutions, because they realize that unless they get that straight, they're not going to be able to build capital markets.

LG: Do you believe that Asia will become more transparent?

Mark Mobius: It has to. They're not going to get the money, otherwise. We as investors are now demanding transparency; we're looking more and more closely at management. Before, we tended to focus more on numbers; now we're looking at the management and their abilities, their conflicts of interests, etc. And we've become much more activist. We're saying to people, "Now look, if we don't think we can do something to change the management, we won't invest in this company."

LG: Are there some countries in Asia that are worse culprits than others?

Mark Mobius: It depends on the degree and the type of violation you're talking about. Each country has its own idiosyncrasies. For example, in Indonesia it's the family interrelated parties and the out-of-company transactions to related parties — that's what you get a lot of. In Malaysia, it's political cronyism; and in the Philippines it's just plain cronyism. In Hong Kong it's family control generally; they tend to have very tight control. So, there are a number of these specific risks that you get in each country. I would say the biggest problem is this conflict of interest point. You have a family that has a listed company and a whole bunch of unlisted companies, and the listed companies do business with the unlisted ones. How do you know where the transfer pricing is taking place?

LG: What changed during 1997? Why did people suddenly get scared?

Mark Mobius: The currency crisis really precipitated that. We knew the market before then was high and we were selling, but we hadn't sold enough and, more importantly, as the market came down by 50% we thought it would be a wonderful time to go in. It looked very cheap because it kept on going down. So, people lost money that way. It was an excessive bear market, and of course it has balanced up since that time just because it went too far.

You have a situation where things look terrible and you think it's a great time to get in, but it gets worse and you lose more money on the way down. Unless you have the fortitude to hang in there and maybe even buy more, you'll be in trouble.

On market timing

LG: How much of your funds are in cash?

Mark Mobius: We now try not to keep any cash. We try to spend every single cent we have, because the condition of the markets is so good for investing now. Things are so cheap that it's not a good idea for us to be out of the market.

We had about 20% in cash when the 1997 crash was coming, but then we put it in too early. In hindsight it would have been better if we'd waited. But that's the nature of the beast: you can't always time the markets. Timing of markets has been a pretty fruitless exercise over the years.

LG: Should private investors hold for the medium to long term?

Mark Mobius: It depends on their age and income. If investors are old, like John Templeton, and financially secure, then they can gamble. They can go into Korea when the market has come down, into Russia and so on. They have that luxury, and ironically they become richer and more secure, but the person who has retired on a very tight pension isn't going to be in a position to do that. The older you get, generally the less you should have in equities in emerging markets because you want to live on this income.

LG: What about people in early middle age? Is that a good time to be gambling?

Mark Mobius: I would say it's a good time, first of all, to get assets outside your own country, globally, and then, within that category, to have 10–20% in emerging markets. Because emerging markets generally will tend to grow faster.

Hong Kong

LG: What do you think the future of Hong Kong is? Do you think it's doomed?

Mark Mobius: No, I don't think it's doomed, but it's going to live a different life than it had under the British administration. The combination of the Chinese immigrants, escapees from communism, and the British administration, the remnants of colonialism, was quite fortuitous. On the one hand, you had the *crème de la crème* of the Chinese entrepreneurs who were unwilling to work under communism; and on the other hand, you had the best of the British colonial rule with the experience that they had, the generations of experience in running a government. So, this was quite a unique combination which, of course, you can't hope to have again. However, there is enough left of the British administrative ethic in the government and there are still the immigrants, they are still there or their sons and daughters are still there and more are coming. Hong Kong can remain a very vibrant place, a very entrepreneurial place.

China

Mark Mobius: China was never really closed, even during the Korean War. Perhaps during the Cultural Revolution it slowed down, but there was always a lot going on between Hong Kong and China. Hong Kong has always lived off China in one way or another. I think that will accelerate, but Hong Kong's future has to be as a service center rather than as a manufacturing center, and we've seen that trend.

China right now is in a big dilemma, which is why Zhu Rongji has made a trip to the U.S. I think he needs American help bad. He needs to sustain a high export ratio to the United States to maintain high growth. He is trying to force reform in China, but he doesn't want to be held responsible and so he prefers the Americans to do it. Then they can openly blame the WTO for it. And they would love to emulate the federal system that the U.S. has, because they realize there is no way they can continue with control through a centralized bureaucracy. At this stage, China needs America more than the other way around. They want to get America in their grips, but unfortunately America isn't cooperating.

LG: Why not?

Mark Mobius: Because of the long-standing U.S. relations with Taiwan. Taiwan is very different from the rest of China. It also has very close relations with Japan. The problem isn't going to go away. To think that Taiwan can become just another province of China is very unrealistic.

Its future would be a function of how Hong Kong goes. The Chinese are really in a dilemma: they need to keep Hong Kong prosperous and happy, so that it's an example to the Taiwanese, while internally in China you have a situation where the formal economy is beginning to crack up. The formal economy — that's the state-owned enterprises and the state-owned banks — is, to all intents and purposes, bankrupt. But the political power of the Communist Party stems from these institutions. If these institutions are bankrupt, it's very, very difficult for them. The only answer, of course, is there will have to be more opening up of the informal economy.

LG: That sounds as if one shouldn't be buying the existing Chinese companies.

Mark Mobius: That's right. We try to avoid buying them and buy Hong Kong companies instead, because they at least have the transparency and the professionalism that's required to work in China and to enable the investors to know what's really happening. The "H" shares of the Chinese companies based in Hong Kong are the ones to go for.

LG: And aren't they all domiciled in Bermuda?

Mark Mobius: No. It's the Jardine companies, as far as I know, and a few others. The reality is their base of business is Hong Kong.

LG: But they picked Bermuda just in case?

Mark Mobius: It's not a bad idea, considering their history.

Latin America

Mark Mobius: If you look at Latin America, Brazil of course dominates. What happens to Brazil impacts the whole region. It's followed by Mexico, Argentina, and Chile. These are the important countries and all the rest sort of follow.

The great news about Latin America is that they've been through it. They've had this terrible time, economic crises, all kinds of crises — inflation, hyperinflation — and they've learnt as a result. They have intelligent people who have learnt many lessons and they've finally rejected a lot of the economic models that haven't worked. They've become much more sophisticated. The other thing is that, probably as a result of their proximity to the U.S. and their own history of revolution against Spain, they've become, over the years, much more pluralistic and much more democratic, which adds a great deal of stability to the region. Latin America really has a lot of the elements, in addition to a very strong northern friend, the U.S., who wants to do more business with them and wants to bring them into the fold. That combination, I think, is very, very powerful.

LG: That seems a remarkably optimistic view.

Mark Mobius: Yes. I think I'm probably more optimistic than other people, but I think it's reasonable, given what's happened and what we see going forward.

LG: Which industries are going to grow?

Mark Mobius: Raw materials, mining, agriculture, power (there's a great shortage of power), telecommunications. You may not think of power generation as a growth industry, but that's exactly what it is in Latin America.

LG: Which countries should you avoid?

Mark Mobius: The ones I would avoid are those that don't have a thriving, liquid stock market, and there are quite a few of those. So, the concentration has to be on places like Chile, Argentina, Brazil, and Mexico, with maybe some Venezuela thrown in, some Colombia, and some Peru. Other than that, most other areas should be rejected because they're just not big enough.

Africa

Mark Mobius: There's a lot of hope in South Africa. In the rest of Africa, with the exception of Northern Africa — Morocco and Egypt — they've got a long way to go. The fact that South Africa now has become a black, or at least a multiracial, nation augers very well for the rest of Africa, because South African money and South African know-how will be feeding into the rest of Africa. As far as we're concerned, as regards to places to invest, the political systems and the institutions are just too immature to warrant much of a look. They're just too small; the reward relationship isn't there.

LG: Are there no more capital controls in South Africa?

Mark Mobius: To all intents and purposes, no. South Africans can only take a limited amount of money out, but for us there's no problem.

LG: And for a private investor?

Mark Mobius: For a private investor coming from the outside there's no problem. Somebody who is already in South Africa has restrictions.

LG: To invest in somewhere like Morocco sounds pretty scary.

Mark Mobius: Actually, it's been very rewarding. Morocco has done very well. In Morocco there is no problem getting invested money in and out, but it must be recorded. Most of the countries in which we're invested, with a few exceptions, now allow this. As long as you register going in and going out, there's no problem.

LG: Is the Moroccan Stock Exchange well run?

Mark Mobius: It has improved a great deal.

LG: In your book you talk about there being only twenty-four countries that you invest in. Has that number increased?

Mark Mobius: It's actually forty now, potentially, but more and more of these countries are beyond the pale in the sense that they're too small. You can invest, there are emerging markets, but it's not worthwhile for us to do so. Maybe for the individual who wants to put a few thousand dollars in Ghana or in Kenya it's fine, but for us, at least at this stage, there are enough bargain opportunities in the big liquid markets that we don't need to go with these other ones. But the potential is there; we've got our eye on about forty markets around the world that we hope will develop and become thriving, open, liquid, transparent, and so forth, but for the time being I would say we're active in only fifteen — twenty at most.

If direct investment in emerging markets seems too daunting to do personally, you could consider one of the many Templeton funds. The group, Franklin Templeton, has offices in over twenty-five countries and manages over US$200 billion worldwide — but not all of this is in emerging markets. For emerging markets information, go to: www.templeton.com.sg/, or contact:

Templeton International
7 Temasek Boulevard
#38-03 Suntec Tower One
Singapore 038987
Tel: +65 338 7177
Fax: +65 338 7677

5

Alfred Steinherr: Making Sense of Russia

Anyone over the age of thirty could be forgiven for feeling a little confused about the world these days. What ever happened to the Cold War? Where's that "Evil Empire" that was going to get us if it could?

The implosion of the U.S.S.R., for most of us, was completely unexpected. Now, a decade or so later, it is plain that the world has changed utterly, but we don't know what it is changing into. Does it mean a final victory for market-based capitalism and a bonanza for international investors? A new era of permanent bull markets? And what about Russia itself? With so much commercial hype and political disinformation around, it's hard for the private investor to assess whether there really are bargains to be found amid its chaos.

In 1997 and 1998 a number of market letters were strongly recommending various Russian ADRs; the basic argument was that they were a commodity play — Russia's vast natural resources would eventually come on to the world's markets and the companies which control them would suddenly be revalued upward by several hundred percent. One minor guru, who shall remain nameless, endorsed a short-term portfolio of Russian ADRs which managed, collectively, to drop by some 50% in value in 1998 before he finally threw in the towel.

Meanwhile, as we shall see below, more sophisticated professional investors managed to lose their shirts in Russian government bonds (treasury bills), which dropped by around 70%

when the ruble dramatically devalued. By the time you read this there may have been more wild swings in this turbulent country.

I felt I needed, along with most other private investors, an objective, overall perspective on what is happening in the ex-Soviet countries, so I traveled to Luxembourg to meet an expert, Professor Alfred Steinherr. Luxembourg is a tiny country sandwiched between Belgium, Germany, and France which used to have a reputation as a tax haven; these days it is the base for several European Union agencies as well as over 200 international banks, and the medieval town is swarming with prosperous financial types from all over Europe. The atmosphere is sophisticated — and secretive.

Professor Alfred Steinherr is Chief Economist and Director General, Economics and Information Directorate, at the European Investment Bank, a non-profit development bank set up some forty years ago by the E.U. governments. He is the author, with Daniel Gros, of Winds of Change *(Longman, 1995), an impressive and highly readable analysis of the transitions that are taking place in the former Soviet bloc. He has been a senior economist at the IMF, has an MS in mathematics from George Washington University and an economics doctorate from Cornell, has been on IMF missions to Tunisia, Senegal, and Niger, and on World Bank missions to Guinea and Brazil. An advisor to the government of Kazakhstan and to the European Commission, Professor Steinherr is also a Mandarin speaker who has held lectureships in Beijing and Shanghai. Here, I felt, was someone with a wide experience of the world who would be able to give me a better understanding of what is really going on in the "Wild East." I wasn't disappointed!*

The European Investment Bank

LG: Could you describe the activities of the European Investment Bank?

Alfred Steinherr: The European Investment Bank isn't an investment bank in the American sense of the word. We are a long-term lending institution. Our shareholders are the governments of E.C. countries and our main job is to complete the market; we only finance investment projects, and whenever we sense that an investment project is economically sound but needs a little help, then we intervene. When I say "needs a little help," I don't mean that we subsidize — we don't.

But we are a non-profit organization. We make loans at the cost of our refinancing and we add a very, very small mark-up to cover our administrative costs. The biggest project we have ever financed is the Channel Tunnel between England and France. We lent them US$3 billion.

We have many projects of considerable size — of a billion dollars or so — airports, fast train connections, and stuff like that. We increasingly lend to private corporations. We don't only lend on infrastructure projects. Ninety percent of our lending is in the European Union, and the other 10% is virtually worldwide. A particular area of interest for us is Eastern Europe.

We are the largest lender of our type in the world. We lend twice as much as the World Bank with one-tenth of the staff, which probably means that we are relatively efficient, but of course the two things are not comparable. Our job is much easier than the World Bank's job — providing US$3 billion to the Channel Tunnel is much easier than accumulating US$3 billion loans in Africa spread over fifty countries under much more difficult conditions.

Last year we lent close to 30 billion euro, which was all actual disbursements and not theoretical deals. We were created by the Treaty of Rome. At that time, of course, market imperfections were widespread. Politicians asked, "How will the North channel money to the South?" Since there were no market mechanisms, they created this bank. Today we would certainly not be created, because the market is integrated in Europe; but on the other hand, we have accumulated over forty years of hands-on experience. Our size sometimes facilitates very large-scale financing. We have a good reputation, so even the signaling is good; certain corporations borrow from us for the signaling effect, not because they need the money from us but because it's always good to be able to say that our conservative bank has supported their investment program with the loan of a billion euro or pounds or deutschmarks, or whatever it is.

I think we are socially useful. We don't cost a penny to taxpayers because we cover all our costs.

On funds and fund managers

LG: Many investors feel that it is safer to give their money to investment managers, or to put it into funds, instead of venturing into emerging markets on their own. What is your view on this?

Alfred Steinherr: I don't have a high opinion of gurus, investment managers, or investment fund managers. In the end, if you look at the performance of the funds they run over an extended period of time, it's totally unimpressive. They underperform the averages and I think that says a lot.

One has to admit that a number of fund managers, notably hedge fund managers, have done extremely well over extended periods of time, partly because they can operate with tremendous leverage. But remember that we have had an extended glorious period in the markets. The real test for any manager is an extended downturn. Today, one thinks extended downturns are a thing of the past, but I'm not so sure. After all, even in the most developed financial market in the world, the U.S. market, the last extended downturn wasn't in the nineteenth century. In the U.S., the stock market declined in real terms from 1973 to 1987. It only recovered its level of 1973 in 1987 — fourteen years later.

Now, that's quite an extended downturn, and a good test is how smart these managers are or their performance is during a period like that. With the crash of 1987, the Dow Jones went down to a little bit over 2000 and now it's about 10,000. Well, that's an increase by a factor of five. It's not that difficult to have a good performance over that period.

LG: But even so, there are some fund managers who have performed outstandingly well. Warren Buffett, for instance.

Alfred Steinherr: If you take ten different strategies, one of them will work well for some time. You may just happen to be a guy who used the strategy and was lucky with it. We can't talk about the other strategies, because they don't exist anymore. What is impressive about Warren Buffett is that he has had success not just for a few years, but for several decades. But during the bad years of the 1970s his investment performance wasn't that impressive. The really big impressive returns came during that extended period of strong growth in U.S. markets.

Some of his ideas make sense: to select growth companies, his special definition of a growth company, his investment in Coca-Cola, and so on. But I don't know whether he was able to forecast, for instance, the fall of the Iron Curtain and therefore the extension of the imperial reach of Coca-Cola into these regions — perhaps there was also a little bit of luck.

It was basically good thinking on Buffett's part to say that Coca-Cola is a brand value that can be sold in parts of the world where it is still underdeveloped — in China and places like that. I think during recent years his success has tarnished a little bit, but for some time you can have success with a particular strategy. It doesn't mean that you can learn from the strategy and replicate it, because even Warren Buffett may not be able to replicate his success over the next five or ten years.

Warren Buffett is always careful, in his famous annual reports, to stress that his future performance may not be as good as it has been in the past, especially now that his Berkshire Hathaway fund has grown so large.

The efficient market theory

LG: It sounds as if you are a supporter of the efficient market theory.

Alfred Steinherr: On the one hand, I take the efficient market hypothesis seriously for stock picking. I don't see any rational basis for an individual to say, "I pick Coca-Cola because it will do well." You and I don't have the information to predict that Coca-Cola will do better than the average of the stock market. It's just a feeling we have, or some confused thinking on our part. If there is something that tells investors that Coca-Cola will do well, then all investors will know it and that will be immediately reflected in the price today. So, in this sense, I don't believe that you or I or investment managers can do a great job in stock picking — and the proof is that 80% of investment funds underperform the market. That's total failure in stock picking.

On the other hand, one shouldn't push the efficient market hypothesis too far. I think there are phenomena — herd behavior, over-shooting, and so on — and these can be identified and exploited. So, an investor like George Soros has a point in saying, "I'm interested in these exceptional market movements when the system is in disequilibrium. I'm not interested in equilibrium, I can't make an extra buck out of equilibrium."

I think he is correct, but that isn't a basic contradiction of the general reach of market efficiency.

LG: Would you say that emerging markets are less efficient and offer more opportunities of this kind?

Alfred Steinherr: Yes. For instance, investors flocked into Russia, until July 1998, more or less blindly. Then, during one month, they all tried to rush out. What has that got to do with market efficiency? What did they know before the crisis? What did they know afterwards?

If you look at the Dow Jones over the last twelve years, the trend is essentially up. From time to time it went down, but there's a clear upward time trend in this series. You can see this in currencies, too — the dollar is moving up and down with wiggles around a trend, but there are time series and trends that you can detect. I think the great era of market efficiency is past.

LG: So, Soros's approach makes sense?

Alfred Steinherr: Yes, of course, because he was trading in much thinner markets where prices don't necessarily reveal as much information as prices in London or New York. Second, when you have a lot of interference, then transaction costs are much higher — which again is a barrier to the processing of information.

You also have corruption and political interference, so certainly the efficiency of the emerging markets is much less than the efficiency we have in our markets. This provides opportunities. For instance, you can do a little bit of financial engineering in order to avoid this sort of local inefficiency.

Profiting from swaps

Alfred Steinherr: Let me give you an example: suppose you have an investment fund in the U.K. and you would like to have a position in — let's take a fairly inefficient market — India, say, and you are appalled by the transaction costs and all the regulations and you may not even get the right to be present on the exchange and trade, and so on.

You talk to an Indian investment fund and they have the problem that they can't invest their money abroad because the Indian government wants all savings invested in their own country. This is, of course, bad for the Indian fund, because there is no risk diversification and it would be nice for them to have part of the funds abroad. When there's a downturn in India that is uncorrelated to the stock exchange in London, say, then if the Indian fund has an investment in London it evens out their performance.

You, the U.K. fund manager, talk to the Indian fund and you do a swap. You take the market index of Mumbai [formerly Bombay] and the market index of London and you make a deal. If, at the end of the year, the London index has an increase of 10% and the Mumbai index has increased by 3%, then you pay the Indians 7%. The following year, perhaps Mumbai has a better time than London and the Indians pay you.

The nice thing about swaps is that there's no investment at the beginning. No money leaves India to be invested in London. In fact, the Indians pay when they are in an easy position, because the return on Indian stocks in a particular year is higher than in London — so they can afford to pay. When stocks don't do well in India but do well in London, the Indians receive money. It's really a good arrangement for everybody and it totally circumvents the stock market. You just look at the indexes.

Of course, the index still reflects a lot of inefficiencies, but at least you don't suffer from restrictions to market access, high transaction costs, the insecurity of counterparties for depositing your securities, and all that. You do have a counterparty risk — both the fund managers in the deal have to pay up if they lose — but you can settle the gains and losses each year, so the most you could lose is one year's win. You can never lose the contract value, the nominal value. This is just one example of how clever financial engineering can get around some of the problems of emerging markets, developing opportunities and good trade potential.

LG: Is this something that small private investors could do for themselves?

Alfred Steinherr: You and I couldn't — you have to be an investment fund, a pension fund, or something like that. But you could do it informally, maybe. You could find a local Indian in New York and say, "Hey, what about making the following bet? At the end of the year you pay me if the Mumbai Stock Exchange is doing better than the New York Stock Exchange." So that can be done, but you have to find a counterparty; you have to make sure that your Indian friend will really pay up, and so on. It's not that easy, but in principle it could be done for small amounts.

Russia's predicament

LG: Does the lack of market efficiency that you talked about earlier apply to Russia?

Alfred Steinherr: It applies to a large part of the former Soviet Union. Remember, the Soviet Union, like all communist countries, had high savings and poor investments. Now the situation is absolutely traumatic. There is virtually no investment at all — they are just running down the capital stock. Their investment isn't even enough to maintain the capital stock. Of course, some capital stock just has to be depreciated, thrown away, but not even pipelines, airports, roads, and housing are being maintained.

Compare this with Western Europe, where most countries have about 20% of their GDPs invested. Of that 20%, let's say one-third is net investment and two-thirds is just maintenance of the capital stock. In order for the former Soviet countries to catch up and transform, they need much more than just that; they must create a new infrastructure, more market-oriented investment, and so on.

The problem is both with savings and with investment, because to the extent that the Russians save, they convert it into dollars and leave it under the bed. If they are larger operators, they bring it out to Switzerland, New York, Cyprus, or wherever. So, there are savings in Russia, but they aren't being invested; they're just being put aside. You have a problem in the transmission channel from savings to investment — in other words, the banking system. The banking system doesn't work. Even before the crisis of 1998, the banking system didn't really make loans — the amount of loans they provided to the economy was something like 5% of GDP.

LG: Why is the level of investment so low?

Alfred Steinherr: It's not just that there's no investment because there's no money. There's no investment because, in the past, it has been much more profitable to invest, for instance, in Russian treasury bills and the like than to go through the difficulty of setting up a new factory, say.

Russia has become a society that economists call "rent seeking" — you know, like the Mafia seeks rents or creates a local monopoly to exploit. The lack of investment isn't only due to the lack of funding; it's also because of a breakdown in law and order. Why don't you invest in agriculture in Russia? Because property rights aren't secure. Why don't you open a store? Because, just as in Southern Italy, nobody opens a small store since there are only two possibilities: either your store doesn't work and you make a loss, or it does work and you have to pay off the Mafia.

In Russia, racketeering is much more attractive than producing honestly. It's the whole institutional framework that doesn't work and therefore there's no incentive to save, there's no incentive to invest, and there's no incentive to bring savings to investment.

The failure of Western aid

LG: We heard a lot about Western aid to Russia in the media a few years back, but much less so recently. Has the West been able to improve the situation?

Alfred Steinherr: Russia and the whole Soviet bloc was something new for the Western institutions involved there. The institutions had experience in dealing with the problems of Latin America and stuff like that, but reforming Russia was a new kind of problem. So, it's natural that we made mistakes.

What isn't so natural is that, more or less, we only made mistakes. The West supplied money relatively late. When it was most needed — in 1991–93 — there were promises but not much official money. Official Western money came or was promised just before the Russian crisis in 1998, but not earlier when the reforms had a much better chance and when the reformers really were in control of things.

One amazing thing, now that the Soviet Union isn't a military threat anymore, is the enormous potential for saving on the West's defense expenditures. There is a good geopolitical argument to treat Russia with a certain degree of generosity, because we would be very unhappy if extreme right-wing nationalists or the communists took over — and part of the defense expenditure we save could be used to support Russia, to stabilize it.

LG: So, why did it go wrong?

Alfred Steinherr: It was strange that we were so reluctant to give Russia money. The advice we gave them was also strange. For instance, with the implosion of the Soviet Union the IMF advised Russia to maintain the ruble. This was a problem, because it implied that the

Russian Central Bank had to pay, without limit, the deficits of the other ex-Soviet countries.

Second, this implosion was a major shock to all these economies because, during Soviet times, they were highly interconnected. You had a factory in Russia that received all the goods supplied by some important factory in Kazakhstan, and another one in the Ukraine and so on. During the break-up of the Soviet empire it would have been sensible to maintain the logic that had existed and make it easy for Ukrainian suppliers to serve the factory in Russia, and so on. And that wasn't done.

An idea of a payments union, as we experienced in Europe after the Second World War, would have been helpful. I will never forget when a leading IMF member of the team of Russia told me, "First best is total free capital convertibility. Payments union and so on are second best, so we aren't considering that."

After the Second World War the war-torn nations of Western Europe kept their currencies overvalued against the dollar. This had the effect of limiting trade and creating an extreme shortage of foreign currency, which in turn forced governments to make their currencies non-convertible. Barter trade (which is very inefficient) became common because of the lack of US dollars, the only currency that was in demand. In 1950 a cross-Europe clearing system, the European Payments Union, was introduced to ease the problems caused by non-convertibility. By 1958 it had succeeded and was abolished.

Alfred Steinherr: It was idiotic to ignore the possibility of implementing a payments union because, although textbooks are patient, populations and countries are less so. I think it was unnecessary to put the Soviet Union through the extreme stress of this supply shock. They have had to go through a lot of unnecessary hassle.

The IMF had also tremendously underestimated the monetary overhang in Russia and, therefore, the inflation that was virtually exploding in 1992 …

LG: Can you explain monetary overhang?

Alfred Steinherr: Yes. If we print more money in the West, then people have more to spend; and if they have more to spend but certain goods cannot be increased in supply, it just means the price goes up.

In Soviet Russia they had price controls, which meant that when people had more money in their pockets or in their bank accounts, they couldn't get more goods. So, over many years, even during the Brezhnev years, there was an accumulation of monetary holdings because there weren't enough goods. Then prices and markets were liberalized, so that in theory you didn't have to queue up — you just had to agree to pay a little bit more and you could get everything. Then this monetary overhang, by which I mean all that money that had accumulated involuntarily, was put on to the market and prices increased dramatically.

The trouble with globalization

The dramatic push toward free markets and globalization during the last few years has greatly stimulated investing abroad, but is it really the best solution for all developing countries? I asked Professor Steinherr how he viewed this trend in the light of disasters such as the Asian currency crisis of 1997 and the Russian collapse in 1998.

Alfred Steinherr: The problem is this extreme — and I would say, primarily American — ideological belief in three things: first, private ownership — that one has to privatize quickly; second, free capital flows; and third, that one has to create financial markets, the stock exchange and the like, as quickly as possible.

Now, the Russians have privatized relatively quickly, but in a way that the insiders, the old managers, were usually able to get a large share of the firm for nothing, so there was no widespread ownership. The government didn't get real money for auctioning off its firms, and what does it mean to have a privatized firm when the institutions aren't there so that a firm is under the rule of law and has to pay taxes, maintain books that are checked by auditors, and so on? I mean, it makes sense to privatize, but this sort of "Wild East" privatization has just produced tremendous chaos.

I think it also created a lot of injustice, which is a basis for social discontent. All the robber barons are now billionaires, or at least very rich by Western standards, but if you are an average Russian you cannot applaud such a development.

Russian accounting practices

LG: From what you say, it sounds as if it is very hard to believe the published accounts of Russian firms, even the large ones that are quoted as ADRs in the U.S.

Alfred Steinherr: Let me give you an example. Recently, I was considering the purchase of a bank in the Ukraine. I looked at the balance sheet and the profit and loss statement and I really tried to evaluate each item — what each one really meant. There was a big real estate item on the asset side. This was the building in which the bank had its headquarters. The manager of the bank, who was also its major shareholder, was a Member of Parliament and he had obtained the right, free of charge, to use the building, which actually belonged to the state. Now, how do you evaluate such a thing? As long as this man is in political power, you have a big asset for free. As soon as he's out or he's selling up, then it's worth nothing.

It was fairly difficult to discover this, because there are no public registries for real estate. It was only through an indiscretion that I found out that the building didn't belong to the bank. It looked in the accounts as if it belonged to them. The refurbishing and all of that was paid by them, so it looked as if they were investing in their own building. How do you find out that it isn't their building? Where is it written down? There is nothing written down, so the guy put the building on his balance sheet.

All these companies are extremely difficult to deal with. Over time, the larger firms will follow Western standards and will be audited by Western accountants. At the moment, the principals can do what they like — some money floats back to Moscow, other funds float to Switzerland. Take false invoicing — if a company sells goods that have a world market price, it's easier for an outsider to monitor; you can easily check to see if the books tally. The trouble here is that most of the inventory that they sell in Russia is well below world market price. For some of it they will never be paid. Do they have accounting provisions for that? Of course not. They don't know what will be paid or what won't be paid. Even the largest company in Russia gives you a balance sheet and a profit and loss account that is totally meaningless.

Foreign investment losses in Russia

LG: So, what were Western investment firms doing in Russia? How did they lose all that money in 1998?

Alfred Steinherr: Let me first say that the West hasn't made a lot of direct investment in Russia. Very few Western firms bought up Russian firms. There have been "political" investments in the energy sector; for example, the German Ruhrgas has bought a few percent of Gazprom's capital, Western oil companies have invested, and so on, but basically very little overall.

There was Western financial investment; most of it went not into shares but into Russian treasury bills. In a way, it was irresistible. You had interest rates of 40–50%, the ruble had been stable for some time, and everybody was optimistic about the vast potential of Russia.

Investors said to themselves, "If the exchange rate depreciates, I'll just get out beforehand." People did buy shares, yes, but in dollar terms much less was invested in shares because we all knew very well that the profits would be sucked off first by the managers or other connected people before we Western shareholders ever saw a penny.

The people who invested in Russian treasury bills expected that there was no default risk — that Russia is too big to fail and the IMF will support it. The only perceived risk was of a devaluation, but Russia had stabilized at around six rubles to the dollar. The idea was that you just watch it and you know that at a 50% interest rate, even if you hold the paper for a year and you sell when the ruble is 10–20% depreciated, you still have a high return. You make 40% or 30% instead of 50%, and that is still much better than making 4% or 5% on European paper. So, it made sense.

LG: How much did they lose?

Alfred Steinherr: One should not always believe what investors and bankers tell you, but they lost substantially — the ones who got stuck and couldn't move out in time.

The ruble now quotes at twenty-two to the dollar. It went from six to twenty-two. If you had, say, US$100 invested, it would have been worth 600 rubles. Your 600 rubles are now worth not even $30. Two-thirds has already gone just there. If you hold the paper to redemption, you will get perhaps even the full amount of rubles back but at a time when the ruble isn't twenty-two anymore but is, say, forty. I believe that the Russian government will pay up, but in rubles at a time when they have depreciated even more.

Déjà vu?

LG: This has happened before, hasn't it? Didn't a lot of Western investors get burnt in Russia before the 1917 revolution?

Alfred Steinherr: Before the First World War Russia had some glorious years, particularly in the 1890s. Russia always had a problem of collecting taxes and, in a way, some of the problems they have now are really old problems in Russian history. They always tried to squeeze the peasants to the maximum, but they also had to borrow abroad in order to finance their expansion. And it *was* an expansion. Russia was growing very rapidly up to the First World War, so they had twenty good years, except that they also accumulated a lot of debt. Then the war came and all the fruits of their investments were gone.

I think the largest Western buyers of the Russian debt back then were the French. In France, one still meets families who bought this paper which is now worthless.

LG: So, wasn't the 1998 crisis predictable?

Alfred Steinherr: I wouldn't say that one could have forecast the recent T-bill crisis if one had studied history better. After all, the communist régime, which lasted several decades, paid its debts.

The problem in Russia now is the total absence of law. If you have a government that doesn't behave lawfully and defaults on its debt, it is just the result of not being able to do anything else. Let's face it, we should have known that the Russian market is in total dynamic disequilibrium. If you pay interest rates of 40% or 50% a year, the growth of your debt is just excessive.

I think it was Western advice to create the treasury bill. It was part of the Washington ideology. If Russia hadn't opened up its markets, the interest rates would have increased earlier and gone much higher because there weren't enough savings to be channeled into the T-bill market and the whole thing would have stopped earlier.

Russia is more or less cut off from the Western markets now. I'm not on the political left, but we in Europe have plenty of experience of capital controls. We were very highly developed when we still had capital controls. The U.K. had capital controls virtually all through the 1970s and 1980s, yet it wasn't a totally inefficient economy — London was the center of the world financial market.

But to these poor beginners with very undeveloped institutions, we recommended, and to some extent forced them, to adopt free markets. We forced the Asian countries and Russia to open up, and that, I think, was extremely bad advice.

LG: Are Western governments revising their ideas in the light of what has happened?

Alfred Steinherr: A crisis always has the nice by-product of providing a lesson. The U.K. Finance Minister, Gordon Brown, had an idea that was also pushed around by the Republicans in Congress, namely that the IMF should only support countries that have totally liberalized capital flows.

This is an ideological thing. What is interesting is that not just the

Republicans, but even [the socialist] Gordon Brown was pushing it. I don't think he would say it now, because in general most experts are now ready to admit that there should be a proper sequencing. Free capital movement should be a long-term goal, but one needs to have a financial sector that is properly monitored and has a solid basis first. It's now accepted that first comes domestic stability, then opening up. Russia didn't have domestic stability when it opened up, nor did the Asian countries.

LG: So, how long do you think it will take for Russia to stabilize?

Alfred Steinherr: That I cannot say, because I think it would take something very dramatic to bring about stability. Right now, there's no light at the end of the tunnel. This is a missed opportunity. When you have these powerful oligarchs there, when the Mafia is so widespread and so powerful, it's much more difficult to eliminate all that than to set up a new system where all these things don't exist.

You know, in the south of Italy no government has been able to eliminate the Italian Mafia. I suppose that in Russia it will be even more difficult. I mean, the Russian mafias are now more powerful, perhaps, than the state. So, it's much more difficult now than it was six or seven years ago.

Russian oil

LG: One of the stories promoted by various market newsletters that were bullish on Russia was that its oil companies would do well. How do low oil prices affect the country's economy as a whole?

Alfred Steinherr: It's a big problem, certainly, for Russia, because oil is the major export item and Russia isn't Saudi Arabia — it has a much higher cost of production. If the price of oil falls to US$5, they would sell at a loss. Now, in addition, they are already selling much of it at a loss internally. There's some potential because the domestic market needs to be properly organized, people have to pay for energy, and then there's the potential of saving a lot of energy that is currently being wasted. Probably half of the current Russian energy production costs could be saved and either be exported or production could just be cut. One could maintain present exports and still cut production by something like one-third to a half. By saving energy domestically they could close down the uneconomic pits.

Oil in Russia needs a lot of investment and I think it would be a good idea to bring in Western oil companies as serious partners. If we wanted to help Russia, it would probably make sense to first invest in their energy infrastructure because right now the pipelines are in bad shape. The loss of energy, such as gas, in transport is extremely high, and also there is the environmental risk. So, investments like that would probably make sense — to modernize the whole pipeline system from Siberia to Western Europe.

Modifying globalization

LG: You've said that the drive toward liberalization of the world's markets and so on has created problems in Russia and elsewhere. Do you have any views on how the system could be improved?

Alfred Steinherr: After the war we created a system of worldwide concerns with the World Bank and the IMF. In recent years the system has become over-stressed, because there are very big demands on a regional basis and the world community doesn't always have the same interests. When, for instance, there's a problem in Mexico or in Brazil, that probably concerns the United States more than Europe; and similarly when something happens to Asia, perhaps Japan is more concerned, while Eastern Europe is more a European thing.

In pure economic terms this global economy isn't that global. Look at the trade structure of Eastern Europe; most of their trade is with Western Europe. The United States accounts on average for something like 5% of Eastern Europe's trade, and Japan doesn't count for more. All the rest is with Europe. In this sense we clearly have a greater interest in Eastern Europe than we have in Mexico, for instance, and I think that this should be reflected in the distribution of tasks. There should be a regional dimension. My view of re-doing the architecture of the world is to give more responsibility to regional organizations, which doesn't mean one should do away with the World Bank and the IMF, but they don't have enough resources. Instead of just beefing up their resources, they should be complemented by regional organizations that would be readier to cough up money to pursue interests that are closer to them.

A very good example was the crisis in Mexico in early 1995 when the United States requested Camdessus [the head of the IMF] to sign up for a deal and it had to be done quickly. So, Camdessus committed the IMF because he didn't want to say no to the Americans — after all, the IMF is heavily influenced by and heavily dependent on the United States. The Europeans weren't very happy. They had to approve a bailout operation for Wall Street banks. I'm not saying that was something one shouldn't have done; I'm just saying it illustrates the difference in the regional interests of the great economic powers.

As I said earlier, the American ideology of free capital movements is what they prescribe and what they make as a condition for American support all over the world, and of course that creates more risk. Our European experience has been totally different. In fact, countries like Italy, Spain, and France only eliminated capital controls in the early 1990s, and therefore our understanding about the relative merits of free capital movements or floating exchange rates is a different one. We could therefore play a different advisory role in Eastern Europe than the Americans.

I think one problem right now is that international issues are dominated by the United States. This isn't a negative criticism, because who else is there? The Europeans don't feel responsible, no European country has the weight to do something, and together we don't have a consensus. In a way, everything is left to the United States — and the United States knows its own system, and therefore believes in its own system, but that system may not work in other countries.

One good example is the Asian crisis. Americans would argue that the problem in Asia is that governments are corrupt and that the financial system isn't solid. OK, if that is the case, then don't flood Asia with money through free capital movements. Recognize that they're not ready, they're corrupt, and so on, and don't superimpose the conditions which are very good for the United States and now for Europe, but not for Asia.

I believe that the free capital flows to Asia didn't render Asia a service. The Asian economies have the highest savings rate in the world. Their savings rate is up to 40%. In the West, we have difficulties in ensuring that 20% of GDP is well invested. Imagine how difficult it is in Asia, with poor institutions, to make sure that 40% of GDP is well invested. Add to this, as was the case for instance in Thailand, 8% of a current account deficit. Instead of investing 40%, they were investing 48% of GDP. I don't have to go to Thailand to tell immediately that a lot of this investment is just not efficient. It cannot be otherwise.

As I've mentioned, even economic theory tells you there are some optimality conditions, and one optimality condition is that investment is close to the distributive share of capital in national income. That distributive share is something like one-third of GDP everywhere. So, if you invest more than one-third, you can say immediately that it isn't efficient.

What the capital flows to Asia did was to add to the problem. They didn't allow a more rapid growth. The whole idea of free capital flows didn't serve them. They weren't ready for it and there was no need for it. When the Asian crisis broke out in 1997, it hadn't been foreseen although the inefficiencies could be identified, but I think one should not criticize the IMF for not having acted immediately.

The question is whether the IMF is the ideal crisis manager. Ideally, a liquidity crisis has to be managed like a house on fire. You can't negotiate for months on how to intervene; you have to intervene quickly.

In the meantime we had the second problem — this American conviction that flexible exchange rates are such a good thing. But what people mostly forget is that the tendency of flexible exchange rates is to overshoot. Take Indonesia. From a macroeconomic point of view it was more solid than most European countries. It didn't have a major current account deficit, it didn't have a government deficit, it didn't have high inflation. Then you have a crisis in Thailand that infects Indonesia; Western investors, for very good reasons, suddenly reversed their initial optimism and their readiness to invest in particular banks. They drew out all the loans they had made only months before. The rupiah dropped like a stone.

Is there a European economy that could survive with, say, the pound going from three deutschmarks to forty pfennig? No company would survive that shock. If you only had a little bit of foreign debt, all your profits — and probably all your equity — would be wiped out. This overshooting in Asia shows the problem of flexible exchange rates, but it also illustrates the difficulty when you have the IMF that flies in and promises to come up with a program in a month's time. In a month's time things have changed, so you must revise the program, and then the government isn't immediately ready to accept all that. The IMF asked for anti-corruption measures to improve democracy — for God's sake, you can't change the whole political organizational structure of a country within a few months!

We knew for thirty years that Indonesia was corrupt and had a totally corrupt presidency, and we all did business with them. Suddenly there is a crisis and they're supposed to change it all. It doesn't make sense.

Certainly, in the long run one should find ways of dealing with corruption, but it cannot be a precondition for helping a country out. The crisis was a liquidity crisis; we could see that, with this highly depreciated exchange rate, they couldn't even increase exports. Firms couldn't find finance locally or externally to produce and export. So, the whole improvement in the Indonesian current account was achieved through depressing national demand and thus the demand for the imports.

If the problem is a financial one, then an exchange rate depreciation isn't helpful. It worsens your conditions because all the firms, as I've said, who had a reasonable level of dollar indebtedness were de facto bankrupt after an exchange rate devaluation of such magnitude.

We have to find another way. One way of doing it is to require that countries should, during good times, negotiate credit lines. That's what has been done by the Argentinian Central Bank. The central bank could negotiate credit lines with commercial banks as Argentina does, but also with other central banks. The bank that is most cooperative and sensitive to such an initiative would obviously be an important regional central bank. The risk that, say, the Bank of Japan would take in providing the credit line isn't that large, because such credit lines could be renegotiated on a monthly or quarterly basis and the renegotiation would send a useful signal to the market — it would do all the stuff the IMF cannot do. If a crisis breaks out, the credit lines are there, so you don't have to wait for successful conclusion of negotiations with the IMF; you can immediately draw on your credit line and deal with the problem.

If the problem isn't one of liquidity but is structural, it can be seen well in advance and therefore the Bank of Japan wouldn't provide the credit line, or only with certain conditions. So, if a crisis breaks out, then it will be of the liquidity type. I could imagine Europe taking care of providing Eastern Europe with credit lines, and America doing it with Latin America.

The European Community and Eastern Europe

Alfred Steinherr: The Europeans realize that they will have the most responsibility for Eastern Europe. There is a contradiction because, from a cultural point of view, Eastern Europe isn't only interested in Europe but also in the American way of life. The textbooks they are using are American textbooks. In economic terms, though, the central European countries want to be members of the European Community.

This implies a need for the reform of our European institutions. We know that already a lot of the stuff we do doesn't make sense — the agricultural policy, the way the European Commission is managed, and so on. So in our own interests we should reform, but it is frightfully difficult. If we don't manage to have really meaningful and very far-going reforms, then Eastern European support will be correspondingly costly for us. The current beneficiaries of our European largesse, who are already inside the E.C., aren't so happy with Eastern European support.

It's probably reasonable not to expect that the only payer for Europe is Germany. At present, there are essentially two net payers and by far the largest is Germany. If we are unable to reform and

Europe retains the same support structures, who is going to pay for it? Germany. And Germany has made it clear now that it's not so eager to assume the cost of this operation. On the other hand, they are unable to make convincing alternative proposals.

LG: Which central European countries are the most attractive places to invest in the medium term?

Alfred Steinherr: The most dynamic places are Poland and Hungary. Hungary, in particular, has had a very successful reform of its banking sector. (All the leading banks in Hungary are now foreign-owned or foreign-controlled.) They have probably the most efficient banking intermediation now. All the others have hang-ups about selling their national assets.

Poland has certainly been dynamic and has created the conditions for small and medium-sized enterprises to prosper. The Czech Republic in a way had the best starting conditions, but they tried to maintain employment and were very reticent about real reform of the banking sector. Now they are suffering from that. I am not saying the Czech Republic isn't interesting — the Slovak economy is also interesting. For investors, these are good places.

Immigration from the East

LG: Is there much danger of a mass immigration to the E.C. from the East?

Alfred Steinherr: The United States is always much smarter than we are about this. They have been able to attract Eastern European talents very quickly. As soon as these people could leave, they were offered research positions or professorships in American universities. The U.K. also has a number of Eastern European scientists. But the Continental system is too rigid. All the chairs we have are filled by nationals. Professors are still civil servants, so you must fulfill a certain number of conditions and universities don't have the autonomy to say, "Oh, it would be great to have world-class mathematicians who would be willing to come from the East — let's create the chairs." No. Governments decide how many chairs there are to be. That's the trouble with our government-run national education.

That is an opportunity for firms; if you need mathematicians, physicists, and people in informatics, here is a marvelous opportunity to tap a resource in the East, but on the Continent they don't want to have this competition from newcomers.

We also have a problem with our immigration laws. The Germans, in particular, have the largest inflow of foreign labor in Europe. It's a system based on national origins, so any Russian who can prove that his family goes back four centuries, or whatever it is, to a German ancestor has the right to get German citizenship and the immediate right to a pension!

Americans don't bring in people to pay them Social Security; they bring in people to work. In Kazakhstan they had a very large German population that was transferred to Kazakhstan during the Second World War. Younger Kazakhs of German origin are not really leaving any more — it's only the old people, and they come to Germany in order to draw a pension.

Give them the right to come, but don't offer them a pension and Social Security support. To some extent we get the kind of immigration we don't want — all these old people — but that's perhaps a German particularity. All the criminal part of German society has been taken over by Russians. Russians run the street girls and so on.

What has not come yet is the massive inflow, the hundreds of thousands that just stream in and you don't know how to get rid of them. Probably they will never come. If now, after the onset of the August 1998 crisis, Russians haven't emigrated to Western Europe, then I think we can put aside that fear.

LG: Why haven't they come?

Alfred Steinherr: That's a good question. In a way, migration is a very costly enterprise; you leave your friends, you may leave part of the family, all your social connections (the social capital), and you come to a country where real job opportunities only arise when you have skills and when you master the language.

I think that in the East, word of mouth has it that when you come to Western Europe it isn't easy to find a job. If we had American conditions where it is easy to find some job, then I think there would have been more Russians and Poles coming over.

We have a lot of Poles all over Europe doing black market work. Anyone who wants to construct a building hires a few Poles. These people haven't entered the statistics yet, but they are here. Some of the very dynamic entrepreneurial craftsmen do come.

Europe's common agricultural policy

One of the more bizarre features of the European Union is its "common agricultural policy," an enormously costly subsidy system for farmers. I asked Professor Steinherr whether it might be abolished if some of the Eastern European countries are allowed to join the E.C.

Alfred Steinherr: We have known for decades that the E.C.'s common agricultural policy is silly. It's a system of fixing prices. Initially the idea was to fix prices in such a way that Europe covered its own agricultural needs. And, of course, it's difficult to fix prices so that demand and supply is equal. In fact, prices are fixed at levels such that we have had over-production. What do we do with the over-production? Partly we destroy it and partly we sell it, but we can only sell it at subsidized prices, which poses a problem for the efficient producers, including developed countries like Australia and New Zealand, Argentina, the United States, and Canada — but for many products the poor countries are also efficient.

The E.C.'s common agricultural policy is harmful to efficient producers and to agricultural producers in poor countries. It's also silly because, why should we aim at autarky? We would never do that in industry.

There's a notion that we have to support agriculture because otherwise our small and inefficient producers will leave and the

European countryside will be depopulated. But if that were the objective, then it would be better to do what the English have done for a long time, which is to provide direct income transfers rather than fixing prices.

The difficulty of reform is huge, because the most powerful voices in national farmers' associations are the voices of the large producers. They would lose from subsidy cuts and therefore we have a system that only marginally benefits the small producers. If you're a small producer you get less; if you're a large producer you get more. So, the whole system isn't in line with its declared objectives. It's a fairly costly system for a population that, in some of our countries, represents only 3% of the total population. Any way you look at it, it doesn't make sense.

LG: Is it likely to be reformed?

Alfred Steinherr: Intervention prices are being lowered, but over a period of, I think, six years, by amounts much less than initially proposed. One idea that was thrown around is to give part of the support responsibility to national governments. Of course, those countries that benefit most from the subsidies, such as the French, don't agree with it, so it's frightfully difficult to reform it. Again, the problem is that once you have a bad system, it's much more difficult to eliminate it than it would have been not to create it at all.

LG: How would it be affected if Eastern European countries join the E.C.?

Alfred Steinherr: There is a huge potential in Poland, Hungary, Romania, and Bulgaria to step up agricultural production. If they received European Community prices, then they would dramatically raise their production, which would make the cost of subsidy more expensive. We would have larger surpluses to throw on to the world market and then we would run into difficulties with the Americans and the Australians, and so on.

The optimum size of the E.C.

LG: There are fears that increasing the number of member states within the European Community may somehow "dilute" its effectiveness. In your book *Winds of Change* you discuss the optimum size of the E.C. Are you suggesting that the E.C. will have difficulty in absorbing Eastern European countries?

Alfred Steinherr: No. The argument is that the optimum size is a function of the organization of the Union. I would say that the E.C. is already, at fifteen members, beyond the optimum. Structural funds which are now grants could be transformed into loans at market interest rates — perhaps with a small subsidy.

Another problem is the way the European Commission is managed, and how many commissioners are appointed. There is the problem of our languages — we would be adding Polish, Czech, Romanian, Bulgarian, and Hungarian. The most reasonable thing would be to have one working language, which obviously would be English. The French don't accept that, and since the French don't accept it, neither do the Germans, who want German as the working language — and the Spaniards say that Spanish is one of the most important languages in the world, and so on. In the end you can't reform anything.

We could certainly go further and have a larger membership if the E.C. succeeded in making deep reforms. In principle, Central Europe and the Baltic states are relatively small, and hence their membership looks manageable. We should, however, make sure that decisions are being taken on the basis of majority voting, because with all these small countries you could imagine that, for instance, all the Eastern European countries would form a coalition. A coalition of that size can block decisions such as reforms of the agricultural policy.

We could accommodate Eastern Europe, but not the bulk of the former Soviet Union. Once we think about bringing in, for instance, the Ukraine, for which there are good political reasons, we can see big problems. The Ukraine has fifty million people and its economy is still far less developed than the central European economies. If we extended the common agricultural policy to the Ukraine, it would really have a major negative financial impact. The Ukraine may be a candidate for membership in twenty or thirty years — geopolitically, it would certainly make sense — but right now the E.C. couldn't handle it.

America probably doesn't have a problem with the expansion of the Europe Union to the East and the supporting satellite countries. America also operates a satellite system — Mexico and Canada have 80% of their foreign trade with the United States.

European socialism

LG: But socialism is a powerful force in Western Europe. How far can this move go?

Alfred Steinherr: We Europeans always say we cannot totally adopt the American model because we believe more in social justice. Americans would probably reply that they are interested in creating job opportunities, whereas Europe throws people out of jobs and then gives them state support.

Now, what's the better model? On the Continent the majority of the population doesn't believe in more competition and less of a welfare safety net. They still think that the state is responsible for the welfare of people, and I think this is the problem. It is often said that the German Chancellor Kohl was voted out of power because people were tired of him, but the Social Democratic Party that supplanted him was elected on a platform of fairly old-fashioned socialist ideas: to give more family allowances (the more kids you have, the more money you get); to increase Social Security; to make sure that pensions will be paid by the government; to tax business more, and so on.

Germany is a country that has the highest cost of labor, the highest cost of energy, and one of the highest taxation rates in Europe. Happily, though, we have free competition in Europe. It obviously limits the scope of action of individual governments.

LG: How?

Alfred Steinherr: Let's say I'm Allianz, one of the largest insurers in Europe. I have my headquarters in Munich, but I can have my headquarters anywhere. I don't have to administer and manage global operations out of Munich. So, if the tax laws are pushed further, I can threaten the government that I will build up our operations elsewhere. Most journalists in Germany would say that this is unacceptable, that governmental policies are being dictated by business, which is nonsense, but it shows that the government has realized that there are constraints on what you can do. This type of market pressure served to reverse the policies that the new socialist government, with Finance Minister Lafontaine, wanted to pursue.

One example that I find quite interesting was when Mitterand and his socialist party were elected in France in 1980. Being ideological and inexperienced, they launched their new demand-driven policy to create jobs and more growth. Two years later they had to reverse their course completely with devaluation of the French franc, putting everything into reverse gear. Eventually the socialists were out. This was extremely important for Europe, because I think without that experience we wouldn't have had that convergence of economic thinking that allowed monetary union.

It essentially means you have to put aside the idea that with a little bit more inflation, you can buy a little bit more growth. In the end that made it possible in the E.U. to share a common outlook on what is possible, what is feasible, and what is desirable.

We may go through a similar experience with the new socialist government in Germany. Lafontaine, who is the representative of the left wing, has already been pushed out. It could well be that within a few years we will have a reversal of policies as happened in France in 1982.

Inefficiency in the E.C.

Among Europeans who are wary of further integration (the "Euroskeptics") there is a view that the E.C.'s supranational bureaucracy is riddled with corruption, cronyism, and inefficiency. I asked Professor Steinherr if he thought this was actually the case.

Alfred Steinherr: I'm not saying the European Commission is less efficient than national administrations — probably, it's more efficient. Certainly, London has a much larger number of civil servants than the European Commission and perhaps so does even a medium-sized city such as Manchester or Birmingham. The European civil service is quite small. Obviously, some civil servants are overpaid, but even if they're overpaid by a factor of two it would still not amount to a large sum.

There are inefficiencies, as in all administrations, but I cannot think of any national administration that can claim to be more efficient than the European Commission.

The other problem is, of course, at the top. As long as most countries send the politicians they cannot use at home to Brussels, what do you expect? Happily, most of the real decisions aren't taken by the Commission; they are taken by the Council and if the Council cannot reform the agriculture policy, don't blame the Commission for running it.

Corruption in the emerging markets

LG: You've described a disastrous situation in Russia — and we hear dramatic tales of Western executives paying off racketeers there, and sometimes being killed. Do you think that both corporate and private investors should completely avoid countries in such circumstances?

Alfred Steinherr: What's important is political stability. There is no point in investing in a country where everything seems to be very promising and then a year later there's a coup and the rules of the game have changed. Ideally, you would also have a transparent and fair legal system, but that's much more difficult to create.

If you don't have a legal system that protects the investment, a corporate investor might make a present of 10% of the shares of the investment to, say, a member of the Suharto family in Indonesia and that replaces the rule of law. That protects you. Now, that's relatively costly, but the opportunities in Indonesia are huge — a big domestic market of 200 million people, cheap labor, cheap natural resources, and all that made it worthwhile to pay the transaction cost or whatever you want to call it. Something like 10% or 20% of the investment went into the pockets of the Suharto clan. That was a way of ensuring there was macro stability and that the investment was protected, because you had the Suharto family as shareholders.

LG: What do you think about the anti-bribery legislation in the U.S. that forbids American countries from paying bribes abroad?

Alfred Steinherr: It's the right piece of paper to produce, because it sounds good. But it is fairly ineffective. You don't do any major business anywhere in Asia or Latin America or Eastern Europe without bribery. No American company that operates in those countries can afford not to pay bribes. So, you just have to make sure you're not caught.

The alternative is to be out of the market. We all make brave faces, and of course we really believe that bribery isn't the right thing, but if you want to do business in China or anywhere else in Asia, you have to pay bribes.

I would be interested in knowing — and we will never know, neither you nor I — how, for instance, British arms are being sold abroad. My hunch is that many contracts require bribes.

I have an ex-student who works for an American company that sells special cables for nuclear reactors, transatlantic telecommunication items, and so on. He told me that typically a contract is concluded after a weekend in an expensive resort where the company pays all the expenses and every room is equipped with a top-class call girl. Without that, no contract is signed — and that's an American company picking up the tab.

These are the realities of life. I'm not pointing at any country or company, in particular. They all have to do it, and therefore, although I can very well understand anti-bribery laws, the practical application is very difficult.

Successful investors often make only one or two really big coups during their lives — even the skinflint Benjamin Graham, father of stock analysis, admitted as much. You go on investing, year after year, making your modest gains, trying to beat the averages, and then, suddenly, either by luck or good judgment, an investment pays off big time. As Professor Steinberr points out, the places where you are most likely to make unusually large gains are in markets which have "disequilibrium" — in other words, where nobody is sure what is going to happen next and prices are yo-yoing like crazy. In such places an investor with superior knowledge or judgment may be able to strike it rich.

But how can an armchair investor do that? One approach is what you could call "the patient predator"; by educating yourself about a market and watching it for many years, there may come a time when you feel an inner certainty that you should make a move. That's why it makes sense to follow markets like Russia's, even if you don't feel good about investing right now. Perhaps one day the time will be right.

Another approach is to take advantage of what Professor Steinberr calls "overshooting." Just as you can tell that a market must be overheating if more than 33% of the country's GDP is being invested in it, you can also be optimistic that after an institutional panic, stocks will be too low and there will be a bounce back. That's not necessarily as hard to gauge as it sounds; in mid-1998, after the currency crisis in Asia, I invested in several South Korean blue chips. After a visit to the country, I'd become convinced that Koreans were not going to let their industry go down the tubes, despite all their problems. To my delight and amazement, my Korean stocks were up by between 70% and 100% within nine months. Risky? Maybe — but maybe the little guy can make good judgments too, sometimes!

6

Dean LeBaron: Poet of the Numbers

Many highly successful investors have unconventional personalities, and Dean Francis LeBaron is a perfect example. He has been called "the absent-minded professor type"; he is fascinated by new inventions, and in his time he has owned amphibious cars (most recently a Dutton Mariner) and a fully operational flight simulator (the kind that real pilots use, not the PC game!).

His investment approach has been equally unorthodox. He develops a collection of generalized approaches — at one time seeking out companies that were buying back their own stock, and at others, for instance, looking for low P/E companies, asset-rich concerns, or recovery situations. Once he has picked his strategies, he uses computers to make all the decisions to buy and sell!

Is he crazy? Not if you give any credence to academic theories about the "random walk" of stock prices, which regard prices in the market as being "efficient," in the sense of always reflecting what is generally known about the companies they represent. On page 187 LeBaron refers to equity investment as perhaps being an "iterative game of chance"— so perhaps you can see why he might regard statistical techniques as being the most valid investment approach. To have your computers actually pick the stocks that fit your criteria makes sense, if you think that the personal touch adds nothing to that part of the process.

He founded his Boston-based firm, Batterymarch Financial Management, Inc., in 1969 to actively manage U.S. institutional

equity assets. In the 1970s he became one of the first U.S.
professionals to invest in Russia, China, India, and Brazil.

A pioneer of the use of computer-driven models, Dean LeBaron is
recognized as being a "futurist." When I approached him to give an
interview, he asked if I would draw on the video interviews he posts
daily at his website from his homes in Switzerland and New
Hampshire. I was skeptical; opinion published on Internet home
pages is often on the bland side, especially when it comes to actually
discussing investment intricacies. Once I'd viewed his site, however, I
realized that this one was different. Not only are LeBaron's comments
a rich mine of useful investing insights, but also he is something of a
poet — hence the title of this chapter. His pioneering work in the new
mathematical approaches to investment has left him humble (unlike
many younger "rocket scientists") and full of a fascination with
meaning and possibilities. His excitement about the potential of the
Internet, for instance, is more like that of a teenager than a
distinguished professional investor.

Dean LeBaron: We are playing a great game of "institutional chicken"
now. Most funds I know of are run by fully invested bears — people
who believe that we are at extraordinarily high valuation levels, totally
unjustified by modest, low-confidence estimates of what the future
could bring. And the mantra of the day is to run disciplined portfolios,
where discipline is a "cover" for staying close to whatever the
benchmark may be. In other words, not to reflect one's judgment,
concerns, or even enthusiasms, if one happens to have that about an
investment's outcome. Discipline is a better word than uncertainty,
and it is a better justification than saying, "I'm doing something I don't
believe in, because otherwise I might be fired."

We are all going to reach for the wheel at the same time, and we
are going to have some outcomes that will embarrass the best of us. It
is uncomfortable to watch.

Managers "run" money. They "achieve" results. They "identify"
errors and "correct" them. All these macho steps should produce
superior, controlled investment results. I wonder if that is how the
investment world works. The physical world doesn't.

Instead, we may be in an iterative game of chance during which we can assess the odds used by other participants in this game and, when we find variance with "reality," attempt to exploit the hypocrisy or stupidity of our opponents. All in real time. No wonder investment management was once described to me as "an exercise where you make major decisions on the basis of flimsy information in a system largely governed by chance, when you may be wrong slightly more than 50% of the time, publicly, and … you have to go back and do it again." Most sensible people don't expose their careers to such a capricious system.

One of the uncomfortable facts that efficient marketeers like to remind us of is that batteries of analytical tests have produced no evidence that the past movement of stock prices can be used to foretell future movements. For example, testing price changes of a particular stock in one period with those of the same stock in another period has shown that the correlation of past price movements to present and future price movements is almost zero — in other words, sequences of price changes in a particular direction are random, in the same way that a run of heads when you flip a coin is random.

Dean LeBaron: There is never a present in market terms, only a past and a future. Nothing can be said to be "working" or "going on," because markets operate in discrete time, quanta, or bursts, without an assured tie to the past or the future. Most market participants make their forecasts of the future based upon the naive, but logical, assumption that the past foretells the future. But that is still a forecast and not an observation of current events.

How long can the bull run last?

Dean LeBaron: Let us examine the bull case for U.S. stocks. It is always worthwhile to examine both the bull and bear cases. Of course, we know there is virtually no inflation. We know the economy is good, surprisingly good. If you pick up the "Help wanted" section in the newspaper, employment is at an all-time high. Money is freely available. You can finance almost any kind of business project. And the U.S. economy is dominant in the world, as the U.S. itself is dominant in the world.

Even the optimists among us have to be impressed at the market's power. Its momentum is outstanding. It overcomes bad news in the technology sector, bad news in Asia, with an increasing period of withdrawal and isolation and nationalism around the world. And yet the market power is strong everywhere — Europe, Asia, the United States. Money is flowing into equity funds. Short-term money flows are occurring without any transparency in ever-increasing amounts. We have to be impressed with all of this.

This is the best sign for a durable bull market. Of course it is. We've had it for a decade. Why shouldn't it be durable?

Perhaps we should keep in mind that there is a very strong momentum buying into stocks. The public has learnt over the past five or six years that every time there is a market decline they should go in and buy on a dip, even a minor dip, because things will go higher. That is now a conditioned response, as Pavlovian as anything we have ever seen. And the most important thing of all, absolutely the most important, is: we can't forecast anyway, so if you have money to invest, why bother to forecast? That's the bull case. What do you think?

Precisely the same evidence may be used to support a good market tone or a bad market tone — a bull market or a bear market. For example, prices are not rising as you would expect at this advanced stage of a business recovery. It could be good or it could be bad, because inflationary forces are building up and they are extremely destabilizing, as we are learning from Asia.

Rates are attractive for borrowing and money is plentiful, and that is very good for business … or it may well be bad, because it means that a great deal of money is flowing in from overseas to the United States as the last fortress of capital. Similarly, the public — almost everyone — continues to buy on debt. Is that good, because it means confidence? Or is it bad, because it means that there is such a strong psychological undertone to the market that, when it cracks, nothing will bring it back? Further, we have the quality stocks doing much better for the past several years than the broad market averages. Good leadership? Or bad, meaning that there really is a low level of confidence, and this is just speculation in well-known names?

Finally, earnings are good. Yes, they are. On the other hand, the majority of the surprises are on the down side, not just this quarter, but in preceding quarters as well. There appears to be a deterioration in terms of build-up of disappointments. The same news. It can be seen as good ... or as bad.

In times of volatility in so many factors, it is worthwhile to stand back, gain perspective, and then, on issues, one by one, dig deeper to get your hands dirty with the data, and come back up. This used to be referred to sometimes as a pattern of inference reading for news. It is rather difficult to do when you are involved in day-to-day affairs, but it is essential to do it when you want perspective.

Today, the mantras of the past fifty years are being broken one by one. The mantra of "the Japanese miracle" which drove so much of the post-Second World War period is broken and probably won't return until China takes over as the leader of Greater Asia and Greater China well into the next century. The mantra of "small is good" is broken. Now companies are rushing to merge, to get bigger and bigger, in order to build up liquidity and cash in on the market's favoring now of larger companies.

Business, presumably, should be thinking long-term, but most proposals I see are extremely short-term and extremely equity-driven. We used to hold that capital was good to be poured into emerging market countries. Now the evidence is fairly strong that that has helped those people within the countries who had access to the financial system, but it hasn't done much for anybody else. Russia is an example of this, and the early moves of capitalism have exacerbated the split in income inequity around the world.

Globalization is giving way to nationalism, which is putting at risk a whole variety of institutions set on the global model. The UN, the IMF (which probably is out of money), and NATO are just three among the many at risk. Finally, of course, we have labor unrest over work rules, not over pay. We will see some real union militancy coming up in the United States in the next few years.

So, these mantras are being broken, one after another. What does that mean? It means we should go down into each one, get our hands dirty in the data, and see what implications they have for our investment decision-making in this rather extraordinary era of volatility, change, and questions.

Emerging turmoil

Dean LeBaron: ADRs give the U.S. investor a convenient way to buy shares in leading companies of emerging markets. Recently, emerging markets haven't been a very attractive place to be. Markets are down, probably 10% overall, and many by a lot more. There have been notable, well-publicized collapses in Asia, more recently in Russia, and on the subcontinent in India and Pakistan. Investors in emerging markets are worried and reminded of the risks of being there.

I think this is quite properly so, because the risks this year are in the form of nationalism — not necessarily reforms, but rather how foreign investors are going to be treated. And since ADRs reflect a flow of funds into the larger companies, rather than into the smaller companies which are more broadly representative of the local markets, they are highly influenced by the flow of funds of foreign investors. I would thus expect that this year, for the first time in years, the ADRs and the leading companies — the larger companies in emerging markets — will underperform the broad local markets. I would treat ADRs with care and distance. This forecast has been wrong thus far in 1999 — there has been only a little buying off the bottom in emerging markets, perhaps by institutions maintaining their asset allocations, but it has gone into the leading companies. ADRs have been standouts thus far.

Each emerging market considers itself unique in attempting to solve its own problems. However, the problems seem to be quite common. Most emerging markets have borrowed heavily in dollars, in this capital-plentiful period, in order to rebuild their economies. Investors have also invested dollars in those economies and now plan, at higher rates, in higher markets, to take them out. And even if not at higher levels, they plan to take them out anyway, because emerging markets on the whole look like a considerably less attractive place to invest than they did five years ago. This is a worldwide phenomenon, and isn't just limited to Indonesia, Russia, and Latin America.

China may be different in the sense that it has a high surplus of dollars with its very positive trade balance with the U.S., but for others, perhaps, it is quite different. And I think we can expect that there will be continual turmoil in these countries, promoting more nationalism, more separation from the international community, and yet more necessity on the part of the developed nations, especially the United States, to support them. These countries are the countries that have a very positive trade balance (in most cases) with the United States. And they buy what we produce. It is a tough, tough dilemma and will produce more turmoil.

Throughout the Asian financial crisis, we kept hearing the pleas for more transparency. This reminded me a great deal of Heisenberg's uncertainty principle, which, by its extension, suggested that the role of the observer in an experiment was very critical in determining the outcome. Accounting information and financial information are subjective. You can see pretty much what you want to see — within some rules, to be sure — but at least in the short run, less than five years or so, there is a fair amount of flexibility as far as reporting profit, not necessarily honesty, but profit. You can find out pretty much what you want. The market really determines its own support and background, rather than the background determining the market.

The Russian stock market

Dean LeBaron: In 1998 the Russian stock market, which had previously been one of the best-performing of the emerging markets, crumbled by over 80%. Infusions of cash from the IMF and re-dedications of the new government to economic reform hardly caused a hiccup in the dramatic decline, most of which occurred on very little volume. In 1999 there has been a market recovery exceeding two times on low volume with little structural change. The earlier crisis conditions have abated because of credit extensions.

The fact that the Russian economy functioned at all after this decline shows how little the stock market is actually involved in the real economy in Russia. The stock market is of interest mostly to foreign investors, because domestic investors are involved with the managers of the enterprises who control the cash flow. So, foreigners see the stock market as a way in which they can judge the health of *their* investments in the economy. And, with the rise of nationalism, I fear the stock market reflects the opinion of international investors for future prospects, not necessarily for the domestic health of the economy.

The lesson of the financial collapse in Russia isn't related to Russia, although that is significant with somewhere between 26,000 and 30,000 nuclear weapons potentially at loose in the hands of terrorists around the world. It is a lesson for the IMF, which is no longer effective on the global scene. The IMF is out of money.

The U.S. Congress, among others, refuses to give it more money, and so it cannot stop the flow of crises from Asia, to Japan — a different kind of country than others in Asia — to Russia, potentially back to China, Eastern Europe, and maybe even back to the United States, which continues to build up its trade deficit even while we are greatly enhanced economically.

The system is broken, and I doubt if we can fix it at the same time we are putting out fires. It doesn't relate to a particular country. It's a global issue and it will take a global solution.

Using the Internet

Dean LeBaron: Can the Internet survive capitalism? I'm a great fan of the Internet … it's magic for me! I have been an early adopter since the 1970s as far as computer equipment is concerned. And I'm an early adopter because it is magic and I want to get the magic going as early as possible. Of course, I have found a number of things I don't use, and I either give them to someone or throw them away. But when I find something that absolutely works, it's terrific.

Lately, capitalism is driving the Internet, and it has to do with financings and deals and mergers. It's not the old days where there were just a few hackers getting together to try to do something, with a remarkable new tool, that provided them with some personal satisfaction. Now, Wall Street has hold of it.

The quality of the products that are coming in is going down quite seriously. I hope it doesn't affect things, but I fear, now that the Web is getting involved with telephony and with TV, that we will have regulators and more capitalism and financings, and the geeks are going to take a back seat. I'm afraid we are all going to lose.

Several years ago when I began studying the application of the Internet, it seemed to me that the Internet industry was very similar to the emerging markets of five to ten years earlier, with the excitement of discovery, with the glamor of seemingly unbridled growth and almost infinite demand. And markets were completely attracted to emerging-market countries, because little was known about the risks or any of the eventual outcomes. Not so in the emerging markets now. We are going through a period of increasing maturity and sobriety.

The Internet, on the other hand, is in the stage the emerging markets were in three or four years ago, with enthusiasm that seems completely unchecked. The latest is on portals and home base. It seems somewhat silly, because the Internet arena for retailing and commerce will go through the same stages as outlets and shopping malls have gone through in the United States and elsewhere. At first, people wanted the convenience of going to the same place all the time. But then they wanted to make sure that there were competitive stores in a given shopping mall, and they only went to malls that had more than one so-called anchor store. Similarly with portals, except now the shopping will be done by bots and intelligent agents, so portals will actually be of no value whatsoever. And yet, they seem to be important now.

Yes, I use Lycos as a typical portal; others use Yahoo!; and I was probably one of the earliest customers of Amazon.com, but I can be perfectly well persuaded to use Copernic to choose among all of the booksellers on the Internet and have it do the buying for me. Yes, the Internet is the emerging markets all over again, and I suspect it is going to follow exactly the same path. We are on the upside now.

Investment research on the Web

Dean LeBaron: The Internet is especially useful for conducting investment-related research. Through the Web, knowledge gathering is dramatically easier, better, and more cost-efficient. Essentially, the knowledge accumulated at huge expense by the Western world is available now to anyone who wants to find it.

Basic news is readily available on the Web. The Web carries around 2500 of the world's leading daily newspapers, most of which you can get automatically. The Microsoft news service, which is an alliance with NBC as msnbc.com/, is also quite useful. Financial information is also readily available on the Web and has been effectively mimicked by America Online. Most of the stock exchanges have a presence on the Web, and they offer links to companies listed on the exchange that have a presence on the Web. Industry associations, including AIMR, are there. The Market Technicians Association has an extraordinarily good site, including a huge amount of shareware.

Brokers are now on the Web. They can transmit material via the Internet without clogging fax machines, and getting the material isn't dependent on whether the machine is out of paper.

The Web contains a wealth of information on countries, which makes doing research quite easy, particularly for those countries that are hard to visit. Take Cuba, for example, which I think is going to be an attractive market. Activities there are quite easy to follow on the Internet through about 100 home pages from Cuba. You do have to be careful when you search for Cuba, however, that you don't get all the "scuba" sites. For Americans who cannot travel to Cuba, these home pages are a wealth of information.

Iran is another country that Americans don't know very much about — or else, what they know, they don't like — but it's a large country that I want to start following. Iran has about fifty websites, although some of the better sites originate outside of Iran, away from the censorship. China has about 2000 home pages in various places. Russia has about 500 sites in Russia, but, if you cast the net wider, a total of about 1200 sites on Russia are available.

Another important attribute of the Web is that you can contact people whom you might find hard to contact otherwise. Before the Web, when I traveled to a country, I tried to meet representatives of the opposition political party, face to face, which was always difficult. In Argentina several years ago, for example, I wanted to meet some Peronistas, but no banker would admit to knowing any Peronistas. Similarly, I had difficulty meeting any Zulus in South Africa. Now, I can find Zulus on the Web. Almost every South African university and even several high schools now have a presence on the Web.

Does the Internet really help poor countries?

Dean LeBaron: The Internet seems made for countries like Nepal. All of a sudden a remote land with no money is hooked by computer to the best of the world's knowledge, at a price which is free, at a time which is instantaneous, and where distance is immaterial. You would think it to be ideal. A friend of mine sent me a review of conditions in Kathmandu, which suggests that my optimistic framework is less than realistic. Even so, Nepal's Web presence is growing.

In the first place, much of the news on the Internet is U.S.-based, or so they find with the *New York Times* and MSNBC and so forth. They haven't explored the other news sources. Next, it is in English, or at least 85% of it. Certainly, English is the *lingua franca* of the commercial world, but, for most of the people in Nepal, it doesn't help them very much — although English is the language of the intelligentsia of that country. And finally, it is extremely expensive. There are only three Internet service providers in Kathmandu and they charge, as a percentage of national income, a horrendous amount.

So, it doesn't always work, but at least it's better than nothing, and at least it is competition for the postal service, because email works. Well, it works most of the time ... when the country has electricity!

On stock market forecasting

Dean LeBaron: As financial analysts, we are professional forecasters who have a pretty dismal record. Our results are usually no better than chance, and when you take into account our expenses incurred in achieving these results, they come out a little bit less than chance.

But we can make our forecasts more useful, even though not necessarily better, by labeling them. Let's follow the truth-in-labeling law, which is done on food packages and everything else, and call it what it is. Let's describe what kind of forecast we are making.

For example, if we're going to use back testing, let's use back testing, but say that's exactly what we are doing. Back tests come in two varieties. One is momentum — that is, the forecast is derived from our view that the past momentum will continue in roughly the same direction (a straight line, often) as it has in the past. Another form of back testing is regression to the mean. That is, we think things will go back to average conditions, not back, or up or down, but return to average. It's like a coin flip that goes ninety-nine times in one direction, and we think the next event is related to the preceding one.

Or, we can say that our forecast comes from our own insight or novelty and label it that way until we know that it's essentially out of our head and creativity (or lack of creativity) which we will know in time. Sometimes different techniques, like high-frequency forecasting and so forth, come from this. Or it can come from news, our response to new news. I won't call this "insider information," but let's say it is news that's not necessarily generally recognized by others. And that is a form of forecasting derived from information.

Finally, which is the most common of all, I fear, is that we waffle. That is, we do benchmark-investing, or we stick to the middle, because we don't know what else to do. That's perfectly all right, but let's label it as such. Let us *say* that is what we are doing, so that people can understand what they're getting when they listen to us. Most of the time, waffling is the right thing to do, but at all times we can make our forecasts better by correctly labeling them.

Investing with Artificial Intelligence

Dean LeBaron: Batterymarch first set up the firm as a large Artificial Intelligence (AI) system in the late 1970s. The ethic of machines mimicking the intentions of humans, and of machines, not the people, organized by hierarchical organization charts, was counter-intuitive. I can recall a trustee of a large university endowment who made a due diligence call on Batterymarch just before we were to be assigned a substantial portion of the fund. Upon noting that no-one "worked," he commented that the Puritan ethic was just the opposite and he would ensure that none of the university's money was managed through such beliefs. He succeeded.

Today, uses of AI incorporate dynamic learning features. Models *learn*, rather than operate rigidly, as we did several decades ago. Individual agents carry the same simple codes that we used, and can be used to combine into complex systems just as we did.

Most clients cannot tolerate the unforecastable outcomes of portfolios that might be produced at the most rewarding, yet most risky, tails of the distributions. There is a desire to impose limits at the system level, usually "optimizers" built on the assumption that market characteristics follow linear relationships. Of course, such limitation undoes the very value of an emergent system. But if one lets the system evolve, the power of machine assignment of tasks can free humans to do creative tasks. And much better math tools are available today.

I fear that more harm is done by the misleading information in performance figures than by any other statistical evil. And I am partly responsible. The Financial Analysts Society, predecessor to the AIMR, appointed a small panel of wise seniors (of which I was one) to recommend reform measures for all investment firms presenting performance numbers. We determined rather quickly that commingled results had to include all accounts, with no convenient dropping of those which left to go elsewhere; had to follow, in general, mutual fund accounting; and, ideally, would be certified by an outside audit. These proposals were adopted and were the basis for a new industry of software practitioners and performance attribution specialists.

If people were as numerate as they are literate, investment professionals would never make mistaken claims and investors would be less willing to believe them. Take fund performance, for instance; if I manage ten funds and every few years I merge the bad performers with better performers and also start new ones, it's easy for me to make all kinds of positive claims that are misleading. It's like the store that says "established 1888" when it has had sixteen different owners, each with different goods and policies, in the intervening period.

Dean LeBaron: Should we be proud of our work? I fear we should not. The resulting numbers look more reliable and, after all, have the AIMR stamp of approval. But they fail standard statistical tests of significance and very rarely can be projected forward. Our proposals were rather like encouraging cigarette factories to sweep the dust from their floors, giving recognition for the new cleanliness to be put on the cigarette pack.

We could have included a range of significance to the numbers. We did not, because it would uncover that most had no meaning.

When investment analysis began to be highly quantitative twenty to thirty years ago, problems of modeling had to be broken into small, manageable pieces to be studied and then reconstructed into a whole to run. In the investment world we have demanded so much precision in our data, so-called clean data, that all the benefit of a favorable surprise is gone. Just think of charts and how often we see equal units of time on the horizontal axis. But is all time equal? Not in the physical world — some time is more important than other time when things are happening.

Perhaps analytical synthesis lost the important interconnections and complexity which are inherent in an organic market world. Just breaking out of our concept of time may release our minds and models from the bonds of false assumptions about how the investment world operates.

Several centers of study are attempting to move the new mathematics of complex, dynamic systems into application to analyze data, verify its validity instantly, correlate its relation to other data, and provide a risk assessment.

Market simulations can be forward-looking rather than backward. Just as we have flight simulators to train flight crews, comparable tools are becoming available for investment practitioners today. Trading models using "high-frequency" data. Neural networks and genetic algorithms. New techniques of visualization, like virtual reality and multimedia data displays, providing insights into data equivalent to what the electronic microscope did for images that could only be seen by optics. You can "sense" data in addition to analyzing it — and in real time.

Market forces that can only be imagined can be tried on traders before they happen in reality. Emerging markets, or any markets that have idiosyncratic features, can be modeled, studied, and mastered before expensive lessons are learnt with real money. The simulations can be used as default decision-makers. In a world which demands new risk control tools, they are at hand in the market models which move instantly along complex lines taking into account rapid external forces.

This world is inherently complex, organic, adaptive, and nonlinear. It follows no rigid patterns, but it does have a pattern — it's just different than we have been taught to expect. In physics, around the turn of the century, experimental data from new laboratory machines challenged and eventually overturned Newtonian principles. We may stand at the same place in investment thinking almost a century later.

One of the slightly sick jokes I remember reading in the *Journal of Portfolio Management* made a very profound point. A new researcher, a freshly-minted Ph.D., came to work at a brokerage firm from academia and was told that he would do numbers, problems involving addition, subtraction, multiplication, and division — but not to worry, as division wasn't used very much. The point of that story was that what passes for quantitative analysis in the investment area is frequently static, simplistic, and does not meet the rigors of statistical tests that can be used with today's instruments and today's demands.

The new tests are dynamic, often involving complexity analysis and destructive statistical testing to determine the limits. They are very demanding of time scales and frequently are so large and so demanding, such as high-frequency analysis, that they can only be done on supercomputers. In today's investment world, quantitative analysis must be the very best, not the most used.

We live in an age of measurement. We want to measure everything — how high, how heavy, how much … We are trying desperately to improve our ability to have accurate measures. We need measures in order to be able to forecast, because how can we tell anything about how much, how many, how heavy, for the future unless we know the base from which we leave — the initial conditions? And yet, as we improve our data (which we do) but don't improve anything to do with the measures — the models to which they move — in the end, we come out with nothing that is any better.

Technical analysis — who needs it?

Dean LeBaron: We've had a sixteen-year bull market in the United States, and the Dow has gone from 1000 to 11,000 — it has doubled in the last three years. Why would you want to have a tool, which, even if successful, got you in and out of the market during that time? The thing is to be in, in fact, even in an index fund which has outperformed most active managers who have tried to do better than the average of other managers — or better than the average of the market (which might be an index).

Technicians are in the doghouse. And yet, they may have their day. Let me suggest a couple who might be useful to you. I'm involved with, and am an investor in, a high-frequency data processing firm in Zürich called Olsen. Their website is www.oanda.com/. They use very advanced mathematical techniques to forecast currencies. My favorite of the traditional and extremely good market technicians covering equity markets is my friend Walt Deemer at www.4w.com/deemer/.

Walt and some other technicians feel that the U.S. market is getting a little "toppy." Not the end, but "toppy." Will we ever know when the end is? But what a fantastic ride!

Misinterpreting financial data

Dean LeBaron: Investment people frequently confuse coincidence with causality. With any two sets of finite data we can find correlations which will satisfy a statistical test. Once we find those correlations, especially if they are plausible, we tend to enshrine them as causality, cause and effect, and assume that the very conditions which produced those circumstances, coincidences perhaps, in the past are projectable into the future where conditions can be entirely different. And even if they were the same, the result might not be the same in a complex adaptive system. And once we project into the future, we further attribute leads and lags that are quite predictable — or we think they are predictable — and ascribe those to the system that we have produced.

It is a tissue of assumptions, of implausibility, and produces a result that is highly prone to flaw, failure, and excuses. We even go on to be prescriptive in the cause and effect, to say that if we do this, that will happen. For example, we say if interest rates are increased, that will make the stock market go down ... not necessarily if the market interprets that move in entirely the opposite way, as being a very strong economy or as something else. But it's not a one-to-one relationship. There are new tools that are very infrequently used which don't promise as much — fuzzy data, high-frequency data, adaptive systems, simulations. We should look at those as being at least more honest than what we do now.

I would estimate that almost all investment research puts some measure of performance risk, adjusted or nominal, or something on the left side of the equal sign in an equation. And then there are a number of dependent variables to be examined: factors, economic variables, sunspots, what-have-you. Not surprisingly, the researcher finds some correlations across the sign and attributes causality. Bad.

It may just be a correlation and no more. In fact, that is the likely case. This trap was pointed out by James March of Stanford in describing the foremost errors by his junior students. (It reminds me of first-year medical students who learn that they have the symptoms of almost all diseases.) It is a curse of most of the senior research of investment firms.

We have most of our data from non-outrageous conditions. Risk measurement is built up of lots of data close to "normal." (There really is no normal, ever, but there is usually tolerable.) These measurements are often extended, linear or otherwise, to the extremes where we get worried. But these measurements have nothing to do with the extremes and, when we get there, we know no more than we did before (for example, tactical asset allocation) — but we have higher and unjustified confidence.

I remember the admonitions of a junior high school science teacher that students should not record measurements to a greater degree of precision than our crude instruments could resolve. Although we could interpolate between the marks on a scale, we added error rather than greater precision by writing down numbers that were unsubstantiated. It seemed counter-intuitive at the time, but that observation has guided me countless times since with investment numbers, especially in the days of computers with their appetite for numbers to the right of the decimal point.

There are two levels of significance for investment numbers. The first is, are the numbers produced significant and/or predictive? Performance numbers are particularly subject to this scrutiny. They are almost always statistically insignificant and most likely subject to initial conditions that are unrepeatable. The second is, do the numbers imply greater merit than is warranted by the underlying limitations of the measurement technique (the junior high example)?

Investment numbers that fall short in these areas can be harmful, yet they are widely evident. And when seen they suggest a disregard of basic academic standards for the expediency of doing what is required by convention.

The trouble with "clean" data

Dean LeBaron: Many investment managers pride themselves on working only with clean, accurate data, thinking that careless errors are reduced. Yes … but. As in science and signaling, the techniques to clean the data must be used sparingly and with full knowledge of what is lost and what is gained. The real world is messy and emergent; never like what just happened, which will never happen completely the same again, with all the ramifications. When we model, we set up simplifying assumptions that try to capture the essence of the real world; we pretend its exactitude for study, understanding, and, if we are lucky, predictability. Real data is inherently dirty; model data is usually scrubbed.

The errors introduced by demanding clean data are many. The foremost is time. To get clean data demands that more time is introduced between the last bit of relevant data collected and the time at which it will be used. And time in markets involves, always, the activity of feedback loops that undoes the value of the measurements we have made. The second error is competitive. If we wait for clean data, knowing that our competitors do as well, we find the answers from that data just when everyone else does, often in the same manner, increasing the likelihood that we arrive at the same, discounted conclusion. Third is sample size. To get clean data, we often discard the suspicious measurements, and these may well include the most advantaged (even if startling) and potentially rewarding insights. Fourth is tools, like percentiling, interpolation, curve fitting, and test of significance. These may be correct and helpful, and they may be just as misleading in assuming regularity, linearity, and serial correlation.

And then there is synthesis: separating a characteristic of the data from its associations, studying it as if it were a member of a closed system, and attributing the results of the piece back into the whole system. Most research contains all of these potential flaws. Is it any wonder that looking at historical data always produces wondrous suggestions for investment action, and application of this same process often produces humbling results. The careful researcher tries to handle data in the rawest form possible.

Good research is more likely to produce a surprise than to confirm suspicions. The classic Hawthorne study in the 1920s was attempting to confirm the *a priori* that light level in an assembly operation (phone handsets) was positively related to output. Industrial engineers in white coats with clipboards and stopwatches roamed the plant to confirm that there was a relation between higher light and higher output. The study, if done by many investment organizations, would have stopped there (the data was tortured and confessed). But young F. J. Roethlisberger wanted to confirm when it wouldn't work. He reduced the light level, fully expecting output to fall.

However, it rose. Lights went still lower and production soared. What is happening? Clearly, the original specifications of output as the dependent variable and light level as the independent variable were swamped by something else, perhaps people in white coats paying attention to the workers.

The careful scientist looks for the surprise, looks for the non-working conditions, is sensitive to transient effects, and generally treats research like porcupines making love.

To find out more about Dean LeBaron and his work, you can access his website at www.deanlebaron.com/, where you can download a number of his books, including the fascinating Climbing Falling Walls, *about his experiences as an investor in Russia and China. He has recently written, with Romesh Vaitlingham,* Ultimate Investor *and* Ultimate Investment Quotations *(Capstone, 1999). He also provides numerous useful links for those who wish to deepen their understanding of state-of-the-art quantitative techniques, including the two mentioned on page 200: Olsen at www.oanda.com/and Walt Deemer at www.4w.com/deemer/.*

7

Marc Faber:
Bursting Bubbles

He's been called "Dr. Doom," "the Prince of Pessimism," and "Cassandra" — and that's by his friends! Despite the evidence to the contrary, Marc Faber, Ph.D. isn't really a permanent bear. He's simply someone who speaks bluntly and feels comfortable holding uncomfortable views. He makes few allowances for investment newcomers (you won't find any saccharine reassurances here), but much of his analyses are of great use to serious investors.

I went to visit him at his offices on Hong Kong Island, a few streets up from the Kowloon ferry. Marc Faber Ltd's premises are quite a surprise after the anodyne steel and glass you see everywhere in upmarket Asia — shelves of antiquarian books vie for space with busts of Mao and Chinese revolutionary art. It's an unconventional office for someone who manages US$120 million on behalf of Asian clients through his BVI-based Iconoclastic International Fund, yet it's reassuring. Here, one feels, is an investor who really does know his own mind.

The Michael Milken days

The scandal and eventual imprisonment of "junk bond king" Michael Milken at the end of the 1980s was seen by many to be symbolic of a decade of financial excess. Milken, an employee of Wall Street firm Drexel Burnham Lambert, specialized in "junk bonds," corporate bonds that are too risky to be rated by Moody's and Standard &

Poor's. Persuading investors that these bonds would produce superior returns, Milken gradually developed a substantial degree of control over the whole junk bond market, earning massive advisory fees for helping companies to issue more junk bonds.

Using his network of clients, which included Savings and Loan and insurance companies, as a pool of money with which to exploit the leveraged buy-out craze, Milken was able to finance the corporate raiders of the day. Each year he presided over a conference, dubbed "The Predator's Ball," which attracted high-flyers such as Rupert Murdoch and Sir James Goldsmith. Secretly, however, Milken was colluding with arbitrageur Ivan Boesky to manipulate markets and trade on inside information.

Marc Faber also worked for Drexel in the 1980s, so I asked him about his involvement in the eighties' junk bond scene.

Marc Faber: I started working on Wall Street in 1970, for a firm called White Weld. In 1973 they sent me to Asia. I left the firm after they were absorbed by Merrill Lynch in 1978. At the time, Merrill Lynch wasn't particularly keen for me to work for them, and I wasn't very keen on the idea either. Then I opened the offices for Drexel Burnham here in Asia and subsequently worked for them until 1990 when the firm went into Chapter 11.

When I joined White Weld, I was told that there was a very brilliant guy there named Mike Milken who was doing great things. When I met him in Los Angeles in 1978 he had just started to deal in junk bonds and wasn't yet doing any underwriting.

Milken had invested in a lot of REIT securities because, after 1973, the REITs were decimated and the bonds were trading at deep discounts. There were lots of other securities that were trading at these discounts because, at that time in the 1970s, basic industries and real estate weren't doing as well as, say, oil and gold. They were still withholding tax on the interest received on U.S. bonds — it was lifted in 1986 — and I had some clients in Asia who had a tax-exempt status because they were charitable institutions.

I had the opportunity to buy high-yield bonds early on, on behalf of those clients. We bought some high-yield bonds in the late 1970s and early 1980s, with mixed success, because after 1982 the whole bond market rallied very strongly. The long-date treasuries, thirty-year treasuries, performed the best, as yields fell from close to 15% to around 9% in 1987. Today, they're 5.5%, so basically, over that period of time, it was more profitable to be in long treasuries, if you had rolled them over, than to be in equities.

But we bought junk bonds called high-yield bonds. I was one of the few foreigners that bought them, because of those tax-exempt accounts I had. Nobody else in the Drexel network had this ability, and people abroad weren't interested in high-yield bonds.

So, I built up a very friendly relationship with Mike Milken's department. He was growing very rapidly and then, in 1985 and 1986, I saw the excesses developing. In 1986 I started to write negative articles about the high-yield market. Then came the 1987 crash and the difficult period for high-yield bonds up to 1990.

Basically, I saw that a lot of excesses had been building up and that it couldn't go on forever. I also saw some danger in Drexel Burnham borrowing short and lending long in relatively liquid securities. To be fair to Drexel, they went bankrupt not because of a negative network at the firm; they just had difficulty in rolling over their short-term borrowings, and nobody bailed them out because of the legal problems they had. Nobody could ascertain the liability. By going into Chapter 11, they kind of got rid of a lot of legal problems and the shareholders then got much more out of the liquidation than anyone had ever dreamed.

To answer your question about my involvement — yes, I was quite involved from the beginning and then I turned negative when I saw the excesses that were occurring.

LG: Did you get into trouble for turning negative?

Marc Faber: I think that had I not been a buyer of the bonds earlier on and supportive of the department, they would have sacked me — plus the fact that my office was actually the only profitable office out of all the overseas offices. They said, "OK, Marc is a nut-case. Let's not pay too much attention to him."

I have to give Mike Milken great credit in the sense that he was an individualist — that was the philosophy of Drexel. As long as people did their business, they could have their own views and Drexel left them more or less in peace. Everybody was able to do whatever he wanted to do as long as it made some kind of commercial sense, but I think that had I not known some of the important Drexel clients, who were supportive of me in America, they might have sacked me.

LG: Many people say that Milken was picked on unfairly. What's your opinion?

Marc Faber: He made a lot of money. He gave some back, because he paid a fine, and also went to jail for two years. Others in that department didn't go to jail or give anything back. Was Mike Milken's department breaking the law? I think in some cases they did break the law somewhat, but everybody else probably did so as well. In financial booms, such as we had in junk bonds at the time, there's a lot of funny business that goes on. For instance, there was this whole business with the Savings and Loans [S&Ls]— the government permitted the S&Ls to make all kinds of investments — so a lot of abuses occurred at the time.

I find it very difficult to be a judge of regulatory issues, because every law will be circumvented somewhere, somehow, and smart businessmen may be able to circumvent it without being convicted while those who are less fortunate get caught. Sure, Mike Milken cut some corners, but I know of others who cut many more corners than he did and didn't have to pay a fine or go to jail. So, my judgment of him is basically that the government was after him, period, and they nailed him.

They nailed him, so they should have nailed a lot of other people as well, which they didn't. I think if Drexel hadn't gone bankrupt in 1990, they would have done unbelievably well until 1995, the year of the Mexican crisis. I think the Mexican crisis wouldn't have brought them down, but I'm sure that the emerging market crisis in 1997 would have finished them because their own success would have become that much bigger and the firm would have been that much more powerful. Sooner or later, I suppose, their arrogance would have led to some major mistakes.

On corporate arrogance

Marc Faber: I think we have to analyze why that arrogance arises. Frequently it arises because the demand for a financial asset exceeds the supply, and this puts the people who supply that asset in a very powerful position.

We have observed this in the case of junk bonds and later on in Japan. The Japanese brokers were a prime example of *arrogance par excellence* in 1989. We also had it here in Hong Kong in 1997 during the red-chip craze, and I guess now in the United States.

Most successful people would prefer to attribute their success to some unique skill they possess, rather than just to luck. This is frequently a great error. If one considers that there are six billion people in the world, then it's not so unusual that some of them will win the lottery. They do well not because they are smarter than you and me, but because they are lucky. Many of the CEOs I meet have some skills or good qualities perhaps, but they don't have much knowledge or education.

LG: People management skills?

Marc Faber: Maybe they are ruthless. Often when I meet people who are in very senior positions I scratch my head and say to myself, "Maybe they're there because they joined the company twenty years ago and they were good at company politics and have moved up."

The same applies when you look at democracies and the kinds of officials they produce — and when you look at diplomats and see what kind of people they are. In Switzerland, we say that the stupidest farmers have the biggest potatoes. You can't assume that the Sultan of Brunei is a smart fellow just because he's the second-richest man in the world. It's just accidental that he is in the position he's in.

Supply and demand

LG: Could you talk about how supply and demand work in equities?

Marc Faber: People are tempted by what is hot. Suppose you open two identical restaurants next door to each other. They have the same menu, the same décor, and the same manager at the entrance. If, during the first ten days after opening, you paid people to line up in front of one of the restaurants, I guarantee that that one would be packed with diners all the time and the other, identical one next door, would be empty, because people have a tendency to rush where others are.

Many economic models assume that the markets are rational, whereas markets typically are totally irrational. It is totally wrong to assume that as prices go up, the demand shrinks and the supply increases; and that when prices go down, the supply shrinks and the demand increases. This is the famous demand and supply curve where you move toward a point of equilibrium. There are markets that move that way, and probably in the very long run they *all* move that way, but in the short run rising prices or rising popularity can lead to more demand, and falling prices and falling popularity to less demand.

If you have a restaurant that is continually full, you can be sure that more people will want to go there. If one day the business goes down, people will just exit and not come back — it's over. The same goes for financial markets, particularly in the manic phase — as more and more people participate, those few who haven't joined in feel compelled to do so.

People are attracted to what is popular, and the most popular things are those that people know the least about and where the profits are highly elusive. This is true now of the Internet. Frequently the demand side is underestimated — the demand turns out to be greater than expected, as was the case with cars at the beginning of the century.

The question is about the supply. If the supply increases significantly, then the pricing deteriorates, the margins come off, and you can't have a thriving industry. An example of this is the railroads between 1830 and 1873, when the industry grew exponentially. Later, in the 1890s, most of the railroads went bankrupt. Another example is the electric utilities, which had their boom in the late 1920s and then didn't make a new high until 1965.

LG: The airlines?

Marc Faber: Airlines haven't been a particularly good investment in the very long run. Lots of them went bankrupt. For any new technology, the growth curve looks the same — accelerating growth at the beginning and then the growth flattens out. Every new fad industry has more participants that go out of business than stay in business.

There are great profit opportunities — and, obviously, high risks — in a bubble. If you advised someone not to buy, say, Yahoo! at more than US$100 and offers subsequently go to $300 or $400, you've told them to get out too early, or perhaps you convinced them not to participate at all in what turned out to be a bonanza. On the other hand, maybe the stock suddenly drops by 90%.

The problem with investments is that, in a mania, everybody will have been right, but at different times. The bears are going to be right, because obviously speculative markets eventually do go down. The bulls will also have been right because, during the mania, the markets soared.

LG: So, how do you value stocks?

Marc Faber: In general I would say there are still some valuation criteria that count in the real world, like price/earnings ratios, price to sales, and price to book. Of course, it can go on above or below the trend line for a while, but I would still look at the historical norm as being something important to consider. It tells you roughly if the company is expensive, since if it is expensive it is more vulnerable to bad news than if it is cheap. If a concept is widely accepted and you have symptoms of speculative activity such as heavy volume, heavy day trading, a flood of new issues, and public focus on that investment scene, then you know it's not a very healthy market.

On long-term growth

Marc Faber: I think that performance thinking in America has come up largely because the markets have been rising since 1982. Essentially, the indexes have compounded rates of return of over 15% per annum, but that is an unusual period of time and it won't last forever.

There will be a time when the preservation of capital will become more important to investors than making money. As a bull market unfolds, people become less cautious and prudent, and in a financial mania, such as we have now, caution is thrown aside.

Until two years ago foreigners weren't large buyers of U.S. equities, but just in the last eighteen months or so European accounts have been very heavy buyers of U.S. equities.

LG: So, should we be looking for long-term growth?

Marc Faber: In the U.S. we have around 10,000 listed equities — worldwide we have tens of thousands. With hindsight it's easy to say, well, all you had to do was buy Coca-Cola at the beginning of the century, IBM in 1950, Compaq in 1983, and Microsoft in 1986. Unfortunately, the world doesn't work quite like that. In 1900, the majority of equities listed in America were railroad securities; there were very few industrial shares. Then came the automobile companies, most of which eventually went bankrupt, then radio stocks. Even RCA went down 90% between 1929 and 1932. That's why I'm very skeptical about long-term statistics on index performance.

It's meaningless to look at an index from, say, the 1840s and then to say that stocks have appreciated by so much since then. In the last century you had only canal shares, turnpikes and banking shares, then railroads; only very late in the game, around 1890, did you get into industrial shares. The first batch was pretty much worthless. They didn't perform well, and most of them eventually went out of business or had to be refinanced and restructured. The nineteenth century wasn't a particularly good example of the strong performance of equities. There were many more shares, many more companies, that went bankrupt than survived.

In the nineteenth century, foreigners lost a lot of money in America because it was quite a corrupt country and many investors vowed never again to touch an American security. To have performed well, we would have had to rebalance the portfolio at the right moments; in other words, we would have to have bought canals, but got out of them just before the crash of 1836, then bought railroads, but got out of them just before the crash of 1873, and then shifted into, say, GE and some industrial shares, but then got out of them in 1929, and so forth. After 1950, we would have had to rebalance the portfolio into stocks like Xerox and IBM and avoid the dogs like Woolworths and International Harvester; and then again in the 1980s and 1990s we would have had to rebalance the portfolio again into technology stocks like Microsoft, Dell, Cisco, etc.

The selection of stocks isn't so easy. In retrospect you can always say you should have bought something, but it's very difficult to know today which company is going to be the next Microsoft — maybe there won't be another one. Maybe the capitalistic age has reached a stage where it will be more difficult for companies to become as successful as Microsoft has become.

Remember that in 1900 a global investor had alternatives, not just America. At the time, Argentina was as promising as America; Russia was a favorite destination for investment; so was Egypt, and even some Asian countries. In 1900 someone who had a lot of money wouldn't have put it all in America; he may have put some, maybe 20%, in America, and maybe 20% in Russia and the Ukraine, maybe 50% still in Europe and maybe some in Egypt, in Argentina, and so forth. In early 1917, the Ukraine and Russia went to zero — that was the favorite investment destination of the French. Then we had the First World War when the stock markets closed for a while. Then the crash in 1929 and the Depression years.

After the Second World War, in 1945, Egypt was the third-largest stock market in the world. In 1954, Nasser came to power; in 1956, when he nationalized everything, it all went to zero. In the whole of Eastern Europe, everything went to zero. I may add that Shanghai and Manchuria, home to 90% of all foreign investments in China, went to zero in 1949.

People don't realize, when they hear that stocks do well in the long run, that one of the very few markets that has done well in the long run is actually America. Now, will that be the case in the future? Who knows — maybe not.

During the first millennium after the birth of Christ there was practically no world population growth. Both population growth and world GDP were stagnant. Then, between the year 1000 and 1800, there was a fourfold increase in world population and about a sixfold increase in global GDP. But between 1800 and today, a period of just 200 years, the population has risen six times and world GDP forty times. In other words, there was essentially no growth, or very little growth, between the year zero AD and 1800, but since then we have had a volcanic eruption in the world in terms of both population growth and economic growth. This economic growth seems to have accelerated in the last thirty to forty years. We now have containers which enable goods to be shipped very quickly. An entire factory can be shipped overnight in a Boeing 747 between, say, London and Shanghai, a journey that took four months by sea before the opening of the Suez Canal. Now we have instant communications. You can have a shortage of semiconductors this year, and a glut next year. A shortage of Internet providers this year, and a huge glut next year. Or you can have everybody buying stocks this year in emerging markets and the following year they take their money out and cause an economic crisis. What I want to say is that, in terms of long-term historical perspective, the economic development and population growth between 1800 and today is without precedent.

If you had come to me in 1990 and asked, "Look, communism is falling apart, the policies of isolation and self-reliance in countries like India and Pakistan are breaking down, and interest rates are declining, so where should I invest my money? Should I be in the high-cost, high-priced European and American stock markets, or should I buy securities in the emerging economies?" I would have told you to go and buy in the emerging economies because my assumption would have been that in the Western world we have high prices and saturated markets, and in the emerging world we have low prices, low wages, and unsaturated markets.

But the funny thing is that exactly the opposite has happened. Western stock markets, especially those in Europe and the U.S., have gone up, say, five times, and the emerging economy markets are down to roughly the level they were at in dollar terms in 1985 and 1986. So, you have to ask yourself, why did it all happen? What happened after 1990 is that basically the industrialized nations, specifically the multinationals in the industrialized nations, including Sony, Nestlé, Unilever, Procter & Gamble, Boeing, IBM, Microsoft, and the rest all built up a huge and growing trade surplus with emerging economies starting in 1990 until about 1997.

More recently, these trade surpluses have diminished, and in some cases collapsed, because there has been no demand in the emerging economies since the recession. The prime beneficiaries of this new world order following the breakdown of communism weren't the emerging economies but actually the industrialized nations who found a dumping ground for the products for which their own markets were essentially already saturated.

My feeling is that we are moving into a reversal period which will see a lot of countries question the benefits of free trade. The multinationals, the IMF, the World Bank, and the Western governments were very good at promoting the idea of international trade and the benefits of a global market to the emerging economies. For instance, they went to Indonesia and said, look, you've done well, but you could do so much better if you opened up your markets for capital flow, and freed up foreign exchange and foreign investments. Do all this and we will invest in your country. The problem is that the developing countries are buying goods and machinery whose prices have stayed relatively stable or are high, and what they're selling are low value-added products or commodity-type products, such as raw materials, oil, coffee, cocoa, wheat, corn, garments, textiles, shoes, Nike shoes, and electronic components, which have all gone down in price.

Since the 1970s there has been a tremendous increase in the size of financial assets and the volume of transactions using leverage.

We have monetary and credit inflation where the total investable funds in the world are up from something like US$3 trillion in 1970 to

$55 trillion now. Nobody ever questions anything. Until the bubble burst in Japan, nobody ever questioned anything, but thereafter, many unusual transactions and fraudulent practices came to light. I think in the U.S., once the bull run is over, a lot of abuses will come to light in the fund management industry, in the brokerage industry with all this online trading, and in the corporate world which is actively engaged in what I would call extremely creative "financial engineering."

The truth about growth?

Dr. Faber makes the startling, yet obvious, point, that wealth cannot be accumulated indefinitely (that is, for centuries). I asked him what implications this has for investment strategy.

Marc Faber: I think, in general, it is very difficult to beat compound interest. If you had invested money at the time of the birth of Christ at just 5%, you would have a higher net worth today than that of the entire world. From time to time there are disruptions through wars, revolutions, state expropriations, extortion, theft, natural disasters and so forth, and investments can become worthless.

Of course, we didn't have a stock market 2000 years ago. However, we had a number of cities, many of which have now totally disappeared or are totally insignificant, so it wouldn't have been wise to have invested in those cities. Most of the cities that survived, such as Rome, have been sacked several times. To assume that a company — or a country — that is powerful today will still be powerful in a hundred years would be foolish in the extreme.

History has taught us that cities and civilizations have risen and fallen. I don't know of anything that has permanently kept its value. The only things I can think of that have a permanent value are philosophies and religions, because they are based on ideas and morals. You have Islam, which is 1300 years old, Christianity, which is 2000 years old, Buddhism, which is maybe 3000 years old, and so forth. Apart from this, wealth has come and gone for all people, all nations, all enterprises.

The big business in the Middle Ages was the spice trade. What is the spice trade today? Coffee and tea were once a much bigger thing than Coca-Cola. And companies like the East India Company and the Dutch East Indies Company were huge enterprises for their times but have now vanished.

LG: But there's long term and long term. Don't you think that the U.S. has got another hundred years, at least?

Marc Faber: When Robert Prechter published his first book in 1978 about the Elliott Wave, he said the Dow would go to 2300 and they thought he was a loony. Then he revised it to 4000 and so forth. In 1990 the Dow was at 2000 — now, there is always someone making crazy predictions, but who would have thought it would go to 10,000? Nobody. And in Japan in 1989, when it was at 39,000, if you had said to someone that ten years later it would be down 70% from that level, they would have said you were crazy.

In my opinion, we're not moving into an age of certainty and of stability, but one of unbelievable instability and uncertainty, and therefore I find it quite ludicrous to pay the P/Es we're paying now. Therefore, I think that the valuations in America are unsustainable and I'm convinced that the Dow will come down 80% from the peak, easily. I mean the Dow is at 10,000 — it will be at 2000. Possibly, it will rise further — to say 12,000, or even 15,000 — and then fall by 90%, so it will still eventually fall below 2000. There is also the possibility that the market won't fall but that the U.S. dollar will collapse.

Most bear markets in this century in America have given back at least five years of previous capital gains. In Asia we've given back ten years, so in 1998 we came back to the level of 1986 or 1987. In America after 1929 we gave back sixteen years of previous capital gains. If it gives back five years of previous capital gains, then the Dow will fall to its 1994 level, at around 4000. And that will be a minor decline, given the rise we had before. But I'd like to see the look on people's faces when Microsoft, Intel, and IBM all drop 50%. And they would still be selling at forty times earnings!

I can assure you that the Internet stocks will be down by more than 90% if this happens. So, this is the threat facing the global economy: that this huge bubble, where so much of people's wealth is tied up, is being deflated.

I wouldn't rule out the possibility that this is the biggest bubble in history. Once it is deflated, it is also going to deflate the capitalistic system. I don't know exactly how it will happen, but whenever something goes wrong, people have to blame someone. At the moment the entrepreneurs are heroes, but I'm not sure that they'll be heroes when the thing comes apart. Maybe society will then go back and say, "Well, capitalism is fine, but we cannot have disorderly capitalism. We have to have a more regulated capitalistic system, the way we had it, say, up until 1970, where lots of agencies were regulating industries."

LG: So, do you see a long, slow decline in equities?

Marc Faber: Once it is deflated, it will go quickly. It will go, poof! The markets will collapse by 80% in one or two years, either in nominal or real terms, which would be the case in a hyperinflation environment and is something we cannot rule out given the incompetence of central bankers.

Should you retire abroad?

The benefits for Westerners who choose to retire abroad have been growing for some years, as costs at home increase and health facilities abroad improve, yet very few investment professionals are willing to talk freely about this issue. As someone who made the psychological leap of moving to Asia, Marc Faber is well-placed to discuss the pros and cons of making the break.

Marc Faber: If I can give one piece of investment advice, I would say maybe the best thing isn't necessarily to invest in an emerging economy but, as an alternative to ending your days in cold New York, London, or Munich, deprived of any help, you could retire in a community in Thailand, North Africa, the Caribbean, or in Latin America with, say, three servants. I'd take the servants any time …

Let's take a Swiss who has a pension of, say, Sw.Fr. 50,000 when he retires, which is not uncommon. He can go and live in Shanghai or Portugal or Africa and live very well. But the Indian who retires at age forty-five with another five years' life expectancy has nothing — he has no choice. In Switzerland Sw.Fr. 50,000 won't go very far, because you have to pay the gardener $50 an hour. But you do have the option to leave; the other guy doesn't have that choice.

If we adjust for purchasing power parity, a lot of workers in Europe are barely surviving, and they're not happy because they can't afford very much. They just manage to meet the car loan repayments and the rent. They can only afford to go out maybe once a week. If they have children, they can't afford to send them to private schools. Of course, the government steps in and helps: they have Social Security if they're sick, but it's still kind of an under-class. They can afford to go to a bar once a week, but so can many people in India and the Philippines.

Take the case of my mother. She is eighty years old, has driven a car all her life, and lives half the time in Zurich and the rest of the time in St. Moritz. She travels back and forth independently, and she's used to having no help in the house. Even if she could get used to having a servant around, the flat she lives in isn't equipped to accommodate a servant. It's not like in Asia where we have servants' quarters. If she needed full-time care, it would be unbelievably expensive. Most people eventually wait for death in a home for the elderly unless they are lucky and have a fatal stroke or heart attack.

If you told me that I would end my days in a home for the elderly when I was eighty, I would say, "No, thanks. I'd rather die earlier in Thailand, the Philippines, Indonesia, Cuba, or wherever." It remains to be seen whether society will have enough money to support all the elderly in the long run, because a society depends on productive people and if you have fewer and fewer productive people as a result of demographic changes and more and more elderly, one day there'll be a revolution — not between different social classes, but between the young and the old. The young will say they don't want to pay for all these old people.

LG: In many Western countries there is very strong propaganda against retiring abroad. You're told that it will be disastrous, even though that's probably not true. The state doesn't seem to want old people to leave with their money.

Marc Faber: Yes, I'm sure.

LG: Do you foresee a period where you won't be allowed to take your money with you if you tried to do that?

Marc Faber: I think we're going to move again toward more protectionism and eventually we will have foreign exchange controls in the world or limits on capital transfers, so yes, I would imagine that this is a possibility. I think it would be a tremendous restriction of personal freedom if it happened.

LG: But people will be told that it's not.

Marc Faber: Some people might say that in northern Thailand, for instance, you don't have the medical attention you have in New York, but I don't care.

LG: It's not exactly true, either.

Marc Faber: Yes, maybe you have better attention in the sense that you have a doctor who is nice to you and you have some nurses who are nice to you, whereas if you go to a hospital in the West nobody cares. There I see some potential for wealth transfer from the rich countries to the poor countries, in that people will indeed move there because it's so much cheaper.

There is the security aspect, too. My mother lives in Zurich in one of the best areas — not the best, but one of the best — and they have a lot of crime. The old ladies get mugged all the time.

In countries like the Philippines you have compounds that are fairly well guarded. You have, say, fifty houses and a guard who walks around.

Surviving capital controls

One of the specters that the possibility of an era of protectionism raises is that it may become difficult, or even illegal, for Westerners to take their money abroad when they retire.

LG: How would we get around future capital controls?

Marc Faber: Getting around capital controls isn't all that difficult. First of all, before they were introduced there would be discussions and so forth, so people would take precautions.

LG: What kind of precautions would we take?

Marc Faber: Well, if you have a local savings account at the bank, you could transfer your funds outside your jurisdiction.

LG: And then be forced to move it back when the new laws came in?

Marc Faber: You could then choose to bring it back or move it elsewhere. In some emerging economies it has been the case that if people moved abroad, they couldn't take their money out of the country. So it could happen in the United States. Until the interest equalization tax was lifted in America, Americans also had difficulty in moving funds abroad. I suppose if it was done, it would be done as a tax on capital transfers.

    Theoretically, you could save your holdings, take the cash, and physically bring it over the border. Ideally, you avoid being caught.

LG: It was a big problem for South Africans, for example, wasn't it?

Marc Faber: Yes. Many people have had to leave their jurisdictions and they couldn't take their holdings along with them.

LG: So, would you say that the time to be doing it is now rather than later? You should get some money out; maybe hold stocks in the U.S. through a bank in Hong Kong or Singapore, or something like that?

Marc Faber: As a rule of life, you should always try to hide your possessions. You should hide your possessions especially from your partners, your wife or husband, and maybe from your children. Also, you may have a business but you want to have your reserves removed from your business and in a place where you could operate in a relatively free environment.

Take Switzerland. Of course, it could be invaded by Russia, but as long as Switzerland is in its present form, the bulk of the money in Swiss banks comes from overseas and is invested overseas. Ninety-nine percent of the money in Swiss banks is invested around the world again, so the Swiss government couldn't say to anyone, "You have a bank account in Switzerland. You can't take the money out." In an environment such as this, it is of course much less likely that your funds will ever be frozen.

If you're Mr. John Doe, you live in Seattle, you have a securities portfolio at a bank in Seattle, and you've paid tax all your life, on your income and on your assets, then everybody knows there is this $200,000 sitting there in that account. If it is in Switzerland, nobody knows except you and your banker.

LG: The trouble is that if you're a U.S. citizen, or a U.K. citizen, if you open a secret bank account in another country you're supposed to declare it. You break the law if you don't, and that's a strong deterrent to a lot of people.

Marc Faber: I would have no moral dilemma or bad conscience about having a secret bank account somewhere, because it's my money. I paid tax while I was earning it, so I don't see why the government should have anything to do with it. Maybe other people have different views on the subject.

LG: Perhaps many people hold your view but are afraid.

Marc Faber: If, on each trip out of the U.S., you took $10,000 cash and after, say, two years your bank account was depleted, and a tax guy came to you and said, "What the hell have you been doing with your money?" you could say, "I'm a compulsive gambler. I also have an expensive mistress in Europe. I spend my money on gambling and on my mistress, and that's that." Now, if he's unpleasant he can start to look at you very closely, but it would be very hard for him to prove any wrongdoing if you did it slowly.

Of course, if one year you have a million dollars in your account at your local bank and the next year there is nothing, the tax authorities are likely to want to know what you did with it. You can't say, "I lost it all on commodity trading," because then they'll ask you for statements, but you could gradually deplete your assets in one country and build them up somewhere else. There are many ways of doing this. I would suggest that anyone who has this opportunity should do it.

LG: These are matters that never get talked about but which everybody really cares about. Can you talk a bit about bearer bonds? That seems an ideal way to take money around, but can you be sure that they'll be accepted?

Marc Faber: Let's say you walk into a Swiss bank and you bring in US$20 million worth of bearer bonds. The bank will have to ask you where they came from and so forth, and do the due diligence. Different banks will react to a $20 million account differently. The big Swiss banks, after the kind of problems they had with the Holocaust victims, are probably going to be more careful, but the smaller banks may take it. You can always say you inherited the money from your grandmother, who sold some land in Thailand ... Is it their duty to be policemen?

LG: Can you trust Asian banks? I'm just talking about if you put money in an Asian bank, will it be there in twenty years?

Marc Faber: Yes. It depends a bit on which one, but in general I would say "yes."

LG: If you were a U.S. citizen, would you go for an Asian bank that didn't have branches in the U.S.?

Marc Faber: Yes, but anyone in the world could form a BVI company or one in the Cayman Islands, and then open the account. That company opens the account with, say, an Asian bank, or he could go to an Asian auditor and the auditor opens the account. I would imagine that for people in Europe there will be increasing pressure on Swiss banks, Luxembourg banks, and Austrian banks. I think the pressure on Asian banks won't be all that huge. I would say if you open an account with the Bank of China, they won't tell anyone. I haven't tried it, but my guess is that they wouldn't ask too many questions about where you got the money from.

Actually, the whole art market is thriving because it's an ideal outlet for all kinds of people who want to wash money. They buy a piece of art and then they can re-sell it and get clean money.

LG: I've heard of something called chop banking. This is where you make a deposit with a Chinese moneylender in, say, Hong Kong and he gives you a counter. Then you go to San Francisco and draw the cash by presenting the counter. Are you aware of that, and can you say anything about it?

Marc Faber: I know that it exists, that it's done, but I haven't done it myself.

LG: It's not something that Westerners are likely to be able to take advantage of?

Marc Faber: I guess if they knew where to go, sure.

Investing in the Internet

By the time you read this, there may well have been a shake-out in the group of stocks related to the Internet. Although everyone agrees that by "conventional valuations" these stocks are very high, no-one knows how the industry is going to pan out and who will be the big winners in the long term. At the time of our interview, Marc Faber was clearly concerned that they could be the last bit of froth on what he sees as a massive equity bubble.

LG: Would you mind talking a little bit about the Internet stocks for posterity?

Marc Faber: The Internet companies are a phenomenon just like the railroads in the last century, radios in the 1920s, or PCs early on. There is a huge potential, but the profitability is vague. Some companies may make a lot of money one day, but in my opinion most of them will never make any money. In a way, the enthusiasm is overdone because it's not as great an advance as, say, railroads were in the last century. Railroads were an unbelievable invention because they enabled goods, people, and news to travel faster. Napoleon couldn't move his armies any faster than, say, Alexander the Great did more than 2000 years earlier. But after the railroad came along, you could move goods and people at, say, fifty miles an hour!

The Internet can deliver news quickly and cheaply, but if you order a pizza through the Internet, someone has to get it from the kitchen, pack it, put it on a bicycle or in a car, get to your house, go up to the seventh floor of your building, and so forth. So the advance of the Internet isn't so huge. It's just a continuation of the information and communication revolution that began with the telegraph, but in terms of delivery of goods, with the exception of delivery of information, it hasn't brought any progress.

I don't see a huge difference between receiving the Sears Roebuck catalog or the Walmart catalog, filling out the form and sending it in, and ordering the same stuff through the Internet.

I think the people that will make a lot of money are the users of the Internet. Before email, if, say, you wanted a soft copy of something I wrote, I either sent you the file on a diskette, or I faxed it to you and you had to re-key it. Now I can send you the whole file by email and you can print it out. It's a tremendous advantage for both you and me.

LG: Yes, indeed. It cuts companies' overheads.

Marc Faber: Yes, hugely. We can download information instead of going to the library; instead of buying a book or a newspaper, we can call it up and read it onscreen. We can call up stock quotes. But if people believe that the Internet will make the world much smarter, then they're probably wrong. Did radio make the world much smarter? Did TV? On the contrary, they have made us *less* smart. Consider the following: if information and news becomes freely available, how much value can it have? It is possible that it will be so contaminated by rumors, sensationalism, half-truths, and filth that it won't have *any* real value, and that it will in fact be more productive in terms of investments to avoid such sources of "information" as CNN, CNBC, *USA Today*, Street.com, etc.

LG: I think it has already happened. So, you're bearish on Net stocks?

Marc Faber: I think it's a question of valuation. They have a much higher valuation than anything I've seen before in terms of price to earnings, price to sales, and so forth, and you have this flood of new issues. I think this is the icing on the cake of the big stock market mania of the 1980s and 1990s, and when this breaks it may be over. Also, how much is the producer of a free commodity — news — going to be? Nobody knows, but I suspect that the Internet stocks will make textbook examples of a mania and become as famous as the tulip mania in the seventeenth century, with the exception that a nice tulip, then, may still have won the heart of a beautiful young lady.

LG: If I couldn't hold myself back, if I knew that the valuations were crazy but I wanted to try to get out at the top, what signs would I look for to find it?

Marc Faber: As a group, maybe they've topped out already. Now they're buying each other. The new issue calendar is now mainly Internet stocks. When the new issue calendar was just oil servicing stocks in the 1980s, it was very close to the end. I mean, I think the writing is really on the wall.

Sometimes they have new issues that, on the first day of trading, trade four to five times the number of shares they just issued. You have to ask yourself, if companies are issuing a share at $15 and in a day it's at $80, is the underwriter so dumb, or are the people who buy it dumb? Somewhere, someone has to be wrong.

I just can't see how they're going to make a lot of money, even out of e-Commerce. The Amazon.com people say the diversification is great and so forth, but if the book business was so great, they would have stayed in the book business. Now they're going into lots of other things and they're becoming another huge department store. Now, they may have a brand, where the others have less of a brand, but I don't think there's going to be huge loyalty. The advantage of Walmart is that they already have customers and warehouses, as well as established distribution and sourcing channels — it's a tremendous advantage. If you buy something you don't like, you bring it back to the store. The problem when you buy something on the Internet is that if you don't like it, you have to ship it back.

A lot of shopping is still a social experience. Why do people go to restaurants when they can eat more cheaply at home? They go to restaurants because they want to see and be seen and they like the atmosphere. The principal buyers of goods in the world are women, not men. Why do women like to go shopping? They go to meet their friends, to have coffee, they go because they know the salesgirl, they want to meet a man, they want to find some company, they want the social interaction — there are a hundred reasons. That won't change.

I agree that a fellow living in the countryside may find it more convenient to order a fishing rod through the Internet than have to drive to New York to buy it, but he could have ordered it through a catalog. So, you tell me whether this is such a huge revolution.

The people who use the Internet are the same people who are buying the Internet shares, and they make it sound as if it is the greatest invention ever. My view is that it's just a continuation of what we already had.

LG: So, are you a value investor?

Marc Faber: In general, I try to buy things that are inexpensive and sell things that are expensive — but, with the exception of commodities which have never been lower in this century in real terms, in the last few years everything has become expensive. I believe that eventually the divergences in valuations between highly priced U.S. financial assets and real assets such as commodities and agricultural land, and the price level in emerging economies will be corrected.

Commodity prices are unbelievably low by historical standards. Inflation adjusted, they're just incredibly low. On the other hand, you have financial asset prices that are in the sky and I guess that there will be a reversal eventually.

I don't know whether this is a trend that has already started, but just recently commodity prices have started to move up somewhat, bonds have started to act heavy, European stocks are no longer participating, the U.S. market has a very narrow leadership, and Japanese stocks have started to move up and Japanese bonds to move down, so maybe something is happening.

I think that the downward wave in commodity prices and interest rates is now coming to an end. Will the bottom be in three months or three years? I don't know, but let's say that the big downward wave is already over. I think what still has to happen is debt liquidation somewhere, somehow, because normally before you can get into the up-swing again you need to clean the system, and that hasn't happened yet.

So, returning to the question of value investing, the difficulty is that value at different times is different. You could argue that Yahoo! and Amazon.com are very cheap because they're no longer selling to a regional market but to the whole world and they have a brand. A guy in, say, Shanghai can't go to Walmart in America, but he can order a book from Amazon.com. To some extent I agree with this, but equally it would seem to me that the entry into this business is also very easy because the guy in Shanghai, if he's smart, can start a website and sell books. I'm not yet sure exactly who is going to make a lot of money, because of the ease with which you can enter e-Commerce.

LG: By value investing I was thinking of the pure Benjamin Graham approach of really just finding things that were cheap relative to their asset value and then selling them when they went up.

Marc Faber: First of all, we have a deflationary environment, and maybe in a deflationary environment you don't want to own assets because they depreciate.

In a deflationary environment corporate profits will eventually go down. If your stock sells at 100 times book value, then in a deflationary environment maybe one day it will only sell at twenty times book value. I'm not sure about how to measure value, but certainly if traditional measures have any validity, which I think they do, then obviously technology, not just the Internet, is grossly overvalued. Dell is an assembler of PCs — I don't see any difference between assembling PCs and assembling washing machines. Why would one sell at the market cap of US$100 billion and not the others? If you take traditional value measures, then really the whole U.S. market for these so-called stocks that have driven the index is grossly, unbelievably overvalued.

LG: What sectors do you like?

Marc Faber: I don't particularly like any financial assets. I think bonds are probably going to be OK, but even there I have some reservations. I think gold and commodities are very inexpensive.

Time to buy commodities?

LG: How would you buy the commodities?

Marc Faber: You can buy a basket of commodities — the commodity index. You could buy some commodity-related shares — you could buy forest companies, say.

LG: Would you buy gold-mining companies?

Marc Faber: Yes. Actually, I just wrote a report on buying insurance policies. I think people should buy, with about 5–10% of their assets, something not related to financial assets and that would be gold. Of course, you can buy coffee, but that's more difficult to store than gold.

LG: Not oil?

Marc Faber: I don't know. I was very negative about oil in the early 1980s when it was above US$30, because I visited the Middle East regularly and I saw that they could produce oil at a dollar a barrel, so in my opinion it had to come down. Now at this level I'm less negative, because I think we will one day no longer need oil. Basically it's an inelegant solution that you dig a hole somewhere in the world, take the oil out, then it goes through a huge pipeline, it's then put in a tanker, the tanker goes from A to B, it's unloaded into terminals, then the trucks come to the terminals, it's put on the truck and the truck brings it to the petrol station, and then it goes into your car. It's a crazy process that will be eliminated one day through new technology.

It's not going to disappear overnight; it could take years and years and in the meantime, as countries develop, they will need airconditioning, electricity for light, for their stoves, for their stereos, for the TV, for their PCs, and so on. The energy needs in places like Asia and the emerging economies are huge.

At the same time you have, because of productivity, improvements in resources. You have a lot of supply. I'm not wildly optimistic about commodities, but if you asked me to choose between putting all my money into the Dow Jones today or all of it in a basket of commodities, I'd choose the commodities. I would suggest that gold is now out of favor for a variety of reasons, mainly because the central banks have been selling it, but if you count all the gold that is above the ground that has been found since King Solomon's time, it is worth roughly US$1.2 trillion.

LG: Is that all?

Marc Faber: Yes, it's not very much and the annual supply is US$25 billion. Now, US$1.2 trillion is essentially the market cap of Microsoft, IBM, and Intel. You have as much value there as in all the gold that has ever been found by mankind. Over longer periods of time the supply of gold is increasing, but I can assure you that the supply of bonds —

and of paper — is going up dramatically too. Now if, say, the world woke up one day and didn't like Internet stocks, they would drop 90%. If, one day, every man, woman, and child on the planet bought one gram of gold — one gram of gold is about US$9.20, and, if 950 million Indians can buy 800 tons of gold, it's not a totally unrealistic idea — then the total demand would be three times the annual supply. If the whole world decided to buy one ounce of gold per head, then the demand in that year would exceed all the available gold in the world. Gold isn't a commodity that is widely available. I think, therefore, that in our lifetime we'll see significantly higher gold prices.

LG: Aren't there any hidden reserves in Russia or anything like that?

Marc Faber: Yes, there's a lot of gold under the ground. There's a lot of gold in homes, too, but that's all in this US$1.2 trillion I mentioned. You can mine more, but you can't double the production of gold in one year. In any event, never in the history of modern capitalism could you buy as many ounces of gold with one Dow Jones Industrial Average as you could buy today. As we speak, with the Dow at over 11,000, you can buy more than forty-three ounces of gold! May I remind you that in 1980, you could buy just one ounce of gold with one Dow Jones Industrial Average point.

Hong Kong

A long-time resident of Hong Kong, Faber has spoken publicly of his doubts about its future. I asked him what life was like now that it is part of China.

Marc Faber: You can have all kinds of odd experiences, like bad experiences with the Chinese police, but I think that the administration has gone out of its way to ensure that foreigners don't feel that they are harassed in any way by the local authorities. In terms of personal freedom, I think you may have more freedom today than you had under the British. Under the British I was never a permanent resident. You couldn't become a permanent resident unless, as a

Briton, you had the right to live here. As a foreigner, every two years you had to go and get a new visa and they could decline to extend your visa without giving you a reason.

If I had written something very negative about the Governor, or someone important in the administration, maybe they would have refused to renew my visa. Today I'm a resident; I have the right to live here forever. Even if I move away for a whole year, I have the right to come back and stay here. So, they can put me in jail for insulting the government or whatnot, but they can't kick me out.

I'm not entirely sure how Hong Kong will play itself out, but I'm convinced that if the optimists are right about China then cities like Shanghai, Beijing, Tianjin, Dalian, Chongqing, and so on, will develop very rapidly and gradually either rival, or more likely overtake, Hong Kong. From a cyclical point of view, I'm negative about China; in the long run, however, I'm relatively optimistic about economic development, at least in some cities of China, some industries, and some regions.

In 1990, if you went to Shanghai you were practically the only foreigner; Beijing was the same. Today there is a very big foreign community in Shanghai. I think in about five years' time life in Shanghai may actually be more pleasant for foreigners than in Hong Kong. Shanghai has a special atmosphere, it is very dynamic, and the government in China is very pro-Shanghai. The geographical location of Shanghai *vis à vis* China is better than that of Hong Kong *vis à vis* China. The flights to Europe are faster from Shanghai than from Hong Kong, and the flights from Shanghai and Beijing to the U.S. are shorter, so the major airline hops will be in the north anyway. Therefore, I think that the major financial, commercial, technology, and undoubtedly the cultural centers of China will be in Shanghai and the corridor north of Shanghai toward Tianjin and Beijing. The major educational institutions in China are there, as are the major cultural institutions because the south speaks the wrong language (Cantonese, not Mandarin).

Overall, I think it's only a matter of time before Hong Kong will be overtaken by Shanghai. Shanghai was the dominant city in China anyway before 1949.

If someone had the choice of buying a small, empty flat in Hong Kong or a large luxury flat in Shanghai which would include a nice concubine and still cost less than the pigeonhole in Hong Kong, I would advise them to buy the one in Shanghai. It will have a much better price appreciation in the long run than the one in Hong Kong (albeit, depending on the demands of its occupant, a higher running cost).

LG: So, should we be buying China?

Marc Faber: The problem is on the micro level. Since 1989 when they started to launch the stock market, most companies that were listed were still state-owned companies — they're not the entrepreneurial companies. There aren't many great investment candidates. Some of the state-owned companies may become better over time, and since these Chinese stocks have declined by roughly 80–90%, they're now reasonably interesting. I'm not sure that this batch of companies will be the best performers. Maybe the best-performing stocks in China are ones that aren't yet listed.

The legal system was extremely vague initially and still is, so unless you have very well written memorandums of understanding, it is very easy to be ripped off. Also, what is the value of a shareholders' agreement in China? I don't know, but it can't be much!

If you are a multinational and you want to launch a new product, you can achieve, maybe, a 50% market share if you invest US$200 or $300 million. In the U.S. you couldn't do that! And maybe in ten years' time this 50% market share of China with a population of 1.2 billion people is going to be worth a lot of money. Nowadays, if you want to list your product in a department store anywhere in the world, you pay listing fees for the shelf space. China is also at present charging shelf space fees and so on.

The problem with China is it became fashionable to invest there. We had Tiananmen Square in 1989, but by 1992 things were starting to improve. Then everybody was saying that a billion people will need all kinds of products. Everybody rushed in and too much capacity was built, and there was more and more competition that developed and depressed prices. People didn't realize that distribution is very difficult in China and that there are a lot of regulations that are constantly changing. The experience has been very frustrating for most Western companies.

It's hard to imagine how it would be physically possible to have the prosperity we have in the Western world in some of these large population countries like China. In general, rich countries have been small countries. China has been lucky in having a large territory endowed with many resources, and they had a head-start in terms of the population that went to America and who are already educated. So, in general I think they are quite lucky; it will be interesting to see whether they can maintain the prosperity in the long run. I doubt that China will become rich, but I think some people in China will become very rich.

Life is uncertain, yet most people seek certainty, especially where money is concerned. It takes a wise investor to accept the basic insecurities of life, and an even wiser one to exploit doubtful situations successfully. We all want easy answers; the trouble is that the easy answers are usually wrong, and mean that we eventually lose out. Unlike the majority of investment professionals, Marc Faber is willing to point out some very harsh truths — but, again, that doesn't mean that the work has been done for you. If you are handling your own investments, you still need to interpret these facts and make your own choices.

One of the most valuable pieces of advice he offered during this interview was the suggestion that you may be much better off in your old age, in terms of your quality of life and purchasing power — which are the real measures of personal wealth — if you retire abroad to a developing country. For many people, this represents a very tough decision. Good advice often does.

Readers who would like to know more about Marc Faber's views can obtain his monthly newsletter, The Gloom, Boom & Doom Report, *by contacting:*

Marc Faber Limited
Room 2705
New World Tower
16–18 Queen's Road Central
Hong Kong
Tel: +852 2801 5410
Fax: +852 2845 9192
Email: contrary@hk.super.net
Website: www.marcfaber.com

8

Robert Prechter: Reading the Runes

Most of us know instinctively that there is such a thing as "crowd psychology" — we learn it as kids. The latest playground craze, the sudden decision by the majority to pick on a particular child, an obviously false delusion taking hold of the gang so strongly that it is unsafe to disagree ... all these are typical features of children's lives. Adults are no better. Convention and consensus are little more than adult forms of group behavior — but that doesn't mean that the majority is always wrong, or that the lone dissenter is sure to be right. In investment, though, unlike most other human activities, it pays to be acutely aware of the crowd's mood, since we can be sure that it will alter at some point, causing massive price changes.

While we all may know this, crowd psychology has not yielded much to science. If there were a true science of herd behavior that allowed one to predict accurately what any given mass of people were going to do next, much money could be made. That's what "technical analysis" attempts to do by studying the charts of price movements to find recurring patterns which may be predictable. When pressed to explain why these patterns might exist, technical analysts usually say that it relates to crowd psychology — prices move in patterns because people, en masse, *behave in patterns.*

Controversial though its theories are, no discussion of the market can be complete without examining the Wave Principle. Discovered by Ralph Elliott, a corporate accountant, in the 1930s, it is, as defined by Robert Prechter, "a catalog of price patterns and an explanation of where these forms are likely to occur in the overall path of market development."

Greatly simplified, the "Wave Principle" is a pattern of three steps forward and two steps back. Each wave combines with others on the same scale to form a similar pattern on a larger scale and so on, so that analysts are able to discover the wave formation in data that occurred over a few minutes, right up to a time-span of centuries.

Figure 8.1 The Elliott Wave

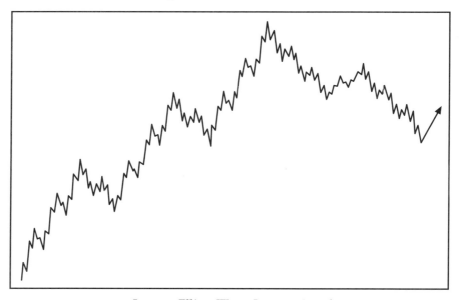

Source: Elliott Wave International

In this idealized Elliott Wave chart, the three-steps-forward, two-steps-back pattern is evident on different scales or "degrees."

Elliott also applied the Fibonacci sequence and ratio to his market studies. Fibonacci, a medieval mathematician, found a curious numerical sequence that seems to occur widely in nature. The sequence is formed by adding the two preceding numbers in the sequence to form the next one: 1, 1, 2, 3, 5, 8, 13, 21, 34 ... and so on. Elliott believed that this ratio could be identified in the movement of stock prices.

Robert Prechter is the foremost proponent of the Elliott Wave today. He rose to prominence in the 1980s with a series of uncannily accurate market predictions; for instance, early in the 1980s he predicted a major bull market with the Dow rising to 3600 after a stop at 2700 along the way.

In his recent book, At the Crest of the Tidal Wave *(New Classics Library, 1995), he argues that a great, and long-lasting, bear market is impending, based on his highly detailed analyses of Elliott Wave forms. His conclusions seem to support what some of the other investors in this book also feel — that perhaps we are on the verge of an earth-shattering paradigm shift that spells the end of centuries of Western progress and pre-eminence in the world.*

Scary? Maybe — it depends on how much you have invested psychologically in the notion of endless Western progress. As serious investors we must be realists and face up to what is really happening, however painful it may be. Pessimism can be addictive, but if you really want to protect your existing wealth and accumulate more, it is important to examine the downside possibilities from time to time.

LG: Could you describe your background and career?

Robert Prechter: I was born in New York State and raised in Atlanta, Georgia. In the 1960s, a major U.S. corporation annually awarded one college scholarship for each of four regions in the nation, and I was fortunate enough to receive their scholarship for the Southeastern region. I went to Yale University and graduated in 1971 with a B.A. in Sociology. After graduation, I played and recorded with a band for four years and had a great time. In 1975, I joined the Merrill Lynch Market Analysts department under Bob Farrell and worked with such luminaries as Bob Nurock, Phil Roth, Steve Shobin, and Dick McCabe, all of whom have become major Wall Street figures.

In 1978, I finished co-authoring, with A. J. Frost, *Elliott Wave Principle — Key to Market Behavior*, and in April 1979 I left Merrill Lynch to start *The Elliott Wave Theorist*. I have published continually ever since. In 1990, I expanded the company, hired a number of analysts, and began providing full-time analysis to institutional subscribers on almost every market worldwide. We have since created the biggest technical analysts' website in the world at www.elliottwave.com/. We have free courses on the Wave Principle, an active bulletin board, a chat room where traders can discuss the S&P's wave structure as it unfolds during the day, daily market commentary, a weekly in-depth interview called "Wall Street UnCut," as well as scientifically oriented papers on the validity of the Wave Principle and its sociological implications, which together form what I call the new science of socionomics.

LG: You've been described as a steadfast bear since the late 1980s (John Rothschild, *The Bear Book*, John Wiley, 1998). Is this true?

Robert Prechter: Yes, though I have been temporarily bullish several times along the way. My main message is that this bull market is the terminal phase of a two-century advance that began in 1784. Consequently, the ensuing bear market will be the largest since the 1700s in England when stock values declined 98% after the peak of the South Sea bubble. That one perspective has colored all of my commentary.

LG: I believe that in 1978 you predicted a bull market in stocks, and that in 1980 you correctly called a halt to the bull market in gold. Could you describe these events?

Robert Prechter: In 1978, Frost and I predicted the great bull market, and in 1982 I called the lift-off and forecasted that the market would go up five times in value, to nearly 4000. People thought it crazy at the time, but in retrospect, I underestimated the potential.

As for gold, silver, interest rates, and the inflation rate in general, if you check the January 1980 issue of *Futures* (then *Commodities*) *Magazine*, you'll see that I called a major top in all of these areas as well as the start of a disinflationary trend that has been in force since.

LG: Have you had any other major successes in prediction?

Robert Prechter: Sure. I think the best forecast I made was for an expanding economy during the bull market but one that would nevertheless expand at a lesser rate than the economy of the 1950s and 1960s. In the 1980s and 1990s, this is how it has developed.

I've also caught almost all of the intermediate term moves in gold and silver over the past twenty years. I also called the peak in several famous people's careers and in my own business in January 1988. However, I think that was only a temporary top! On the other hand, I've been pretty poor at anticipating the action in the bond market. I think that's going to change, though, when deflation sets in.

LG: How does the Elliott Wave work in foreign markets generally, and in emerging markets in particular?

Robert Prechter: It works fine, but that question is probably better put to our foreign equities analyst, Bill Mitchell, who is quite a celebrity in Asia since he called their crash of 1998 and the subsequent rebound. I don't believe in the term "emerging markets." I think it's a fancy phrase for low-quality investment locales that will prove disastrous to those who classify them as "emerging," which erroneously implies great long-term upside potential. To truly find a market that is emerging, one that will assume a major place on the world stage, takes great foresight, and most people don't have a clue about the prerequisites. If they did, they wouldn't have invested in Russia, most of Latin America, or many of the Southeast Asian stocks and bonds.

LG: How do you account for the existence of the wave — is it a natural phenomenon that occurs everywhere?

Robert Prechter: The best way to answer that question is to read my new book, *The Wave Principle of Human Social Behavior and the New Science of Socionomics*. A short answer is that it results from the unconscious herding impulse that all humans inherit from their evolutionary ancestors. So yes, it is natural. What's more, it's extremely powerful, being an impulse of the primitive pre-rational portion of the brain.

LG: Are you predicting a global bear market? Will any foreign markets prosper?

Robert Prechter: There is no question about a global bear market. What surprised me most was the fact that it hasn't been concurrent. Japan led it off on the first day of 1990, other Asian markets joined in last year, and it appears that the West will turn down in 1999 — or at least no later than 2001. I don't believe any markets will be in bull trends once these final major stock markets begin to head lower.

LG: You've written that the Kondratieff Wave was known by the ancient Mayas and Israelites. Could you expand on this?

Robert Prechter: Both the Bible and Mayan texts refer vaguely to a fifty-year cycle of expansion and contraction. However, I wouldn't say that they had extensive knowledge of the cycle such as I think is available now, given the three centuries of meticulous stock price and commodity price records that we have today.

The Kondratieff Wave

Nikolai Kondratieff, a Russian economist who perished under Stalin, proposed the idea that there are recurring cycles of boom and slump in capitalist economies that last around fifty-four years. He believed that, during the upswing, industrialized economies expand rapidly to the point where the primary producers of raw materials cannot keep up with demand; at this point a downswing begins, driving capital and labor abroad to "new"countries (such as Australia and America) and stimulating new discoveries which are exploited in the next upswing, as the "new" countries increase the supply of raw materials. The "long wave," as it is sometimes called, wasn't intended to be applied to stocks per se — it's about the economy as a whole. Conventional economists tend to doubt its validity, arguing that there have not been enough long wave periods since the beginning of the eighteenth-century Industrial Revolution for the idea to be testable.

Figure 8.2 The Kondratieff Wave

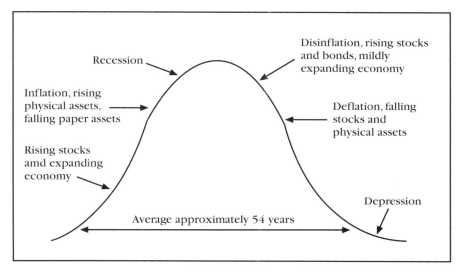

Source: Elliott Wave International

An idealized Kondratieff Wave showing economic conditions
at different points in the cycle.

*Robert Prechter believes that the high point in the current
Kondratieff cycle may be reached sometime around the turn of the
millennium, implying a gradual period of deflation for the next
two-and-a-half decades or so.*

LG: Do the Kondratieff Wave and the Elliott Wave relate to one another?

Robert Prechter: They really don't relate at all. The Wave Principle is a
phenomenon of form and is the reality of market behavior. The
Kondratieff Wave is actually not a wave, but a cycle. Cycles expand,
contract, and disappear from time to time. Or they work from turn to
turn but not necessarily from top to top or bottom to bottom.
Practically speaking, both approaches do relate in the current
environment because they are both calling for the same result into
approximately 2003–4, when ideally the next major stock market
bottom by both methods is due.

LG: What are your views on the explosion in the number of mutual funds in the U.S.?

Robert Prechter: It's a function of the most bullish market sociology since 1720.

LG: What are your views on amateur day trading?

Robert Prechter: I think the phrase is a misnomer. True traders can make money in both directions. The people that the newspapers call "day traders" today are simply stock buyers who focus on the near term. They never sell short for a decline, so in my opinion they're not traders.

LG: Are there any sectors that will do well during the bear market?

Robert Prechter: Not this bear market. The engine of this bear market will be deflation, in which case virtually every asset will decline in money value. The only thing that will gain value is cash, and that cash has to be in safe instruments whose issuers won't go under. It will be difficult even choosing your cash vehicle.

LG: Many investment professionals who don't believe in technical analysis still pay attention to its practitioners — why?

Robert Prechter: Actually, many investment professionals don't pay any attention to technical analysis at all. In June, a money manager on financial television said he never looked at chart patterns. I believe that in a few years from now, he'll wish he had.

LG: Foreigners often remark that people in the U.S. are too fearful of apocalypses (such as nuclear war, tyranny, famine, plague, and so on), perhaps because they have never experienced one on their soil. Would you comment on this?

Robert Prechter: Historically speaking, I would say that most people society-wide are either too fearful or not fearful enough, depending on the time. Rarely does a society accurately anticipate the next major social period of either peace and prosperity or depression and war. People in the U.S. built bomb shelters *after* the Second World War; they are speculating in stocks *after* they have risen 1000%, and so on. What happens next is always what the crowd is unprepared for.

The Grand Supercycle

As mentioned earlier, Ralph Elliott believed that the wave formation is seen on many different scales; he propounded nine of them, from the tiny, short-term "Subminuette" (degree 1) to the massive, centuries-long cycles of the "Grand Supercycle" (degree 9). Prechter has added "Submillennium," "Millennium," "Super-millennium," and even higher degrees. To distinguish between the different scales, special notation is used — so, for instance, the fifth leg of a "Cycle" (degree 7) is referred to by the Roman numeral "V," while the fifth leg of a "Supercycle" (degree 8) is referred to by the same Roman numeral in brackets: "(V)."

Robert Prechter thinks that a Grand Supercycle bull market that began in 1784 has now ended, and that a long process of contraction is under way.

The following, taken from The Elliott Wave Theorist, *issues of April 6, 1983 and April 3, 1984, remains, says Prechter, a "succinct summary of the Elliott Wave outlook today":*

If all goes according to expectations, the last remaining question is, what happens after wave V tops out? The Wave Principle would recognize the 3686 top as the end of wave V of (V), the peak of a Grand Supercycle that stretches all the way back to [1784]. At that point, the most devastating stock price decline in United States history will ensue: a Grand Supercycle bear market that would then "correct" all the progress dating from the late 1700s. It is expected to be so severe that a worldwide monetary and economic collapse will most certainly follow on its heels. The downside target zone would be the price area (ideally near the low) of the previous fourth wave of lesser degree, wave (IV), which fell from 386 to 41 on the Dow. Government bonds and most corporate bonds will then be on the verge of a collapse to worthlessness as the bond market comes face to face with the reality that increasingly greater long term debt cannot be serviced at double digit interest rates, no matter what the government or the economy does. Worldwide banking failures, government bankruptcy, and eventual destruction of the paper money system might be plausible [results of] a bear phase of this magnitude. Since armed conflicts often occur after severe financial crises, one would have to consider the possibility that the collapse in value of financial assets would presage war between the superpowers.

LG: Is it easy to misinterpret the Elliott Wave?

Robert Prechter: Typically, one or two degrees of the trend unfold in an extremely clear manner and you know exactly where you are. The other degrees are often quite difficult to label, at least in prospect. My problem in the 1990s was that the position of the waves at Supercycle and Grand Supercycle degree are unmistakable, but the lower degrees were severely stretched upward, making them difficult to anticipate. One could almost say there weren't any waves, as the setbacks since 1987 have been so mild as to be virtually non-existent. This is apparently typical of the final up moves in Grand Supercycles. Unfortunately, we only had one in history to examine, and that was way back in the early 1700s. The developing bear market will unfold in a similar manner, where the rallies will be minimal. But overall, to answer your question: in the proper light, the Wave Principle is less difficult to interpret than fundamentals and news, which is what most investors rely on.

LG: Would you give private investors some tips on how to survive the bear years?

Robert Prechter: Definitely. Get into cash early and spread your holdings in several countries, but then only in their very safest banks. If you are wealthy, you should get advice from an international firm specializing in capital preservation. You will find information on and the addresses of a lot of these services in the back of my book, *At the Crest of the Tidal Wave*. There are also some practical things you can do.

First of all, convert life insurance to term insurance, because I think many insurance companies will fail as their assets collapse in value.

"Term assurance" is the oldest and simplest form of life cover — it is also the cheapest. The contract guarantees to pay out a sum of money if the person dies within a given time. "Whole of life" insurance, on the other hand, has a quasi-investment element — it guarantees to pay the amount assured on death, regardless of when it happens. In the event of a major squeeze of insurance companies, it is clear that term assurance policies are likely to be safer than "whole of life" policies.

Get out of stock mutual funds. Get out of municipal bonds, as many municipalities will be going under. Don't make the mistake of assuming that this bear market will be like that of the 1970s, when commodities rose. This one will be like 1929–32, when everything fell. Not even gold will be a refuge, as its bear market has yet to bottom, although we are getting closer to my long-term downside target with every passing year.

LG: We are told that stocks always go up in the long term, yet in the very long term all stock markets other than those in the United States have been virtually wiped out. If you could have invested at a 5% annual return (inflation adjusted) for 2000 years or more, you would now be worth more than the world's GDP. Would you comment on these ideas?

Robert Prechter: Stocks definitely don't always go up long term because, as you point out, many of history's stock markets have simply disappeared. Those that haven't disappeared, being in the modern age, have occasionally suffered declines of over 90%. In depressions, many bond issuers are totally wiped out and don't pay. As for investing for a 5% annual return for 2000 years, the idea is ridiculous. Cultures undergo massive upheavals from time to time, when capital is destroyed. There is risk in everything.

The idea that all societies experience periods when capital is destroyed is hardly controversial — so far as we know, it has occurred in every society in history, so why should ours be any different? It's an uncomfortable prospect for many, but perhaps it is better to see it as an inevitability, just as we can be certain that all living organisms eventually die. A devastating destruction of capital doesn't mean that all the people are destroyed, too — the descendants of Southern planters, Anglo-Irish landowners, and Russian aristocrats are still with us today, despite the fact that their families' wealth was destroyed 70-150 years ago. "Old money" tends to try to preserve its wealth within the family indefinitely, but it would appear that eventually all such fortunes are wiped out. Given enough time, a rich family will lose its assets and merge back into the mass of humanity — and so will a rich country.

Robert Prechter: My comment on the ideas that stocks always go up long term and that compound interest can make you rich is that these are mottos for good times. When people are in extremely tense historical times, they understand that neither of these apparent truisms can be taken for granted. You always hear these ideas in the middle and later stages of bull markets; you never hear them in years like 1932, 1949, or 1974. In 1979, for instance, all you heard was that bonds were "certificates of guaranteed confiscation," that stocks were a waste of time, and gold was the only answer.

Such truisms change with the times. The Wave Principle is far more reliable.

LG: Do you expect capital controls to be reintroduced? How can you protect assets internationally in such conditions?

Robert Prechter: I definitely expect capital controls to be reintroduced. Governments always have to appear to be doing something about a crisis, and I have little doubt that governments will try various insane policies to try to stop a human emotional tidal wave that cannot be stopped. The best way to protect your assets in such conditions is to have them in safe places well before governments become concerned enough to take drastic measures to curtail financial freedom. If you delay, it may be too late.

If I have anything to add to all of this, it is the critical point that the investor's worst enemy today is the confidently bullish advisor, broker, money manager, or commentator. He is the one who will ensure that you lose your fortune, fail to protect your assets while you still can, and then miss out on a historic buying opportunity later on. A handful of bears in the world are the ones offering sanity and safety at the peak of what my records show to be the greatest stock mania of all time.

Robert Prechter would be the first to admit that interpreting wave patterns isn't easy. As he mentioned in his interview, you can take courses on the Elliott Wave through his organization, Elliott Wave International, which also publishes a number of newsletters analyzing various markets according to Elliott Wave principles:

- The Elliott Wave Theorist
- Currency Market Perspective
- Global Market Perspective
- World Commodity Perspective

Contact:
Elliott Wave International
P.O. Box 1618
Gainesville
Georgia 30503
United States
Tel: +1 800 336 1618 or 770 536 0309
Website: www.elliottwave.com

His books include: Elliott Wave Principle *(with A. J. Frost, New Classics Library) and* At the Crest of the Tidal Wave *(New Classics Library, 1995).*

FURTHER READING

BOOKS

Bavishi, V., 1995, *International Accounting and Auditing Trends*, Princeton Center for International Financial Analysis and Research

Bernstein, Peter, 1996, *Against the Gods*, John Wiley & Sons

Berryessa, N. and Kirzner, E., 1988, *Global Investing the Templeton Way*, Irwin

Day, A., 1983, *International Investment Opportunities*, William Morrow

Dessauer, J. P., 1986, *International Strategies for American Investors*, Prentice-Hall

Fisher, Philip, 1996, *Common Stocks and Uncommon Profits and Other Writings*, John Wiley & Sons

Galbraith, J. K., 1955, *The Great Crash 1929*, Houghton Mifflin

Gastineau, G. L., 1979, *The Stock Options Manual,* McGraw-Hill

Graham, Benjamin, 1965, *The Intelligent Investor,* Harper & Row

Gros, Daniel and Steinherr, Alfred, 1995, *Winds of Change: Economic Transition in Central and Eastern Europe*, Longman

LeBaron, Dean, 1976, *Ins and Outs of Institutional Investing*, Nelson Hall

LeBaron, Dean with Carpenter, Donna, *Climbing Falling Walls*, available at www.deanlebaron.com

LeBaron, Dean and Vaitlingham, Romesh, 1999, *Ultimate Investor*, Capstone

LeBaron, Dean and Vaitlingham, Romesh, 1999, *Ultimate Investor Quotations*, Capstone

Malkiel, Burton G., 1991, *A Random Walk Down Wall Street*, W. W. Norton

Melton, Paul, 1996, *Going Global with Equities*, Financial Times Pitman

Mobius, Mark, 1995, *Mobius on Emerging Markets,* Financial Times Pitman

Morton, James, 1997, *Investing with the Grand Masters*, Financial Times Management

Prechter, Robert, 1995, *At the Crest of the Tidal Wave,* New Classics
    Library
Proctor, W., 1983, *The Templeton Touch*, Doubleday
Rogers, Jim, 1994, *Investment Biker,* Random House
Schwager, Jack D., 1993, *Market Wizards*, HarperCollins
Schwed, Fred, 1995, *Where Are the Customers' Yachts?*, John Wiley &
    Sons
Smith, Adam, 1976, *The Money Game*, Random House
Smith, Ralph Lee, 1963, *The Grim Truth About Mutual Funds*, Putnam
Soros, George, 1995, *Soros on Soros*, John Wiley & Sons
Staley, Kathryn F., 1997, *The Art of Short Selling*, John Wiley & Sons
Taylor, J. H., 1995, *Global Investing for the 21st Century*, International
    Publishing Corporation
Train, John, 1989, *The New Money Masters*, Harper & Row
Vittachi, Nuri, 1998, *Riding the Millennial Storm*, John Wiley & Sons

PERIODICALS

Asia Cover
AsiaMoney, 5th Floor, Singapore Airlines Blds, 138 HV Del a Costa,
Salcepo Village, Makati, Metro Manila, Philippines
Tel: +63 2759 3488
Fax: +63 2867 3494
Email:asiamony@wlink.net
Website: www.euromoney.com

Analyst
Editor: Jeremy Utton
193 Lauderdale Tower, Barbican, London, United Kingdom
Tel: +44 (0)171 256 2214
Fax: +44 (0)171 256 2213

AsiaMoney
5th Floor, Singapore Airlines Blds, 138 HV Del a Costa,
Salcepo Village, Makati, Metro Manila, Philippines
Tel: +63 2759 3488
Fax: +63 2867 3494
Email: asiamony@wlink.net
Website: www.euromoney.com

Asset Finance International
Euromoney Publications, Nestor House, Playhouse Yard, London,
United Kingdom
Tel: +44 (0)171 779 8146
Fax: +44 (0)171 779 8321
Website: www.euromoney.com

Barrons
200 Burnett Road, Chicopee, Massachusetts 01020, United States
Email: barrons.service@cor.dowjones.com
Website: www.barrons.com

Bond Week
The Newsweekly of Fixed Income and Credit Markets
Editor: Tom Lamont
Institutional Investor Newsletters, 477 Madison Avenue, 5th Floor,
New York, NY 10022, United States
Tel: +1 212 224 3041
Fax: +1 212 224 3491
Email: singhm@iinews.com

The Gloom Boom, and Doom Report
Marc Faber Limited, Room 2705, New World Tower,
16–18 Queen's Road Central, Hong Kong
Tel: + 852 2801 5410
Fax: + 852 2845 9192
Email: contrary@hk.super.net
Website: www.marcfaber.com

Capital Markets Guide
Euromoney Publications, Nestor House, Playhouse Yard, London,
United Kingdom
Tel: +44 (0)171 779 8146
Fax: +44 (0)171 779 8321
Website: www.euromoney.com

Central European
Euromoney Publications, Nestor House, Playhouse Yard, London,
United Kingdom
Tel: +44 (0)171 779 8146
Fax: +44 (0)171 779 8321
Website: www.euromoney.com

China Joint Venturer
Asia Law & Practice, 1st Floor, Chinachem Hollywood Centre,
1 Hollywood Road, Central, Hong Kong
Tel: +852 2842 6950
Fax: +852 2543 7617
Email: asiamony@wlink.net
Website: www.euromoney.com

Commercial Lending Review
Editor: Claire Greene
Institutional Investor Journals, 488 Madison Avenue,
16th Floor, New York, NY 10022, United States
Tel: +1 212 224 3562
Fax: +1 212 224 3527
Email: iij@iijournals.com

The Economist
Economist Publications, United Kingdom
Website: www.economist.com

The Elliott Wave Theorist
Elliott Wave International, P.O. Box 1618, Gainesville,
Georgia 30503, United States
Tel: +1 800 336 1618 or +1 770 536 0309
Fax: +1 770 536 2514
Website: www.elliottwave.com

Emerging Markets Investor
Editor: Melvyn Westlake
Risk Publications, 104–112 Marylebone Lane,
London, United Kingdom
Tel: +44 (0)171 487 0717
Fax: +44 (0)171 486 0879
Email: 100566.3177@compuserve.com
Website: www.riskpublications.com

Emerging Markets Quarterly
Editor: Brian Bruce
Institutional Investor Journals, 488 Madison Avenue,
16th Floor, New York, NY 10022, United States
Tel: +1 212 224 3562
Fax: +1 212 224 3527
Email: iij@iijournals.com

Emerging Markets Week
Editor: Tom Lamont
Institutional Investor Newsletters, 477 Madison Avenue,
5th Floor, New York, NY 10022, United States
Tel: +1 212 224 3041
Fax: +1 212 224 3491
Email: singhm@iinews.com

Euromoney
Editor: Garry Evans
Euromoney Publications, Nestor House, Playhouse Yard,
London, United Kingdom
Tel: +44 (0)171 779 8146
Fax: +44 (0)171 779 8321
Website: www.euromoney.com

The Financial Times
The Financial Times, Number One Southwark Bridge,
London, United Kingdom
Tel: +44 (0)171 873 3000
Fax: +44 (0)171 407 5700
Website: www.ft.com

Global Fund News
Editor: Tom Lamont
Institutional Investor Newsletters, 477 Madison Avenue,
5th Floor, New York, NY 10022, United States
Tel: +1 212 224 3041
Fax: +1 212 224 3491
Email: singhm@iinews.com

Global Investor
Editor: Andrew Cappon
Euromoney Publications, Nestor House, Playhouse Yard,
London, United Kingdom
Tel: +44 (0)171 779 8146
Fax: +44 (0)171 779 8321
Website: www.euromoney.com

Institutional Investor International
Editor: Robert Teitelman
Institutional Investor Inc., 488 Madison Avenue, 16th Floor,
New York, NY 10022, United States
Tel: +1 212 224 3570
Fax: +1 212 224 3553
Email: iij@iijournals.com

International Bond Investor
Editor: Andrew Cappon
Euromoney Publications, Nestor House, Playhouse Yard,
London, United Kingdom
Tel: +44 (0)171 779 8146
Fax: +44 (0)171 779 8321
Website: www.euromoney.com

International Equity Review
Editor: Rosie Sheppard
Euromoney Publications, Nestor House, Playhouse Yard,
London, United Kingdom
Tel: +44 (0)171 779 8146
Fax: +44 (0)171 779 8321
Website: www.euromoney.com

International Investment
Editor: Lawrence Gosling
City Financial Communications, 7 Air Street,
London, United Kingdom
Tel: +44 (0)171 439 3050
Fax: +44 (0)171 439 3070
Email: editorial@invweek.co.uk
Website: www.invweek.co.uk

Investors Chronicle
Editor: Ceri Jones
Investors Chronicle, Greystoke Place, Fetter Lane,
London, United Kingdom
Tel: +44 (0)171 463 3000
Fax: +44 (0)171 463 3154
Website: www.investorschronicle.co.uk

Journal of Financial Crime
The Official Journal of the Cambridge International Symposium on
Economic Crime
Editor: Professor Barry Rider
Henry Stewart Publications, Russell House,
28/30 Little Russell Street, London, United Kingdom
Tel: +44 (0)171 323 2916
Fax: +44 (0)171 323 2918
Email: frasert@henrystewart.demon.co.uk

Journal of Money Laundering Control
Editor: Professor Barry Rider
Henry Stewart Publications, Russell House,
28/30 Little Russell Street, London, United Kingdom
Tel: +44 (0)171 323 2916
Fax: +44 (0)171 323 2918
Email: frasert@henrystewart.demon.co.uk

Latin Finance
Editor: Scott Weeks
Latin Finance (Euromoney), 2121 Ponce de leon Blvd,
Suite 1020, Coral Gables, Florida 33134, United States
Tel: +1 305 448 6593
Fax: +1 305 448 0718
Website: www.euromoney.com

MAR Hedge Fund Report
Managed Accounts Report (MAR), 220 Fifth Avenue,
New York, NY 10001, United States
Tel: +1 212 213 6202
Fax: +1 212 213 1870
Email: 72610.3721@compuserve.com
Website: www.marhedge.com/mar/marhome.htm

The Outside Analyst
P.O. Box 70322, 1007 KH Amsterdam, The Netherlands
Tel: + 31 23 544 0501
Fax: + 31 23 544 0502
Website: www. global-investment.com

Red Herring
Red Herring, 1550 Bryant Street, San Francisco,
California, United States
Tel: +1 415 865 2277
Email: subs@herring.com
Website: www.herring.com

Wall Street Journal
Wall Street Journal, 200 Burnett Road, Chicopee,
Massachusetts 01020, United States
Website: www.update.wsj.com

USEFUL WEBSITES

www.deanlebaron.com — Dean LeBaron

www.elliottwave.com — Robert Prechter

www.global-investment.com — Paul Melton

www.global-investor.com — excellent website for the global investor, providing comprehensive links to stock exchanges across the world

www.ibbotson.com — the website of Ibbotson Associates, providers of useful quantitative data

www.jimrogers.com — Jim Rogers

www.marcfaber.com — Marc Faber

www.peterlbernsteininc.com — the website of Peter Bernstein, prominent economist and author of *Against the Gods* (John Wiley & Sons), a superb book on risk

www.regentpac.com — Peter Everington, Regent Pacific Fund Management

www.templeton.com.sg — Mark Mobius, Templeton International